TO HELL
AND BACK

TO HELL
AND BACK

My Life in Johnny Thunders' Heartbreakers,
in the Words of the Last Man Standing

WALTER LURE
WITH DAVE THOMPSON

Backbeat
Books

Guilford, Connecticut

Backbeat Books
An imprint of The Rowman & Littlefield Publishing Group, Inc.
4501 Forbes Blvd., Ste. 200
Lanham, MD 20706
www.rowman.com

Distributed by NATIONAL BOOK NETWORK

Paperback edition published in 2021. Originally published in hardcover by
Backbeat Books in 2020.

Designed by Lynn Bergesen, UB Communications

Library of Congress Cataloging-in-Publication Data available

ISBN 978-1-4930-5169-4 (hardcover)
ISBN 978-1-4930-5988-1 (paperback)
ISBN 978-1-4930-5170-0 (electronic)

♾™ The paper used in this publication meets the minimum requirements of
American National Standard for Information Sciences—Permanence of Paper
for Printed Library Materials, ANSI/NISO Z39.48-1992

Dedicated to the Heartbreakers—
Johnny Thunders, Jerry Nolan,
and Billy Rath.

May they rest in peace
because they spent their time
in hell.

CONTENTS

ACKNOWLEDGMENTS

Walter would like to thank . . .

Bloodbath—*Albert Sce*, George Reisz, Mike Cefola,
Jim Spaeth, George Karas, John Swenson

The Demons—Martin John Butler, *Eliot Kidd*

The Hurricanes—Barry Ryan, *Billy Rogers*

The Heroes—*Richie Lure*, Barry Apfel,
Charlie Sox, Tom

The (original) Waldos—*Tony Coiro*, Jeff West, Perry,
Matt Langone, Joey Pinter, J. F., *Tom G*

The (current) Waldos—Tak Nakai, Ichiuji Takanori (EZ),
Joe Rizzo

The New York Dolls, the Ramones, the Clash,
the Damned, Siouxsie and the Banshees,
the Models, the Marbles, the Sex Pistols

Nils Stevenson

Ray Stevenson

Leee Black Childers

Gail Higgins

Malcolm McLaren

Vivienne Westwood

Sebastian Conran

Sid and *Nancy*

Hilly Kristal

Tommy and *Laura* Dean

Peter Crowley

Andy Shernoff

Levi & the Rockats

Randy Pratt

Carol Hamilton

Diane DaCosta

Damian and Hillary DaCosta, and Mattie and Ellie

Anna Sui

Linda Ramone

Don Chae

Tony Diaz

Shige Matsumoto

Alain Notz

(Names appearing in italics are sadly deceased.)

Dave Thompson would like to thank:

Our agent Lee Sobel for making it happen,

Walter for letting it happen,

Jo-Ann Greene for rumors and legends,

and Amy Hanson for everything else.

INTRODUCTION

We were seated in Hell's Kitchen—that is, Richard Hell's kitchen, as opposed to the once notorious New York City slum. In truth, however, there was probably little to choose between the two of them.

Hell lived at the time on Twelfth Street, between Avenues A and B, the edge of Alphabet City, and the fringe of the East Village, too. I was never certain whether he chose the geography deliberately, but if you wanted to score drugs . . . any drugs . . . he could not have found a cooler location.

Allen Ginsberg lived in one of the apartments upstairs; we used to see him coming up and down the stairs with very young, pretty boys on his arm. It was a strange neighborhood for such a well-known figure to live in, down-at-the-heels and sleazy beyond belief, but it suited him in a peculiar way. Plus, who knows how much money he actually made, or if he pissed it all away on drugs and sex?

It's what most of his neighbors would have done, given the opportunity.

That was not an issue for me. I knew that the Heartbreakers, the band that I had just joined, possessed a certain *reputation* . . . after all, Johnny Thunders, our guitarist, and Jerry Nolan, our drummer, were former New York Dolls and carried all the cultural and chemical baggage that came with such membership.

The rumor was: it was Iggy Pop who turned Johnny onto smack in the first place, when the Dolls visited Los Angeles in 1973, but he'd scarcely been Mr. Clean Living before that. Even before the Dolls, he used to deal speed, which is how he made his money. But he probably took as much as he sold, and not only speed. Uppers, downers, stay-in-the-middlers—it was said that Johnny devoured them all, even before he joined a band. Fame just gave him access to even more than he normally swallowed.

Jerry, older than the rest of us, followed Johnny's lead on that score, which surprised me because, in most respects, it was Johnny who looked up to Jerry. He was fascinated by fifties rock 'n' roll—the music, the lifestyle, the culture, the lot—and to Johnny, Jerry epitomized that era, that first manic rush of teenage rebellion that finally posited an alternative to the white-bread, picket-fence world to which Young America was supposed to aspire.

Jerry was a good teacher, too. He was six years older than Johnny, three years older than Hell and I, and what he didn't know about rock 'n' roll—real rock 'n' roll, before the sixties diluted it down to pop—could be written on the tip of a needle.

Rather like the one that was lying on the table a few feet away.

Initially, the plan was simply to give the new boy—me—a haircut. I had become a Heartbreaker just days before; since then, we'd played one gig and had a couple of rehearsals, and we'd be running through the songs again later today. But first, the haircut.

Aside from Johnny, who still wore his old Dolls mop with possessive pride, I had the longest locks in the band. Richard and Jerry both showed off their ears; Johnny barely revealed he had shoulders. I was somewhere in between, but the short-hairs were adamant. The Heartbreakers had an image to build—street-fighting tough guys from the Lower East Side—and we weren't going to do that if we looked like hippies or glam rockers.

Jerry, at some point in his storied career, had trained as a hairdresser. So, it transpired, had Dee Dee Ramone, whose own band had a lot less in common with him than we did. Years later, I heard rumors that Dee Dee's greatest wish had once been to become a Heartbreaker—I don't know if it's true, and I doubt that it would have worked. But he was always around, and he was here today. In fact, I could hear him and Jerry conferring as they studied the challenge before them. How to make Walter look like a Heartbreaker.

I had no qualms. Say what you like about the band's reputation (that word again!), but when it came to how they presented themselves onstage, they were deadly serious. That was Johnny and

Jerry's doing, I think—you don't come out of the New York Dolls (and, in Johnny's case, you didn't go into them either) without having an innate sense of style, and no matter how sour the Dolls' universe eventually became, they had never lost that.

Times had changed, though. The Dolls had barely been in their grave four months (David Johansen and Sylvain Sylvain had reanimated the name, but we'll get to that later), but already their old promo photos looked like creatures from another age. "Glam" was dead; glamour was finished.

The new wave of bands that emerged in the Dolls' wake, though grateful to the group for kicking down some doors, nevertheless opted for another look entirely . . . not quite street clothes, because they remained too studied for that. But ripped jeans and leather jackets, torn T-shirts and shirtless suits, that was what the bands wore now, and though they probably still shopped at the same thrift stores and vintage marts, they usually stayed in the men's department.

Maybe that's why the long hair had to go.

I don't remember, if I was even aware, who made the first cut. I just sat there waiting as my tresses tumbled. Occasionally one of them would speak—"Too much?" "Not enough?" "That works." And finally, the deed was done. A mirror was procured, and I inspected their handiwork.

It was a shock, but it was a good shock. I liked it. My mom would like it. My careers advisor back at school would have liked it. The guy who decked me in a bar back in 1966, for no reason aside from the fact I had long hair, would have liked it . . . maybe. It might still have been a bit much for him. But, for the Heartbreakers, it was perfect.

I was about to tell them that, but they had already moved on. I'd had my initial induction into the band. Now it was time for my second. Also on the table, alongside the needle, was a spoon. Jerry held the needle, Dee Dee did the cooking, and I just rolled up my sleeve and stretched out my arm as Jerry tied it off.

I had done heroin in the past, once or twice at college or there-abouts, just to see what it was like. It was okay. There were no fireworks, no flashing lights, no lurid neon signs proclaiming "welcome." I did it, and that was it. I never felt the need again.

This time, I wasn't quite so discerning. Like the haircut, getting high was a rite of passage that I needed to undertake as a member of the band . . . although *needed* is the wrong word. It wasn't as if they said, "You have to shoot up if you're going to join the Heart-breakers."

But the way I looked at the situation was that I'd have to get into it sooner or later, just to see what all the fuss was about. Which, of course, is a really stupid reason, but I wasn't going to let that stop me.

It certainly didn't cross my mind that, having made that dis-covery, I would then spend the next thirteen years exploring it. Or that everything I would experience during that period, but especially throughout the lifespan of the Heartbreakers, would ultimately be refracted through the lens of my addiction.

At the time, it was just what I did. Well, that and play guitar.

Chapter One

FROM FLORAL PARK TO THE FILLMORE

Walter Lure is living proof of Jerry Lewis's influence on rock and roll, on stage he alternates between jerking about like an out of control puppet, only to go suddenly rigid and belt out chord upon chord that were predestined to activate yo' feet."

So declared journalist Pete Makowski in the British music paper *Sounds*, in the issue dated June 4, 1977. And, of all the words that have been written about my music over the years, these are some of my favorites.

For a start, it's funny. Lots of musicians have been compared to Jerry *Lee* Lewis. But Jerry no-Lee Lewis? That has to be a first. It was written at the peak of the Heartbreakers' year-and-a-bit in the United Kingdom, late 1976 through spring 1978, and I still remember the pride I felt when I read it, and the smirk that crossed my face as I flicked through that week's music papers in our apartment in Pimlico, London. But do you want to know a secret?

I never intended to be a guitarist. Never wanted to. I took lessons when I was twelve or thirteen, inspired no doubt by hearing the Ventures on the radio, but I can't say my heart was in it. It was just something to do, and having done it, I stopped.

Music meant little to me at the time, although that's not to say I wasn't interested. The late 1950s and early 1960s were the era of the great teen dance programs, the big national shows that everyone had heard of, *American Bandstand*, things like that. But also a lot that seem to have been forgotten now—*The $64,000 Question*, which often had musical guests; Herb Sheldon's *Studio Party*; *The Sandy Becker Show*, which was a puppet show but was where I heard Ray Charles's "Busted" for the first time, sung by two puppets; and *Disc-O-Teen*, hosted by John Zacherley, "the

Cool Ghoul," and broadcast out of Newark, New Jersey. In fact, I once went to see an episode of *Disc-O-Teen* being filmed, and when I watched it on television a few nights later, there I was standing by the side of the stage.

I followed these shows religiously. Home from school, switch on the television, that was my routine. It wasn't only music, either. There were a lot of shows I liked . . . everything from *The Honeymooners*, which seems to have been a favorite with almost every musician I went on to work with, to *Howdy Doody*. In fact, my mother took me to New York to watch the filming of both of those shows as well, and I remember how shocked I was to discover that the comfortable, well-appointed home that Ralph and Alice seemed to inhabit was, in fact, nothing more than an open space with the audience out front, the crew all around, two painted cardboard walls, and no ceiling to speak of. Ah, the wonders of television.

Back to the music, though. I didn't have a radio at the time, not of my own—transistors were around, but they were still expensive, and of course I was too young to drive, so shows like these became my jukebox. A lot of the music that I liked came from those TV programs, and while much of it was very straightforward pop (Gary U. S. Bonds was probably the blackest singer I ever heard), there was enough good stuff to keep me happy.

Plus, I'd get to see all the new dances, and that was important because that's when I started to get into dancing and parties and stuff like that. Before that, I thought dancing meant standing there and shaking. Those shows taught me different a different perspective. So, although the music scene was still full of passing pop stars and watered-down Elvis, Brill Building ballads and "Sealed with a Kiss," I'd buy the latest 45s and take them to parties to dance to or make out to in the dark.

It was wallpaper, really, and that's how I viewed my guitar lessons. They were something to do, but they were scarcely life changing.

Of course, it might have helped if the lessons themselves had been a little more inspiring. My teacher was some middle-aged guy who worked out of a music store near my home, giving lessons in the back room. And the first tune I was given to learn was "She'll Be Coming 'Round the Mountain," which might be a popular standard, but it hardly sets the heartbeat racing. I don't remember how many lessons I took, but it wasn't many.

If we fast forward five or six years to 1967 or 1968, however, my ambitions were considerably more pronounced. Now I was in my freshman year, studying chemistry at Fordham University in the Bronx. My older brother, William, was into his last year at the same establishment, but we rarely socialized. I had a gaggle of friends my own age, including the students with whom I carpooled every morning, and music was the only thing we talked about. More or less.

A few of them already played guitar, and when I first picked up the instrument again, it was so I could join in the jams that most of our evenings together faded into. The difference is, I never put it down again.

I didn't take lessons, either. I let my younger brother, Richie, do that. He'd come home from the tutor, show me what he'd learned that day . . . and you can bet it wasn't "She'll Be Coming 'Round the Mountain" and "Mary Had a Little Lamb." My first notes, my first chords, my first songs. Richie showed me all of them, and the fact that he was six years younger than I was didn't matter at all. In fact, it probably helped. It meant that we could learn together.

I took the instrument seriously, both the rudiments that Richie taught me and those I was learning to discover for myself, listening to records until I'd worn them out, focusing on what the guitar was doing, trying to figure out how Jeff Beck got *this* sound but Pete Townshend got *that* one, flicking through the pages of whichever magazine was on hand, seeing which guitarist played which guitar.

I'd go to shows and perch myself as close to the guitarist as I could, to watch every move he made. For a couple of years, I was practicing two or three hours a day—even after I graduated college and went to work, I'd come home and lock myself away, playing records and my guitar.

I've always prided myself on a certain degree of dedication—if I set my mind to do something, I want to do it well. Ten years later, I suppose, you could say I did it with smack. Ten years after that, I did it on Wall Street. Right now, I was doing it on guitar.

What brought about the change? Why was I suddenly devoted to an instrument that I had hitherto thrown to one side? It's simple. It was the Beatles.

But not the Beatles themselves. They were great, but I was only a diehard fan for a few months. It was what they made possible that made the difference to me.

As far as I was concerned, the Beatles were like the Dolls in a lot of ways. They kicked down doors that had previously been closed and invited everyone else to come pouring through. (The difference, of course, is that the Dolls sat back and watched everyone pass them. The Beatles ran on ahead.)

It's difficult to explain just what a wasteland pop music was before the Beatles came along, if only because so many of the records from that era are now so firmly entrenched as "golden oldies" that people forget how much they disliked them at the time.

I had a few favorites. The Contours' "Do You Love Me" was a great record, and a lot of the Phil Spector things were terrific. But, as I said before, music was a recreational thing—you'd go to a party and they'd play things you liked, people like Gary U. S. Bonds, and then the Beach Boys popped up, and they'd play things you didn't like.

I liked some older stuff as well. Like Jerry Nolan, my brother William had musical tastes forged in the crucible of rock 'n' roll's first flowering. And growing up listening to the records he was playing, I liked a lot of it well enough.

But it never spoke to me—if anything, I preferred the kind of music our father enjoyed listening to. He loved Broadway musicals, and when we were growing up, a musical was the soundtrack to every Saturday morning while my parents were cleaning house. *Oklahoma*, *My Fair Lady*, all the Rodgers and Hammerstein stuff, *The King and I* . . . and dad didn't play them quietly, either. If anyone ever asks me where my love of loud music came from, I tell them that I can still hear those things blasting the shit out of the house.

So it was only when the Beatles came along that music stopped being background noise and became a lifestyle. And then the Rolling Stones came along, and that was what changed my perspective on pop—the first time I heard them, I was sold for life.

Then came the British Invasion, that unparalleled two- or three-year span during which every new record you heard seemed light years on from the last, and every fresh English import felt a little more outrageous or unusual than ever.

The Beatles with their long hair, the Stones with even longer locks, the Pretty Things, who looked practically female when they first appeared. Dylan—not a Briton or an invader, of course, but he learned from them, as they learned from him—with a nasal twang that no one over thirty would even dream of describing as singing, questioning everything we'd been taught to accept.

The Kinks, the Zombies, the Who, the lot. No longer the soundtrack to a teenage make-out party, music had transformed itself into an ongoing conversation between artist and audience, and its words spoke directly to anyone who listened.

It was a whole new dynamic. You didn't just play records to have something to dance to any longer; you listened to the lyrics and the playing. I started obsessing on the Stones, and when I got to college, of course, the place was filled with like-minded people.

The center of our universe was the college music room, which was where they conducted music lessons and which was dominated by the most enormous stereo system I had ever seen. There was a little alcove at the side, where you put the records on, but the music came through these enormous speakers, so it was a great place to listen.

When I first got there, that alcove was the preserve of the jazz and classical brigade, and the records I'd want to hear were few and far between.

Nevertheless, my friends and I were in there as often as we could be. We'd make requests, we'd complain about records we didn't like, and, gradually, we made our way into the midst of things until, ultimately, we *were* the people in the booth. There was a group of us, and maybe two or three others, a couple of Spanish guys, I remember. We took over, and we'd be playing the new albums that came out—the Beatles, the Stones, the Kinks, all the British Invasion bands as they developed into the musical giants they became.

We were not a wholly exclusive coterie. Every so often a newcomer would enter the room and impress us with either his knowledge of music or his taste. The late Albert Sce, for instance. Over the next few years—close to a decade in fact—Albert would rank among my greatest friends, but the first time I met him, he was this kid from Bensonhurst, two or three years behind me, who would just stand around listening.

He was a good looking kid, with long hair and all the new records; he made friends with everyone, and soon he was joining us in the control booth, helping select the music we'd play, and intriguing me even further when he let on that he was a bass player. A couple of the other guys had musical ambitions, but Albert really seemed to know what he was talking about. Soon, we were hanging out together as much as we could.

Of course other people would bring in new records as they came out—the first California groups, Midwest garage bands scoring their one and only hit, all of that. There was also a little contingent, two Italian kids and a Spanish guy who were the very first junkies I ever met. They liked very different music than we did, as well, so there was a little bit of friction, although it never got out of control. We used to refer to it as "the junkies versus the acid heads."

But we were the ones who controlled it, so if we didn't like a record we'd simply refuse to play it. And that's where I got to meet all the different people who played in bands.

Every spare dollar I had was spent on records—everything the Rolling Stones put out, most of the Beatles, a lot of everything else. At home, I'd play them to my brother Richie because, despite the age difference, he grew up on the same bands as I did, just at a later point in their career. I discovered the Stones with "Not Fade Away" and that moodily jacketed debut album. He found them for "Jumping Jack Flash" and *Beggars Banquet*, and you can bet I encouraged the discovery. I encouraged his guitar lessons, as well.

Or I'd go over to Albert's house to listen with him. And all the while, talking talking talking about the music. What it really meant, what it really said. And how great it would be to go to England, where everyone, we imagined, looked and dressed and talked exactly like this.

I grew my hair out, and even that was an act of rebellion, whether I realized the fact or not. My parents put up with it—like so many, I'd imagine, they decided it was just a phase and I'd come to my short-haired senses soon enough.

For instance, occasionally neighbors would tell my mother, "Oh, Walter looks awful with long hair," but she'd just tell them, "He does what he likes."

My father was less tolerant, however. My brothers and I didn't yet have cars of our own, so we had to use Dad's. Every so often, though, he'd get pissed off about my hair (and other things) and refuse to let me use the car. In fact, he'd grab the keys and go out to sit in the car himself.

That was as far as he would take his disapproval, though. The one time he did kick me out of the house because of my hair, my mother refused to cook his dinner until he let me back in. And if I tried to win him over to my way of thinking by showing him pictures of George Washington and Andrew Jackson with their hair down to their shoulders, he'd say, "Oh, that was the old days."

"The good old days," I'd reply.

Out in the wider world, however, I quickly grew accustomed to hearing shouts or whistles from the people I passed, that older generation to whom anything more flamboyant than a regulation buzz cut was just another symptom of the death of decorum, decency, and civilized society.

Most people were happy to leave it at that—an insult hurled from a passing car, a "get your hair cut" from an old man in a store, a "hello, ma'am" from a witty builder. One night in a bar with a friend from high school, however, I discovered just how far some people were prepared to go to make their disapproval known.

In truth, my hair really wasn't that bad. It was just beginning to get long, and I doubt it was even past my ears at the time. And we were just sitting, talking, minding our own business, when this guy simply marched up to me and punched me in the face. One blow, and he knocked out half of one of my front teeth. (I still have a partial cap there.)

My friend jumped out of the seats to try and grab him, and the bartender threw the guy out. She also gave me a free beer. And I was still sitting there wondering, "What the fuck?" And the fuck was: I had long hair. That's why he hit me.

I saw exactly the same thing ten years later when flying into London the night that the Sex Pistols swore on TV and one of the newspapers reported on the lorry driver who was so disgusted that he kicked in his screen. It was the gut reaction of the gutless moron. He couldn't confront the offense in person and probably wouldn't have dared if he could. But an innocent bystander, be it TV screen or skinny high school kid, that was a different matter entirely. Bam.

In a way, though, you could understand the older generation's disquiet. Overnight, everything that the average American teenager had been brought up to expect from life—or, more pertinently, everything life expected from the average American teenager—had been rewritten.

Particularly if you grew up, as I did, in what was effectively suburbia.

My mother, Eillien, was Irish and one of seven kids, two boys and five girls; my father, who was also named Walter, was half-Irish, half-German (hence the family name Luhr—I changed the spelling when I joined the Heartbreakers), and one of four children, two sisters and a brother who died at the Battle of the Bulge.

He worked as a retail banker, and home until I was ten was Queens Village, in East Queens, New York. Very residential, very middle class. Large, detached homes, big yards, long driveways. Later, in 1959, we moved to Floral Park, which was even more exclusive. But it was just as buttoned-up when it came to "freaks" and "hippies." The only real difference was that instead of yelling at you when you passed them, people would tut under their breath.

"Shouldn't be allowed. Tut tut."

My family was Catholic—very Catholic—and my upbringing followed suit. I was born in St. Mary Immaculate in Jamaica, Queens, on April 22, 1949; my first school was St. Joachim and Ann grammar, and after we moved to Floral Park, I transferred to St. Hedwig's, a largely Polish grammar school whose nuns did their best to teach me their native language, although I've forgotten most of it.

From there, I graduated to St. Mary's Boys High School, and the not particularly tender mercies of a band of religious brothers who thought nothing of smacking us around if they decided we were misbehaving.

None of which sounds especially remarkable, but that's because I don't think I was an especially remarkable kid. I did well enough at school to keep out of too much trouble, and if the brothers disapproved of my love of music, that was balanced by my equal love of sports.

Basketball was my number one, although I started too late to develop into a great player and was too short to play my favorite position—center. That was reserved for the biggest kids, as I routinely discovered when we played. But our team made its way through the local playground leagues, and it was only when I turned eighteen that I found myself playing less and less, primarily because that was the way the game was organized at school.

The younger you were, the more opportunities there were to become involved in competitive playing. But the leagues grew more selective as you grew older, and by the time I was a college freshman, I'd more or less stopped—that was the last year in which I played in any league.

I wasn't happy about it, either. The notion that, if I'd had a little more time, I might have made some kind of career from the sport never really left me. In fact, in London with the Heartbreakers a decade later, I was convinced that everything was grinding to a halt, and the only disappointment I had to compare it to was the end of my basketball "career."

I carried on living at home throughout my first years at Fordham University, carpooling the forty-minute commute to college with a few friends who lived locally. For my junior year, however, I moved into an off-campus apartment with a bunch of hippies I knew and with whom I spent my free time lying on the floor for five hours, completely spaced out.

I had discovered LSD.

I'd taken it a few times with some kids I grew up with in Floral Park, but that apartment is where I got into it on a more weekly basis. I used to get together with one of the guys living there, named George. We'd drop acid and then we'd play those early Mothers of Invention albums, *Freak Out!*, *Absolutely Free*, and *We're Only In It for the Money*, and you would not believe what they used to do to my trips, driving them so crazy that I was convinced Zappa was doing it deliberately. I could imagine him gathering a bunch of freaks together, filling them with acid, and then playing them different things until he got the reaction he required.

Albert was my other partner in acid. Every Friday after lunch, we'd go out to the botanical garden alongside the college, a huge park with a giant greenhouse where they'd stage exhibitions. There were miles of pathways you could walk around for hours, and every Friday afternoon, that was where we'd be, tripping.

From there, we'd head back to campus, to the big music room, where we'd play records till ten, which was when we'd leave for the late show at the Fillmore, deep in the bowels of Manhattan. Then, with our heads full of music, we'd move on to Chinatown at four in the morning for a beer.

So, like I said, a normal kid leading a normal life, at least by late-1960s standards. I certainly never got hung up on anything—a bit of pot, a bit of acid, speed a few times. It was rare that I got screwed up on it, and the few times I did, I'd throw up and be fine.

It was 1968 or so now, which means things had changed considerably over the last few years. The Beatles had released *Sergeant Pepper* and set everyone racing toward psychedelia . . . then the Stones came out with *Their Satanic Majesties Request* and sent a lot of people running away from it again.

The short-lived Summer of Love became a far longer winter of discontent, with student riots in Europe, the war in Vietnam, peace marches in America, the chaos of the Democratic Convention in Chicago, and the assassination of Bobby Kennedy. And overhanging everything, the threat of the draft.

You cannot imagine how it felt to be a teen in those days, going through high school knowing that if you didn't get into college, you'd be going to war. And even if you did get in, you were only exempt until you graduated. It was a shadow that was cast over an entire generation, and all the more so because every time you turned on the television or picked up the paper, the body count was splashed across the headlines.

A few of the kids I was at school with were killed in Vietnam, and I doubt there are many people my age who cannot say the same thing. It was so arbitrary, too. You'd get up one morning and there would be the letter: "Greetings from Uncle Sam, please present yourself at such and such an address on such and such a day . . ." I had friends who spent great swaths of their final school years plotting ways of getting out of the draft—escaping to Canada, announcing they were gay, faking an illness, losing a limb—there was no end to the lengths that people were willing to go to.

I was born in 1949, which means that if I hadn't gone to college, I could have been sent out there in 1967. As it was, the year I graduated, 1970, was the year in which a new method was brought in to determine who should be sent out to fight, and possibly die—a lottery. Every birthdate was assigned a number, and then, with all the razzmatazz of the world's sickest game show, the drawing of the numbers would be broadcast live on TV. First prize—a bullet in the head.

I was lucky. Out of the 365 possible numbers in the lottery, my birth date came out 316th. I was never called up. So many of my friends were not so fortunate, however.

That, then, was the world that music soundtracked, and the great thing was that although the riots and the fighting settled down, the music never did, not for three long years and, in some quarters, even longer.

The Jeff Beck Group with a skinny guy named Rod Stewart on vocals.

Humble Pie, fresh out of the Small Faces et al., Stevie Marriott and Peter Frampton at their hard hitting best. Their *Rockin' the Fillmore* remains the greatest live album ever made, all the more so because I was there the night they recorded it.

Chicken Shack with Christine McVie; Fleetwood Mac with Peter Green and then with Christine McVie. I always liked Fleetwood Mac—not just the Peter Green period but after that as well, when McVie was doing most of the vocals, before Lindsay Buckingham and Stevie Nicks joined. I hated them after that.

I used to wait impatiently for John Mayall to release a new album even though I've never been able to play one of his records all the way through. Fucking awful. It was the guitarists who filed through his band, the Bluesbreakers, who kept my devotion alive—Eric Clapton, Peter Green, Mick Taylor. Remember. American radio rarely played any genuine American bluesmen—Robert Johnson, Charlie Patton, Howlin' Wolf, the true pioneers of the music. These British approximations were the closest we could get to them.

They served their purpose, though.

I saw the Yardbirds out on Long Island, at a place called the Action House. Jimmy Page was playing guitar for them by then, yet there were probably no more than ten people in the room, watching in awe as Page pulled off "White Summer" and so much more.

Ten Years After—Alvin Lee was a great guitarist. Procol Harum with Robin Trower. Savoy Brown. The Kinks, back in the United States for the first time since the Musicians' Union blackballed them back in 1965—their Fillmore gig was really special. Page again in Led Zeppelin, before they had a record out. The Who before they did *Tommy*, and after, for *Who's Next*. Strange how such a great band could interrupt their most glorious sequence of concerts and records by dropping a turkey like that in the midst of it.

You've probably already noticed: my tastes were almost exclusively British. I liked the Byrds a bit, and Dylan (although it took a while and a lot of dedication). Jefferson Airplane had one or two songs, but I never liked the guitar playing. That was about it for American rock. The only guitarists who had the right sound and style were the British ones, and that's what I was excited about.

Even Jimi Hendrix . . . I liked him; I saw him a few times in New York and bought a few of his records. But he was something from another planet, a total one-off. I knew so many other guitar players who were in absolute awe, but I never wanted to sound like Hendrix. He was so strange. I loved his playing and inventiveness, but I never sat down to figure out his solos. They never grabbed me. Not when there were so many other people around.

The concerts I attended, of course, reflected my record collection. Naturally, not every gig was wall-to-wall British brilliance—occasionally you'd be stuck with something else . . . Vanilla Fudge, the Grateful Dead, the turgid dross that was America's answer to everything. I knew so many people who thought the Dead were great; they'd rave about them and they'd sit there for hours listening. I usually fell asleep after ten minutes.

Every time I saw them, I'd do my best to find something I liked about them, but every time the same thing happened. I fell asleep. Solos that went nowhere, these hippy yokel jams that totally turned me off. It was so hokey. The other thing was that they didn't know how to dress at all. Nobody had a cool style.

You'd put up with it, though, because they were simply a part of the bill, and the next band would be along soon enough. Plus it was an opportunity to look around at everybody else in the audience—what they were wearing, how their hair was styled, and hey! There's that kid again. The one I see at every show I go to.

Chapter Two
THAT KID

He had one of those faces that you would probably recognize anywhere, good looking with a goofy grin, eyes that smoldered when he wasn't wearing shades. But it was his style that really stood out—vintage chic crossbred with the latest London threads. That and his taste in music.

He dressed like he had an expense account at Granny Takes a Trip, and not the New York branch, either. He'd made at least one trip to London, I think around 1971, and he did a lot of shopping there as well. We never spoke; we rarely came within less than a few yards of one another. But he was in the front row or there-abouts for every British band I went to see.

Albert and I ran into him all the time. Every concert I ever went to in New York, and further afield as well. The Atlantic City Rock Festival in 1969, with the Crazy World of Arthur Brown, Creedence, Zappa, and Joe Cocker. There he was. The Fillmore for the Kinks. The Fillmore for Humble Pie. And when I went to see the Stones' movie *Gimme Shelter*, I couldn't believe it. There he was again, only this time he was onscreen, raised up on his girlfriend Janice's shoulders, unmistakable, large as life.

I even saw him at Woodstock, and when you consider how many people were there—half a million, covered in mud—that was a miracle in itself. But that was the thing about him. He stood out in any crowd.

Again, we never spoke; we were never introduced. The closest we ever came to that was the occasional nod across the room, kindred spirits acknowledging one another but too caught up in the moment to actually say hello. It was like clockwork, though. If a British band was in town, he'd be there, and every time, he caught my eye.

His dress sense was astonishing. You'd see a photo of, say, Rod Stewart in a pair of sensational flares, and the next time you went to a show, you'd see this kid with even better ones. Marc Bolan would have a pair of cool boots, but guess who'd have even cooler ones that evening. I did my best to keep up with the fashions of the day, and I don't think I did too badly. But this kid could out-dress anyone, which was no mean feat. That stuff was expensive. He managed it, though.

Woodstock itself was an amazing experience.

I went with some friends from Floral Park who I used to smoke pot with in high school, and we were smart about it, too, making sure to arrive on-site a week before the festival began to be certain we had a good spot to camp in.

We found ourselves a place alongside the big pond that lay behind the stage, put up the tent, and had a great time. But the closer the big day came, the more crowded the entire site seemed, until all of a sudden you realized that you couldn't get out of the place.

It was like being under siege, just a wall of mud and filth and stink. The toilets, for example. The organizers brought in an army of portables, and they were fine to begin with. But then the mob descended and the rain started, and those little cubicles became another world. All of them were overflowing, to the point when, on the last night of music, I went into one to take a dump and the shit was piled three feet higher than the top of the toilet! I couldn't even work out how the last few people actually got up there to do it. They must have been hanging from the ceiling.

Hygiene went out of the window. The pond that we thought was so picturesque when we arrived became a communal bath tub, with so many people coming down to wash, that what had once been a reasonably clear pond full of fish was now a stinking hole full of black water and dead fish, killed off by all the soap people were using.

And just to make it all that little bit more disgusting, word had spread around the local farms that hippie women were bathing naked in the pond, so the locals would drive up in their cars and sit there watching, and probably jerking off.

We spent as much time as we could around our tent, because it was less crowded there—everybody else wanted to be out front to watch while the bands changed over. We only ventured out there for the bands we wanted to see; hence, I missed seeing the Who doing *Tommy*, and I was righteously proud of that fact.

The occasions when we did join the front-of-stage melee, however, were an experience in themselves. The whole place stunk because it had rained so much, and the air was choked by the odor of hot sweat, filthy flesh, and, over it all, the moldering sleeping bags that lay steaming on the slope. It was as if someone had decided to stage a concert inside a giant cesspit.

But we saw all the bands we wanted to, including Hendrix at eight in the morning on the final day, and then stayed on in the field for three or four days afterward to give the roads a chance to clear. And in that crowd of half a million kids, most of them coated in mud and filth . . . there he was again. That kid.

I was still attending Fordham throughout this period, but switching my major from chemistry to English had freed up a lot of time.

My original course hadn't been so bad at first. I enjoyed mixing compounds, and the processes fascinated me. But more and more, I found myself spending less time in the lab and more at a desk, tormenting myself with advanced calculus.

English, on the other hand, slipped into the love of reading I'd nurtured all my life. One of the first adult books I ever read, when I was about nine, was *20,000 Leagues Under the Sea* by Jules Verne. I could barely understand half the words, but I was hooked.

Later, I fell in love with *The Iliad* and *The Odyssey* as well as Bullfinch's *Mythology*, and a few years on, in London with the Heartbreakers, I remember the bewildered expression of a visiting journalist when he spotted the copy of *À la recherche du temps perdu* (*In Search of Lost Time*) that lay on the coffee table.

"Is that Proust you're reading?" the writer asked, struggling to reconcile the hard-bitten New York junkie punk with the distinctly high-brow French novelist. I nodded but suggested he didn't include it in his piece. A lot of punks had a hard time even accepting that their idols could read. Proust would have alienated them forever.

My greatest passion, however, was English Victoriana, that great swath of wordsmiths that flourished throughout the nineteenth century, and whose work in many cases remains as vibrant today as it was back then. Does a year go by without another adaptation of Charles Dickens showing up on television?

Some of the authors became an integral part of my studies; others I simply read for fun. But they all contributed to my understanding of my course work.

I knew, at the end of the day, that there really wasn't much to be done with an English degree beyond going into teaching, but that wasn't so bad—my brother William was on course to becoming a college professor, and there were a lot worse things I could do than follow in his footsteps. In the meantime, I'd just carry on with what I was doing.

I took a part-time job—stock boy (and later cashier) at the Cowshed, a little dairy that sold milk, bread, and candy in Floral Park—and I found my first band as well, the immortally named Bloodbath . . . the Bloodbath Revue for the first gig.

Albert was our bassist. A friend from the days of acid and the Mothers was one of the singers we used. He had now graduated from acid to become the first junkie I ever made music with. Mike Cefola joined me on guitar, and the drummer was George Reisz. That was the core of the band. But a kid named Jim Spaeth played bass with us sometimes, and we had another singer we could call upon, John Swenson, who went on to become a successful music writer.

I call Bloodbath "immortal" because I've never heard of another band with the same name, and I still can't figure out why. It was perfect, particularly if you recall the headlines that blazed at the end of the sixties, with Manson and Altamont and the continued slaughter in Vietnam. In fact, maybe that's why we never went very far. But we played a gig at Fordham just before I graduated, and John Swenson landed us some shows at Manhattan College, where he was a student. There were a few small clubs around the Bronx and Westchester, including Yonkers, as well, and though crowds were usually small, it was a good band.

Our repertoire was what audiences demanded at that time— cover versions. I'd sprung for a Gibson SG guitar, had mastered a few Stones numbers, and could turn out a more than reasonable approximation of Zeppelin's "Communication Breakdown."

I was happy, too, because over the next couple of years, in other bands of that ilk, I found myself developing a definite style of my own, simply from playing songs by other people.

Every guitarist finds his way by playing along with records; I just took it further, and there's nothing like a drunken bar full of frat kids wanting to hear their favorite Deep Purple number to let you know whether or not your musicianship is up to scratch.

I graduated college in summer 1970 and took a job as a cab driver in the Bronx. I didn't stick it out for long, though, just a couple of months during which time I was robbed twice, once with a knife held to my throat. That was it for me. Not that I'd ever intended to make a career of it.

Teaching was still a possibility, but I wasn't sure. America was just beginning to drift into recession; jobs were becoming harder to find, and were growing harder to keep as well, as belts began to tighten and employers set out to shed weight.

But I heard that the federal government was still hiring, at least for now, so one day I made my way into downtown Manhattan, to Federal Plaza, and I filled out every job application I could lay my hands on. Then I sat back to wait.

It would be a few months before I heard back from any of them, I was warned, so I took a job as a stock boy at Alexander's department store while I waited. After three months of that, the Postal Service called. I'd been accepted to hand-sort mail from 4 p.m. till midnight in a warehouse in Flushing, Queens, which put a crimp into my gig going, for sure, but it was only for a couple of months, until I was transferred to a regular post office.

Finally, however, the job I'd been hoping for when I filled in all those forms got in touch. The FDA (Food and Drug Administration) had accepted my application.

The FDA is the heartbeat of American consumerism. Every ingredient in every pill you swallow, soda you drink, sandwich you eat, burger you grill—I could go on like this forever!—is there because it has been approved by the FDA. If it hasn't, you shouldn't go anywhere near it.

That's also true about some of the things that *have* been approved, but that's another book. What mattered to me was that although I'd dropped my chemistry major, I had nevertheless accumulated sufficient credits to be awarded a minor. That, and agreeing to take more classes, was enough for me to be taken on at the FDA offices on the waterfront in Sunset Park, Brooklyn, about forty-five minutes from my home. The offer arrived just in time, too. That fall, the government announced a hiring freeze.

I started as a technician, but I would quickly qualify as a chemist on the food side of things, testing different products as they came into the country to ensure they adhered to federal guidelines.

If they did, they might eventually be approved for sale in the United States. If they didn't, they'd be added to the list of prohibited items. It was a fascinating job, if a little frightening, too.

Labeling on products was important. For example, there was this stuff that came from China that was called "mouse wine" because, at the bottom of the bottle, there'd be a couple of tiny mouse fetuses. It was supposed to be really healthy, and the manufacturer made the most outrageous claims on the packaging about how it cured bad dreams, it cured your relatives, it did this, that, and the other thing, absolutely none of which was backed up by any scientific evidence whatsoever. So we'd reject it until they came up with more realistic claims.

I was also astonished at how many chemicals—no, let's be blunt, how many poisons—crept into foodstuffs, even in places like Europe, which would never be permitted onto American supermarket shelves.

It wasn't, after all, merely a matter of picking up the box and reading the list of ingredients. In fact, we behaved as though there was no such list. Everything had to be stripped back to its basic compounds and analyzed from scratch. I would think about that a lot in later years once I started traveling abroad and sampling the local fare. I swear, I ate things in the United Kingdom that would never have passed as fit for human consumption back home.

The process was simple. You'd take a piece of a cracker or whatever, boil it down and mix it up, and then add certain chemicals that could make things float to the surface, which you would then look at through the microscope.

Usually it was bits of beetle or ant parts, or if you were analyzing anything involving figs, it would be bits of wasp. There is actually a type of wasp that lives in figs, and it would inevitably be mashed down into the paste that was then packaged for sale. I think our rule was no more than twenty-five wasp parts per serving. Think of that the next time you're tucking into a Fig Newton.

But that microscope served other purposes, too. I'd gone away for a few days with some friends, staying in a cabin on a lake in upstate New York. I had my own little room and it was great. A week or two after we returned, however, I noticed that my legs and crotch were feeling itchy.

I had a look and couldn't see anything, so I assumed it was an allergy. But it kept getting worse, and a week or so later, I started to notice these little spots appearing . . . and moving around! I grabbed one with a pair of tweezers, put it under the microscope, and there was this little crab thing, with six tiny legs waving around. I was screaming into the microscope, "What the fuck is this?" I'd caught crabs, and it was probably from the bed in that cabin because I hadn't actually slept with anyone for a while.

I was still playing in cover bands at night; one, during the summer of 1972, might have even been the first American group ever to try their hand at Bowie's "Suffragette City" and "Hang On to Yourself," picking them up after hearing them on the radio one day, without actually knowing who—or, given the nature of his bisexual spaceman Ziggy Stardust image, what—Bowie was. The hype that preceded his first American tour was still a couple of months away; they were just great rock songs by the guy who'd sung that "Space Oddity" number a few years before.

At the same time, however, some of us at least were ready for what Bowie offered.

It was late 1971, maybe early 1972, when Albert and I first discovered the Mercer Arts Center on Mercer Street, deep inside Greenwich Village, and it quickly became a favorite hangout.

It was not necessarily the music that attracted us. There were only a handful of bands playing regularly there at the time, with Suicide and Warhol superstar Eric Emerson's Magic Tramps probably the best known among them.

The place was like a rabbit warren. Every corridor and every floor seemed to secrete another room or three, and you never knew what you would find in any of them. Experimental theater, wild poetry, electronic noise , drag acts, sex shows . . . anything and everything that fell beneath the banner of the arts was permissible, and the more underground its origins, the better.

Neither was the Mercer alone in catering for this particular world. There were very few clubs and venues in Manhattan at that time that spared a thought for the truly "unknown" artist—even Max's Kansas City, so synonymous today with the Warhol circus, was making ends meet with the same old same old, aging bluesmen and aspiring folkies, or the latest half-hyped record-company hopeful.

So people were putting on shows themselves, in lofts and basements in the Bowery and Soho, neighborhoods in which it wasn't really wise to walk alone late at night but which you'd venture into regardless if you thought the reward was worthwhile.

Not every event that you risked life and limb to see would, in fact, repay you. As much as an utterly unfettered creative environment allows everybody to have a voice (much like the Internet of today), it does so without editor, filter, or quality control. (Again, much like the Internet of today.)

It was fantastically liberating to realize that *anybody* could put on an exhibition, mount a play, or stage a concert without first having to be ground through the machinery of bookers and gallery owners. But sometimes, you understood why that's not always the worst thing that can happen.

A loft party was probably where Albert and I saw the New York Dolls for the first time. It may have been at the Mercer first, in the tiny Oscar Wilde Room, and the loft show came a few nights later, but I don't think so.

Either way, the Dolls had a loft at 119 Christie Street, above a noodle shop in Chinatown, and you can tell what kind of neighborhood that was because the building looked out over a homeless shelter. In fact, the band had been forced to board up all the windows because of the bricks and rocks that the bums used to throw through them whenever a rehearsal kept them awake.

We found the address, paid a couple of bucks to the girl who was collecting the admission fee (or wasn't, depending upon how well she knew the latest visitor), and made our way into the loft.

It was already full, a potpourri of onlookers that ran the gauntlet between kids off the street who were dressed like we were; a handful of hookers from down the road, who'd come along for the party; drag queens whom the band had encountered elsewhere on their own perambulations; and other denizens of the loft party scene, either repaying the Dolls for visiting their last show or drumming up custom for the next one.

And up onstage with a guitar in his hand, dressed to the nines and a few numbers beyond that . . . there's that kid *again!*

It was strange, though. All the times I'd seen him at every concert I went to, stretching back two, almost three years, I'd often thought he looked like he ought to be in a band. It never ever occurred to me that maybe he already was.

Somebody told me his name was Johnny Thunders, and that made sense as well. Looking at the way he dressed, listening to the way he played, what else could it have been?

Chapter Three

WATCHING THE DOLLS

I wasn't Johnny's only admirer. In his book *There's No Bones in Ice Cream*, his bandmate Sylvain Sylvain recalls: "In terms of looks and what I suppose you'd call 'star power,' he was way ahead [of the rest of us]—the sharpest mover, the sharpest dresser. I swear, he could have been the best designer in the world, because the way he was dressing was so intimate. He would iron his clothes perfectly, and arrange them meticulously in his closet. He might have looked as though he'd just fallen out of bed, but believe me, he knew what he was doing."

As the New York Dolls took their first steps onto the scene, however, he was one of the few who did. The universe into which the band so brashly crashed at the start of 1972 was still New York's deepest secret, deep underground, a world light-years away from the leftover hippie groups, aspiring singer-songwriters, and straight-ahead rockers who percolated around the mainstream.

It was only as the year rolled on, and as the Dolls themselves began getting their name around, that anybody outside their most immediate confines began paying attention. By which I mean the press, the clubs, and the music industry in general.

And other bands, of course. The rise of the Dolls on the New York scene coincided with the rise of glam rock in the United Kingdom, and the Dolls—with two confirmed musical Anglophiles in their ranks, Johnny and fellow guitarist Sylvain Sylvain—traced its trajectory with unfettered delight.

It was not because they wanted to emulate it, or climb aboard its bandwagon. Rather, it was because what they heard in the music of Marc Bolan and T Rex (who, that early in the game, was all that glam had to show for itself . . . even Bowie was still largely unknown) was the same glitter-clad car crash of fifties riffs,

Stonesy grooves and seventies sexuality that they'd been aiming for in their own sound. The fact that two bands, on two continents, had fashioned the same kind of sound independently was nothing more than coincidence. Or, perhaps, serendipity.

Neither the Dolls nor T Rex would be alone for long. In the United Kingdom, bands like the Sweet, Gary Glitter, and, of course, David Bowie, were swift to grab their own share of Bolan's spangled swagger; in New York, the Planets, Queen Elizabeth, and the guys who would be Kiss upped their own game accordingly.

The difference was that, for all their talent and creativity, the British, even Bowie, could only take the music so far. They already had major record deals; they were already looking toward chart success and superstardom.

The Dolls, on the other hand, didn't seem to care. No American record label, we all believed, was ever going to take a chance on this lot, and the Dolls themselves seemed to agree. They dressed however they wanted and found an audience that wanted to dress like them. They brought the three-minute pop song back to the city and then played it so fast that they cut it down to two. They dispensed with the twenty-minute drum solos and the yards and yards of guitar showmanship that mainstream rock had now degenerated into.

The Dolls were really the grandmothers of punk rock, in a sense, because they were the first band to show that kids could pick up a guitar and not know how to play it like Jimmy Page or fucking Yes and could start a band and get popular and have people enjoy the music.

Because they created a scene as well.

It was glam rock after the bomb had dropped. And only roaches and Dolls were left alive.

It would be another couple of the years before the Mercer Street Arts Center collapsed, literally falling into the street at the height of a New York rush hour. But it was so fitting that it did, because what else could it have done? A venue like that couldn't just gracefully close and be calmly demolished. It needed to go out with a bang.

For me, the place became like a drug. A few years later, I told my diary: "Rock 'n' roll is a base art form. Clubs are always in out-of-the-way places and are usually dumps. People don't go to be uplifted, but just to lose themselves. Rock is really a drug for most, an excuse to go out and get drunk or stoned." The Mercer epitomized that notion.

All those floors, all those rooms, all those performances. In one room, Jayne (but then Wayne) County with a toilet seat around her neck and garbage pinned to her wig, wearing shoes shaped like cocks as she replayed the Dave Clark 5 through a wall of sex and sleaze.

In another, Suicide mainlining yelping electronics into scarred and yowling vocals.

In another, Patti Smith breathlessly poet-rapping, while Lenny Kaye's guitar fed back in perfect harmony. Or it might be the Modern Lovers, down from Boston and channeling the Velvet Underground so perfectly it was sometimes hard to tell the difference. Pure Garbage, Holly Woodlawns, and Elda Gentile crashing sixties girl groups into glorious outrage. Warhol superstar Ultra Violet. And presiding over it all, downstairs in the main theater, the Dolls dancing trash, pills, and Frankenstein through a wall made out of riffs and thrift store cast-offs.

All these rooms, all these performances, all these different approaches, a veritable festival of ultra-weird glam. I thought music had been exciting in the sixties. It had barely gotten out of the blocks yet.

Before the Dolls, there was no New York scene. There was the Brill Building set, which was quintessential New York from a musical standpoint. There were a few jazz and folk clubs in the Village. But in terms of a rock club scene or a street sound, there was nothing. It was just local bands playing whatever music they liked, and if half of them sounded like Foghat, then that was just the way it went.

But now there was the Dolls, and when you looked out into their audience, you didn't simply see fans. You saw aspiring musicians watching the show and figuring they could do much the same.

"Wow, if I can start a band and learn three chords, maybe I can be top of the scene overnight."

I used to see Steven Tyler watching the Dolls when Aerosmith was starting, and Kiss as well. It was as though the Dolls had ripped up every rule book they had ever read and told everyone to start all over again. I was no different. Suddenly, cover bands felt inadequate, just a way of marking time. I wanted to find out what else I could do.

First, however, I had a vacation planned.

It was the summer of 1973, and New York was still the most thrilling place on earth—and not only because we'd all got it wrong six or nine months earlier. The Dolls did land a record deal, with a real major label, and now their first album was out.

They'd had their trials. Visiting England shortly before Christmas '72, they lost drummer Billy Murcia to a tragic, traumatic drug overdose. He was replaced by Jerry Nolan, a New York veteran who, if you wanted to talk technique, was probably the best musician in the band.

Maybe the band lost their innocence there, along with that weird shuffle with which Billy's drumming style had powered their best songs. Jerry was older than his bandmates, less prone to spectacle, and more solidly rocking, too. I saw the Dolls before they left for England, and they were still a fucked up art experiment pretending to be a rock band. I saw them again once Jerry had joined, and they weren't pretending any more.

I still loved them, though, and I wondered what Europe had made of them. There wasn't much glam rock making its way across the ocean, certainly not as much as you could read about in those expensive imports of *Melody Maker* that turned up two months late on different newsstands around the city.

Even in Manhattan's hippest record stores, you had to actively search for new music because it was rarely going to be played on the radio. Word of mouth for the most part, courageous club DJs if you were lucky—there were a few, Jayne County among them, who kept a close watch on what was happening in England and raced to be the first to play, say, the new Sweet or T Rex record in America.

But what I had heard still felt tame compared to the Dolls— even Bowie, who name-checked Billy Dolls in a song from his latest album. Maybe when I got over there myself, I'd find out if there was more.

My vacation was not wholly impulsive. After two years analyzing strange foreign foodstuffs, I was being transferred across the FDA, into the drugs division. I celebrated by booking two weeks away.

My own drug use at the time, such as it was, remained at the same social/recreational level as it had been since college. A little pot, the occasional tab, the odd upper or downer, depending upon my schedule. Enough to get through a busy day at work and a late night at a club. In fact, as I packed the belongings I figured would see me through two weeks of traveling, a couple of pills were among the last things I gathered, sewn into the lining of my denim jacket.

I had no concrete plans; it was just my acoustic guitar and I, with a giant backpack stuffed with clothes I would barely wear, going where I went and seeing what I saw. Which, for the first two days, was very little. My first stop was Amsterdam; I arrived in mid-afternoon and checked into a hostel in the center of town. By nightfall I was in jail.

It was a simple process. I checked into the hostel, scored a tiny tinfoil wrap of coke from someone I met there, and then made my way to Dam Square, renowned at that time as the first stop for every tourist who wanted more than a guided tour of the city's mainstream attractions. Soon I was deep in conversation with a couple of Rastas, and I suppose I should have realized that they were actually local drug dealers. I didn't, but the police did. They swooped and I was arrested.

The coke went straight into my mouth, and although I couldn't quite bring myself to swallow it, I did manage to keep it out of sight all the while the cops were talking to me, and transporting me to the police station. Safely locked in my cell, I quickly secreted it in a crack in the wall.

The uppers and downers in the lining of my jacket, however, did not evade detection. Two days I spent in the cell, at the end of which I was informed that I was going to be deported.

But not immediately. I had money, I had my guitar, and they knew I was a tourist. I did have to surrender my passport, but I was given permission to hang out in Amsterdam for as long as I wanted, and then they'd put me on a plane out of there.

So I stayed a week or so, just bumming around, wandering the streets and clubs and attending a few gigs, and then I reported to the police station. The intention, they told me, was to fly me directly back to New York City, but really, all they wanted to do was get me out of the country. I persuaded them to put me on a flight to London instead. I still had a week of vacation ahead of me, after all.

They agreed, so that was my next stop—a hostel in Earl's Court and a few days just touring the city and beyond. I hitchhiked out to Stonehenge and spent a night in Bristol, out in the west of the country.

I rode the London underground and visited the museums. But most of all, I walked the streets, soaking in the city and reliving every book I had ever read in which London was the unsung hero.

I traced the journeys taken by Charles Dickens in his explorations of the Victorian city and those that Sherlock Holmes had scoured as he investigated another mystery. I followed the stories of Henry James and Agatha Christie, recognizing the street names and buildings that they had mentioned. I went window shopping on the King's Road and marched the length of every street market I could find, just soaking in the sheer London-ness of the place.

I wallowed in the history. Phil Marcade, the singer with the Senders, once said I could tell you the exact dates of every one of Napoleon's battles, and it was true, I could. A lot of other things, too. It was one thing to read history, though, and another to stand in its shadow.

I marveled at the architecture, I stared spellbound at the monuments, and—with my FDA training foremost in my mind—I recoiled in horror from what passed as food.

Traveling on a budget, I didn't have the opportunity to actually eat anything decent, so I effectively subsisted on the English equivalent of fast food—fish and chips, which was generally palatable so long as you didn't think too hard, and the Wimpy Bar restaurants, where the burgers tasted only marginally better than the chipped Formica tabletops. They couldn't even make peas! They tasted like cardboard, to go with the potatoes that tasted like mashed candle wax, and . . . and . . . and . . .

It took all my willpower not to amend the menu with quotation marks around everything that was described as "food" in those places, as a warning to fellow American visitors. "Coffee." "Vegetables." And, worst of all, "beef." Food in London back then was the worst fucking food in the world, and I can say that because a few years later (it didn't improve) I would wind up spending another eighteen months still trying to digest the stuff.

But I was having a tremendous time, so much so that, as the second week of my vacation drew to a close, I decided I wanted more. I contacted my supervisor at work and announced that my passport had been stolen, explaining that I was stranded until the embassy could issue me a new one. It would be at least another couple of weeks. And then I hitchhiked back to mainland Europe.

Paris first, and then to Barcelona, sitting with a bunch of hippies on Los Ramblos, in the awe-inspiring shadow of Gaudí's Sagrada Família, playing songs by Dylan and Free. And from there to Morocco, me and a kid I met on the ferry, playing our guitars in the desert in the middle of the night.

I loved Morocco, but it was culture shock all the way. I hate to dwell on bathrooms, after my description of the facilities at Woodstock, but the toilets in Morocco, in their own way, were even more bizarre—holes in the ground with these little places where you put your feet as you squatted over a big hole.

Physically, it's a far more practical way of doing the deed, but I'd hate to have been an old person with vertigo!

The poverty was overwhelming. The bus would pull into a town and the beggars would literally swarm it. They were kids for the most part, many of them deformed in some way, an eye missing here, a leg missing there. But you couldn't give them anything, no matter how badly you wanted to, because then they'd follow you all over town, expecting more. It was a nightmare.

The buses themselves were an experience, people with chickens and cats and baskets of food. There was a roof over your head, of course, but it was almost like being in the open air, with poultry flying around your head the entire time.

It was a whole different world. One time, I was visiting a market with a French kid I'd met up with, and we literally walked into someone's house, thinking it was the local movie theater, or a deli, something like that. We were walking around this big central room, and suddenly women started emerging out of the doorways, shouting at us in Arabic, which of course we didn't understand. I thought they were going to beat the shit out of us.

We were doing our best to explain and I think we finally got through, because all of a sudden the women burst out laughing at us. By the time the menfolk arrived, the situation had been well and truly defused and we went on our way. But we'd be a lot more careful about walking through inviting doorways after that.

Finally, it was time to go home, back to New York, and to my new career as a drug tester.

The prospect of the new job excited me. I'd be working with imported pharmaceuticals, and therein lies one of the great misunderstandings about the FDA. I cannot count the number of times I would tell somebody that I worked there only to be greeted with a knowing smile and a request for free samples.

The fact is that the majority of drugs we were testing were effectively the same ones you could simply buy over the counter. Prescription-only substances would cross our desks, but there are far more dramatically-named placebos and sugar pills being flung onto the market than there ever could be narcotics.

Furthermore, anything illegal, or that was considered addictive, was the preserve of either the Bureau of Alcohol, Tobacco, and Firearms, or the Drug Enforcement Administration (DEA), both altogether different operations than ours—although there would be one occasion when some cocaine found its way into the office and then, very mysteriously, found its way out again.

Everybody who'd had access to it was called in for questioning, myself included, and I never did discover if they found out who made off with it. But my coworkers and I had our suspicions, and I'm sure the higher-ups did as well. Oh, and it wasn't me, in case you're wondering.

My musical ambitions remained high; they had, in fact, grown even more elaborate after my visit to London. In the United States, you could go weeks without hearing anything exciting. In London, on the other hand, those records were inescapable. I don't know how the locals themselves felt about it, but for me, there was nothing better than walking past a boutique and hearing Suzi Quatro, Wizzard, Bowie, *whoever*, blaring out onto the street.

New York, even with the Dolls now in full flight and the rest of the crew piling up behind them, seemed drab by comparison— probably because it was suddenly clear just how parochial the whole scene was. In the heart of Max's Kansas City, surrounded by the freaks and the fanciful, with Johansen yowling "Jet Boy" at ear-splitting volume, it was easy to believe that this was the center of the universe. That everybody dressed like this, talked like this, sounded like this.

But then you'd step back onto the street, and nothing would have changed. The same cabs, the same street lights, the same people shuffling from here to there, the same hookers and homeless, and the same interminable soundtrack of FM rock and AM pop pounding wherever you went.

I wanted something more.

Chapter Four

HEARTBROKEN

It was late 1974. I was still playing in covers bands out on Long Island, and I'd just started seeing a girl from Yonkers named Diane. We were playing a show up there and she was out front, looking gorgeous as she shimmied provocatively. I looked out for her after the show and got her number, and the following night we went out to an after-hours club.

It felt as though things were falling into place. Diane and I would go out, or stay in, depending on our mood, and at the same time I was actively looking for new musical opportunities, going through the ads in various papers and magazines, just waiting for the right one to come along. "Guitarist needed for the best band in the world."

It was a long search through an awful lot of time-wasters. There was one band out in Brooklyn, however, whose ad in the *Village Voice* sounded promising. So did their music. Yes, they wore their influences like a neon-lit jacket, but I'm sure that I did as well. They were writing their own material, though, and we quickly gelled as people.

Let's give it a go.

The band was called the Stray Cats—and no, they were neither the first or last to bear that name. Unlike Bloodbath. The singer was a guy named Chris, but the heart of the band was our two guitarists, myself and this guy named Freddie Bell, whose twin brother, it turned out, was a drummer named Marc, whose own groups I'd seen a few times over the years.

First there was Dust, who was the "next big thing" for about five minutes in 1971; they used to hang out at this bar called Nobody's on Bleecker Street, picking up the action that the bigger names—Robert Plant, Rod Stewart—left in their wake. Then came

Estus, who'd just recorded an album with Andrew Loog Oldham. Later, of course, Marc would play with Richard Hell before becoming a Ramone.

Freddie, on the other hand, never lived up to his potential. When he was good, he was terrific. But he also had mental health issues. You never knew where you were with him, and the medication he received and the treatment he was given to even out his temperament did him as much damage as good.

Soon, and it was very soon after I joined the band, he couldn't even play guitar anymore, so we replaced him with this guy named Marty John Butler—tall, blonde, good looking, and a pretty good player as well.

We did a couple of gigs, a mix of covers and the band's own songs, and they went well. But I knew that Marty was looking elsewhere already, and he seemed to think I might be interested as well.

A friend of his, a singer named Eliot Kidd, was also trying to put a group together, and one day Marty suggested we transfer our allegiance to him.

I agreed. The Stray Cats were okay, but like so many bands at that time, they existed in a vacuum. They didn't really know many people, they couldn't get decent gigs, and they would most likely just hang around for a year or so and then give up the ghost. Which, I believe, is what did happen.

Eliot, on the other hand, was already well connected. He was a familiar face at Max's, as I realized when I met first him, and he'd already written a set full of songs.

Plus, he lived on the west side, 16th and 8th, so he was not only firmly in the heart of the action, he was also in territory that I knew, because that's the area where my friends and I used to go to buy drugs.

Eliot quickly pulled a band together around us—a shag-haired bass player he knew from his hometown of New Haven, Robbie Twyford, and a drummer, Steve Abernathy, also from Connecticut.

Rehearsals were no problem. The Dolls' new manager, a wiry, ginger Englishman named Malcolm McLaren, had just rented them a loft above an off-track betting shop on 23rd Street, right next to the Chelsea Hotel. It was a vast space with huge arched windows and fourteen-foot-high ceilings. The entire street had once been occupied by piano stores, and this had been one of the showrooms—before the Dolls moved in, it had also been home to the funk band Mandrill, so unlike the Dolls' last loft, this place had no issues with soundproofing or electrical outlets.

Because Eliot was always around them anyway, the Dolls were happy to share it with us, and that meant, finally, after five years of seeing him virtually every time I went to a gig, I was formally introduced to Johnny Thunders.

I don't recall what we said to one another at that first meeting; most likely, we simply nodded and mumbled something, and allowed our eyes alone to acknowledge that we'd been spotting one another at gigs for the past six years. Then we both went back to doing whatever it was we were doing at the time.

As it happened, we wouldn't spend too much time with the Dolls. McLaren was hustling them hard—helping them work out a new stage act and look, the "red patent leather" routine that replaced the old glam threads; angling for a new record deal; and warming them up for a tour that would take them down the East Coast to Florida.

They were having personal difficulties, too. Johnny and David Johansen seemed to be at permanent loggerheads, tearing the leadership of the band asunder, even as its rhythm section seemed hell-bent on self-destruction, too.

Killer Kane, their bassist, was having serious drinking problems and would be in and out of the hospital throughout the next few months. Jerry Nolan wasn't doing well, either—like Johnny, he'd become something of a major league smackhead, and rehab was looming for him, too. We went to see the Dolls at the Little Hippodrome in early March, and almost half the band was out of action. Their roadie, Peter Jordan, played bass, and Spider—the drummer with Pure Hell, an African American rock band up from Philadelphia—sat in for Jerry.

I wasn't witness to any of the band's internal problems. Maybe I overheard the occasional disagreement, raised voices in the rehearsal room of wherever, but that is part and parcel of any band. They were great guys to hang out with, though, and the friendships that grew out of those first meetings were built to last—Johnny and Jerry, of course, but McLaren to an extent, while Sylvain Sylvain and I are still in touch to this day. In fact, he was the first person ever to warn me about Johnny putting every dime he made into his arm. We even played a show together in September 2017, a sold-out Dolls tribute at the Bowery Electric. He's a natural-born rocker with a heart of solid gold.

With the Dolls out on tour, the loft was all ours. We rehearsed constantly, and even more than that once Eliot confirmed our first gig, at Club 82, an old lesbian basement bar on East 4th Street (number 82, of course).

The place was originally opened, back in the fifties, by Anne Genovese, the wife of Mafia chief Vito, and framed photos on the walls were memories of how hot the place used to be. Everywhere you looked, among the plastic palm trees and tiki souvenirs, there were old Hollywood stars posing alongside the drag queens.

It had only been open to rock 'n' roll for a couple of years—in fact, the Dolls were the first band ever to play there, and I'd been to a few shows there since then. Getting a booking there was a big deal for us, though, particularly when I looked out into the audience and saw . . . I don't believe it. It didn't matter that we'd already met, already knew one another fairly well. Standing there, looking out at the audience, I still felt a shock of recognition when I realized, it's that kid *again*.

The Dolls had broken up. Down in Florida at the beginning of April, with the Dolls staying in a trailer owned by Jerry's mom, an evening meal turned into a full-scale fight that ended with Johnny and Jerry walking out.

They flew home to leave the band to play a few more shows without them. (Blackie Lawless of WASP subbed for Johnny, although he was still a kid named Steve at the time.) Now they were scheming a band of their own.

They'd already hooked up with Richard Hell, who himself had just left Television—one of the recent crop of bands that was playing a club called CBGB, down on the Bowery. They were pretty good, too; they opened for the Dolls at the Little Hippodrome, but CBGB was one of the shows that we had coming up, too, so that indicates the kind of level any of these new groups were in the grander scheme of things. In terms of pulling power, there really was little to choose between the Ramones, Elda Gentile's Stilettos, White Lightning, and so on.

Only the Patti Smith Group had broken out of the clubs—in fact, they were already in the studio, recording their first album for Arista. Everyone else, and that includes the Demons, was still scrambling for shows, and the news that Johnny, Jerry, and Hell were joining forces meant the scene was about to grow even more crowded.

They were called the Heartbreakers—Sylvain came up with the name, apparently, although Jerry liked to say it was his idea, and they had already done a photo session, before they had even gotten around to rehearsing. Maybe that's why they were already being called a supergroup.

But nobody doubted that they would rise above that mocking term. Johnny was Johnny, with that unmistakable guitar, and Hell had always seemed the odd one out in Television, a ragged spot atop Tom Verlaine's intricately constructed facade, bouncing around with that oddball look while Verlaine perfected his impression of a depressed psychotic. Even if they stuck to the familiar old songs—Johnny's Dolls repertoire, Hell's "Blank Generation," and others—they would be worth listening to.

I wished them luck, and I was just about to say that to Johnny when he pulled me over to the stairway.

"We've got a new band together. Don't tell Elliot, but do you want to join the band?"

I'd heard word that the Heartbreakers had been looking to expand the lineup—Jonathan Paley auditioned with them, as did John Felice of the Modern Lovers, Rob Duprey of the Mumps, and even Chris Stein as he vacillated between the Stilettos and what would become Blondie. None of them got the nod, however, or maybe they didn't give the nod to the Heartbreakers. It's worth noting that not one of the guitarists they tried out was a junkie.

Neither was I. I'd never stuck a needle in my arm in my life, and my few experiments with smack back in my college days just left me feeling sick.

But what could I say? On the one hand, I'd just played my first-ever gig with the Demons, and it had gone down really well. Eliot was a great frontman, and apparently I looked good as well—or so Johnny said. But on the other hand . . . the Heartbreakers!

Nobody had heard a note of their music, but I was keen to find out what it sounded like, and I was keen to become a part of it, too, and help to shape it from the ground floor up. I maintained just enough composure to say yes, and then Johnny was off, leaving me with a time and place to meet up with the band a couple of days later.

I turned up at the rehearsal space, in midtown Manhattan around 28th Street, just one more nondescript block. Jerry I knew, of course, but I'd not met Hell before, so Johnny did the introductions.

Hell seemed pleasant enough. Yes, he was a little standoffish, in that way people can be when they're trying to act cool and tough, but I'd seen him onstage and maybe read some of his poetry—he'd put out a couple of chapbooks, which I'm sure I'd flicked through at some point or another. I could see myself working with him.

Of the others, Jerry was the most down to earth, and Johnny was a whack job. But Jerry was a whack job too—it's all relative.

Later, I'd get to see different aspects to their characters; Jerry's mood changes could be affected by absolutely anything, whereas Johnny's were dependent upon his drug intake.

I've mentioned before that Johnny had always been what you might call a tearaway; he had always had his fingers in the drug trade. That's how he financed not only his wardrobe but his entire lifestyle.

But he was a good kid. I didn't know him when he was first starting out in music, but I was beginning to meet people who did—his fellow Dolls for starters, but other people too, friends and fans alike. And they all told roughly the same story. Johnny, pre-drugs, was the cool kid that every guy wanted to be, and every girl wanted to be with. I've already mentioned that he had a great taste in clothes. He also had a terrific taste in music and an irrepressible sense of humor. He was obsessed with the 50s TV shows we all grew up on and could quote great excerpts from *The Honeymooners* verbatim.

Until heroin came along, his drug use was never an issue. Occasionally he would do speed in the Dolls, and that would make him crazy, but Jerry could usually be relied upon to calm him down. After that, things changed dramatically, and I was astonished by how readily he could change from the quiet, amiable, John Genzale, who wisecracked with his buddies, into the loud-mouthed, obnoxious Johnny Thunders.

The transition surprised me, at first, anyway. But of course I grew accustomed to it.

One of the first times I saw it happen was at one of the Heartbreakers' earliest rehearsals. Someone had bought along a mess of flyers that we wanted to put up around the Village for a show we had coming up. We piled into a van, and our roadie, Max, was charged with actually putting the posters up.

Johnny had been quiet throughout rehearsal, just his normal self. But somewhere between rehearsal and van, he got high, and suddenly nothing Max did pleased Johnny. He'd hung the flyer too high, he hadn't hung it high enough, it was slightly off-kilter, he was moving too slow; Johnny just started yelling at Max, "Do it this way, do it that way, put it here, put it there."

It was a complete transformation. You could be talking with him and he'd be so charming, so smart . . . you'd just be having a great time, joking and chatting, reminiscing, planning, whatever. Then he'd notice someone across the room or wherever. He'd excuse himself, and the next time you saw him, he'd be ranting and raging about anything that came to mind. A total dictator. Drugs gave him self-confidence, although I never really believed he needed that; but they also brought out a boisterousness that quickly turned into aggression. And then there were the times when he was completely out of it, with bubbles coming out of his mouth.

It would make it very hard to plan for the future. But I didn't know that at the time.

We chatted together for a while, and then someone suggested we try out a number, Johnny's "I Wanna Be Loved." They started, I jumped in when I'd got the idea, and we blazed.

Johnny's guitar style had always been a little idiosyncratic—according to Sylvain, who actually taught him how to play in the first place, the only reason Johnny became a lead guitarist is because that's what he told everybody he was. Even when the Dolls were at the height of their powers, Johnny was still effectively making it up as he went along, and things had not really changed since then. It wasn't at all difficult to slip in alongside him, keeping the song's shape together no matter where Johnny wound up taking it. And that remained true throughout the years we played together.

He was not a technical guitarist—in love with chords and progressions, notes and solos—but he was unique. Nobody had Johnny's sound, no matter how hard they tried to emulate it. Jerry used to call it the sound of dinosaurs screaming in the jungle, and he was correct.

Yes, he was limited in terms of chord changes; yes, his playing was very basic. I've heard him described as "primitive" because he didn't have that sophistication of the so-called great guitarists, the Claptons and Pages and Becks. But it didn't matter. What he had, that intuitive understanding of rhythm and sound and pace, he used better than anybody else. There was nobody else in the music scene then or since who could capture him.

Even his sound was so unique, piercing and penetrating, but so exciting. There were no pedals, no effects, no stomp boxes or other devices. These days, guitarists come onstage with twenty different effects boxes to play through. Johnny never used them. Everything you heard was just Johnny.

His solos were the same. They were so simple, but they stood out.

Part of it was his taste in guitars. He mostly used Gibson Les Paul Junior and TV models, and those old pickups definitely played a role in creating his sound. But still he had something that that was indefinably his own. A few times during shows, I would break a string and Johnny would give me his guitar to play while he just sang.

Even using his guitar and his amp, though, I still couldn't come close to producing the same sound he did.

You know what I think it was? It was something about the way he pressed the strings with those stubby little fingers of his.

Nobody ever noticed it, but Ray Charles's "Hit the Road Jack" had a lot in common with Hell's "Blank Generation"—the first time I heard it, in fact, I started singing "Hit the Road."

That song was next at the audition, that taut guitar pattern jerking beneath the vocal; and because we were having so much fun, nobody even needed to ask if we wanted to try out another— "Chinese Rocks."

Dee Dee Ramone wrote it, apparently after Hell announced that he intended to write the "ultimate" heroin song. (Hell would add a third verse of his own, but we stopped using it once he left the band.) He then gave it to us because the Ramones refused to play it. They hated the fact that Dee Dee spent so much time with the Heartbreakers; they thought we were a really bad influence . . . which we were . . . while Johnny Ramone, in particular, didn't want to play any songs that had anything to do with drugs.

Glue, yes; cleaning fluid, yes. But drugs? No way.

It sounds crazy now, but his logic was very simple. Neither glue nor cleaning fluid (Carbona was the preferred brand) were at all cool—in fact, kids were getting really sick from Carbona; it was poison, and if you did too much, it would burn out your brain. If there's a hierarchy among stoners, smack was at the top and glue was at the bottom. The very bottom. And that was its appeal to the Ramones. It was so stupid that it fit with the image they wanted.

They would eventually relent and "Chinese Rocks" would enter the Ramones' repertoire in time for their fifth album, *End of the Century*, in 1980. But they played it so fast that it sounded like Chinese speed rocks. Not many people ever pulled off a decent version of a Ramones song, but we had completely made it our own by that time, to the point where their version sounded like a none-too-great cover.

Jerry's Buddy Holly drumbeat and Johnny's little break in the middle made it such a great song. Dee Dee later said he'd written it about Jerry and his girlfriend, Connie. (She's the one "crying in the shower stall" at Arturo Vega's loft.) The Heartbreakers were all over that song even before I joined.

We sounded good together; and we may have tried another song, "Going Steady," as well. I can't say for certain, but either way, the whole thing felt so easy, so natural, so perfect, and the band seemed to agree with me. Which is why it was initially surprising, then a little disturbing, and then downright disappointing to watch the days and weeks slip by without another word from any of them.

Maybe the audition hadn't been so good, after all.

Chapter Five

ROOKIE OF THE YEAR

Every so often, I'd see the Heartbreakers' name in one of the papers, and I noted that they remained a three-piece, so that was one good thing. They hadn't chosen me, but they'd not chosen anybody else, either.

Over the years, I've read that the three-piece lineup played a string of shows, beginning at the end of April, when they opened for Jayne County at Club 82. Apparently, they gigged with the Ramones at the Coventry, out in Queens, at the end of May. There was also, supposedly, a couple of CBGB shows in June.

I don't remember these gigs, and I don't even remember hearing about them, which surprises me because I should have. In fact, I'd have attended them. I'm not saying they didn't happen, just that if they did, it was far, far below my radar, and that of my friends—some of whom were also Johnny's friends. In fact, the only thing I know for certain that they did was have Bob Gruen take another bunch of photos at the old Dolls' loft on 23rd, right before Malcolm McLaren stopped paying the rent on it.

Things weren't going all their own way, though. The Heartbreakers already had an audience—you couldn't be an ex-Doll in New York City without a few people getting excited, but that also aroused a few grumbles of discontent, the feeling that the Dolls had had their chance and they'd blown it. Now it was the next generation's turn, and they didn't need these washed-up old farts still touting old glories in the midst of things.

Sylvain and Johansen, playing around New York as the (abbreviated) Dolls, were running into many of the same kind of obstacles—more, in fact, as any number of old, faithful fans turned against what they saw as a cabaret-themed betrayal of the original group.

The difference was that the Dolls had no intention whatsoever of starting out again, and if the word on the streets was true, they were actually going out for more money a night now, with what were mockingly nicknamed the Dollettes, than they had through much of the original group's existence.

I didn't feel that way. The Dolls, in my opinion, had never fulfilled their potential, and while they could be faulted for some of that, it wasn't completely their own doing. Management never understood them; their label didn't, either. Later, I'd hear more about the group's internal dynamic from Johnny and Jerry, how ego and money played their own part in wrecking things, and how it often felt like David Johansen was deliberately trying to tear things apart so he could get on with a solo career.

But Jerry hated his old singer with a passion. Johnny wasn't Johansen's biggest fan by any means, but Jerry blamed everything that went wrong for the Dolls on Johansen, whether he was responsible for it or not—everything from their failure to break any place but New York to the fact that the records never sounded as good as the band did live. Funny thing, though: he would make the same complaints about the Heartbreakers later. Nothing was ever good enough.

Right now, though, it was the prospect of life away from the Dolls that had him so fired up about the Heartbreakers. He and Johnny had already suffered every hard knock rock can throw at a band, from inept leadership to inappropriate producers. The only possible way to move now was upward.

That I agreed with. Standing on the outside, I knew that neither of the Dolls' LPs matched the ferocity and fire of the band I'd seen perform so many times. Just as I knew that the music I'd heard the Heartbreakers play at my audition was *exactly* what New York was missing right then. Just as the music the Dolls had played back in 1972 was exactly what was needed then.

New bands were pouring out of the woodwork. If you've ever walked into an inner-city kitchen in the middle of the night, switched on the light, and tried to count the roaches, then you know how it felt. They were everywhere, clambering over one another, skittering across every surface, big ones, little ones, flying ones, vicious ones.

I can't even remember all the names. The Mumps, the Shirts, Luger, the Marbles, the Miamis. The original Stilettos had split, and one of Elda's backing singers, Debbie Harry, was now fronting her own band, Blondie and the Banzai Babes. The Rhode Island art students who would become Talking Heads were having their first rehearsals while waiting for Tina Weymouth to perfect her bass playing. Suicide was still at large and still dividing audiences like no other band I had ever seen. Tuff Darts came through— their first ever shows were when they opened for the Demons at CBGB at the end of June.

Hilly Kristal, down at CBGB, announced that he was planning to stage a Festival of Unsigned Bands. I don't know how many days he initially scheduled, but it would ultimately go on for over two weeks, with more than thirty bands taking the stage. There were probably just as many that didn't make the cut.

Something was missing, however. Exclude the bottom-feeders that are always around whenever a scene gets bigger than a band or two, and each of these groups had its own sound, its own style, its own look.

Not one of them, however, grasped rock 'n' roll by the balls in the same way as the Dolls had done—neither Tuff Darts with their Elvis-on-Mars nor Talking Heads with their quirky rhythms, and certainly not the realigned Television, with their ever-extending guitar solo soundscapes. Not even the Ramones, with their cartoon Archies-on-speed. In fact, in a way, least of all the Ramones.

I was rarely impressed by them. I liked them at first, and they were certainly unique. They used to play these twenty-minute sets, and nobody dared do that. But I saw them so many times that it became boring.

Later, they became iconic, but at the time, there was no difference between any of the songs. They were all fast, they all had the same chords, and you usually couldn't make out the words, so Joey was just making the same sounds throughout. Later, they even had their roadie hiding backstage, playing the solos that Johnny never mastered. It was so basic, so elemental.

In a way, however, that was what made them so popular. They tapped into what was almost a primal scream. People started banging their heads to the music and it was like a button had been pressed in their soul. They grasped the most basic instinct.

But it wasn't rock 'n' roll, to me, anyway. None of it. It was as if everybody was so concerned about somehow sounding "unique" that they forgot that, sometimes, the kids just wanna rock.

That was the niche that the Heartbreakers slipped into, and that was why they'd excited me so.

Not that the Demons were doing so badly. Eliot was writing some great material, the band was tight, and the Dolls' influence was there. We would never get around to recording anything during my time in the group, but a year or so later, a new Demons lineup would have an album released by Mercury, and if you excuse the power-pop production, it's a reasonable snapshot-slash-extension of what we were doing during my time with the band.

Our problem was that we didn't get to do it often enough. Following Club 82, we landed no more than a handful of shows. We played one at CBGB during those days when, as Marty later put it, the place "had fifteen people there, and twelve of them were in a band," and a couple at the Coventry where we would be opening for the Heartbreakers. Which would be my chance, I told myself as I got myself ready for the show, to let them see what they were missing.

I did. I played a great show. But I still wasn't expecting it when Jerry Nolan pulled me over afterward and asked whether I'd liked any of the songs I played with them at the audition.

A little surprised—how could I not have been?—I told him the truth. I loved them. He grinned. "So, do you want to join, then?"

And that was it. I became what Chris Stein would later describe as "The Rookie of the Year."

There was no fanfare or great ticker-tape welcome awaiting me when I met up with my new bandmates once again. Johnny said, "Hi"; Hell might have nodded. It was as if I'd just popped out for a sandwich and now we could get back to work.

My last gig with the Demons was back at CBGB on the Friday of the July 4 weekend, performing in front of about twenty people at one or two in the morning. My first gig with the Heartbreakers, also at CBGB, was the following evening in front of several hundred screaming maniacs, with a line around the block as well. It was a madhouse. I was surprised. The others just took it in their stride. They were the Heartbreakers, after all. What kind of reception should they have received, if not absolute mayhem and adoration?

"Punk" history tends to regard CBGB with a lot more affection than it perhaps deserves. Hilly Kristal himself merits every kind word that has ever been said about him—without him, and his vision, New York would never have seen the musical explosion that followed.

That's true, but for me, mention of CBGB conjured another memory entirely, of the Sunday afternoon a couple of years earlier when a college friend of mine invited me down to a dive bar in the East Village to watch his country band play a show. I went, and it was a dreadful place, the kind that you never wanted to think about again—which, at the time, seemed very likely because country was CBGB's specialty. But it wasn't mine.

Of course, it didn't turn out that way, and returning there for the first time only revealed that CBGB had only gone downhill since my last visit. It was a shithole, and just as you don't think kindly of your cat's litter box, no matter how much you love your cat, that damp, narrow room with its barbed-wire acoustics and broken-glass ambience was a place you visited under sufferance, not for fun.

We used to love going there, though. The place was so disgusting that it fit perfectly into that whole down-and-out blank-generation atmosphere that clung to our music. The bum hotel on top of the club, the drunks on the streets outside. If you had a car, it was easy to park because nobody wanted to be there after sundown. And if you didn't have a car, you'd most likely trip over the dead bum who was invariably lying on the street outside, frozen to death, and waiting for the cops to pick him up.

Inside, it was just as bad. Hilly had a greyhound, and invariably you'd step in a pile of dog shit at some point during the evening and then spread it around the club with every step you took. The stench added to the ambience.

There was an article in the *Village Voice* that mentioned how "London's *NME* called CBGB 'a toilet,' and intimated that the owners kick holes in the walls and urinate just to provide atmosphere." And I remember agreeing with the sentence that followed. "Actually, it's not that exotic."

The stage itself was in the back, a tiny little thing that was about half the size of the room itself, and next to that, on the right-hand side, was the kitchen, with roaches and rats crawling all over everything. I know we never had any food there, and I can't imagine many other people did, so eventually they took out the kitchen, extended the stage, and put in dressing rooms.

The bathrooms were downstairs, and they were the ugliest, most disgusting things you'd ever want to see. The men's room was covered with graffiti, junk, garbage, stuff hanging off the walls, and long smears of shit. There were two or, at most, three urinals against the wall and rarely did they ever work, so people would piss in them and they'd overflow. And if you wanted to take a dump, there was no door to the stall, so you'd be sitting bare naked in front of everyone. And you wouldn't have any toilet paper, anyway.

The ladies' room was slightly better; it was still disgusting, but there was a sink that usually worked, and the stalls had doors, so we used to go there, especially when we wanted to get a fix. There might be a girl or two who would come in to use the facilities, but we rarely noticed them, and I doubt whether our presence perturbed them in the slightest. Unless, of course, they wanted to use the stall that we had crammed ourselves into, in which case they might have a long wait.

That was CBGB, sleazy and derelict, with the flimsy old tables and the chairs that used to break when you sat on them. Later, once it started to attract tourists and journalists, they fixed it up to a degree. I even met Frankie Valli there one night, when he dropped by to see this new scene for himself. He was talking with Hilly, who made the introductions, but I can't say it wasn't a shock to see him there. The epitome of sixties American pop, standing at ground zero of seventies punk dissolution.

At the very start, however, it was vile.

I didn't care. I used to go to CBGB a lot, and not only to see bands. I loved hanging out there because my friends were there.

Hell was a big fan, as well.

Part of his attachment, maybe, was sentimental. It was Richard Lloyd of Television, back during Hell's first days with the group, who is generally credited with discovering CBGB, just a couple of months and a handful of gigs after Hilly opened for business.

It was there, in fact, that Television built the reputation that they still exploit today, endless nights, eternal residences, watching as word went around and the crowds grew bigger, until they reached a point where a split in the ranks—Hell's departure to link up with Johnny—actually made the pages of the *Village Voice*. It wasn't "Paul leaves the Beatles" or even "Johnny quits the Dolls," but people cared all the same.

Hell had a genuine affection for the place. He was also close with Roberta Bayley, the girl who worked the door while her career as a photographer got underway.

For Johnny and Jerry, however, after two years playing theaters across the United States and beyond, it was little more than a closet with attitude. I wasn't that jaded, but there's definitely a reason why we played CBGB almost twenty times during Hell's time with the Heartbreakers, and no more than four in the years thereafter.

That first night was special, nonetheless. It was July 4 weekend and the opening night of the Festival of Unsigned Bands. We headlined, of course, and it was incredible standing there, having had just one quick rehearsal that afternoon, watching the place fill up. Twenty-four hours ago, I couldn't help but reflect, I'd been playing to an all but empty room. Now it felt as though half of New York was watching, and the other half was on the street outside, trying to get in.

That was also the night Johnny introduced me to possibly the ugliest man I had ever met. It was shortly before we went on; I saw Johnny approaching and, truly, his companion was hideous. His face was so pockmarked that it looked like oatmeal with raisins; his hair was stringy, he walked like an ape, and I was just thinking, "God, what a fucking monster," when Johnny introduced us. "I want you to meet Ace Frehley."

I couldn't believe it, but of course, I'd never seen him without his makeup on. At that time, not many people had. Now I knew why.

The place was jammed. It was seething. You could see people buckling in the heart of the crowd and feel that heat rising to the stage. We'd barely played one number and we were already soaked in sweat. It was unbelievable, and even better, we'd be repeating the exercise in a few nights time, knowing that everyone who filled the place tonight would be back with a friend or two.

In the meantime, we had another rehearsal scheduled. It was time I had a haircut.

Chapter Six

CASH IN, DOPE OUT

Somehow, somewhere, I had come into possession of an eight-ounce jar of pure quaalude powder and, to put that into perspective, let's just say even a quarter of an ounce is a fatal overdose for most people. (Hardened users can probably double that.)

Obviously it was way too much for me to get through, so in the spirit of band camaraderie, I brought it along to the next rehearsal. We all took a little, and we barely dented the contents of the jar.

It dented us, though. We were scheduled for a three-hour rehearsal. I think it lasted all of ten minutes because, after that, we were all stumbling around not knowing what to do.

As we were packing up to leave, Johnny pulled me to one side and suggested he take the rest of the jar away to sell. Of course he'd split the money with me.

Fine. I knew that Johnny did a little dealing on the side—had been, in fact, since he was at high school. I once asked him whether he'd ever held down what you'd call a real job.

"Yeah, I had one," he replied. "I was a soda jerk when I was fourteen." Apparently he made killer egg creams.

I handed over the jar and off he went. A few moments later, as Jerry and I were leaving, he asked where I'd stashed the ludes.

"Oh, I let Johnny take it. He's going to sell it."

Jerry looked at me as though I had two heads. "You did what? Are you fucking crazy? You never give John drugs like that! He'll be dead in the morning."

Oh shit. Every time the phone rang that evening, I was convinced it would be someone calling to say Johnny had ODed. But I made it through the night, and so did he.

The following day I was supposed to pick up Johnny from the house in Queens where his sister Maryann and her husband Rusty lived. We had set up a photo shoot—my first as a Heartbreaker—with Hell's girlfriend, Roberta, behind the camera.

I called him on the phone to let him know I was on my way, and as soon as Johnny spoke, I knew something was wrong.

He sounded like shit, as though he were speaking through swollen lips and bruised cheeks—which, as it transpired, was exactly what he was doing.

"I got into a fight with Rusty last night. I may look a little strange."

That was an understatement.

The fight did not surprise me. He was a small guy, wiry and thin, but he had a temper, and depending upon what he'd most recently taken, anything could set it off.

He didn't just start screaming on the spot; something would have to provoke him. But once he got going, he could be ruthless. I saw him once get into a fight with James Chance. In fact it wasn't even a fight. We were up in James's apartment to buy drugs or something, and James started talking nasty to his girlfriend. Suddenly Johnny just hauled up and punched him in the face.

Or, we'd be on the street and Johnny would start screaming at passersby. If anyone got in front of him in the line at the deli. Bumped into him by accident backstage. Looked at him wrong while he was playing guitar. He would just fly off the handle, and he didn't care what the consequences might be. I don't think I ever saw him get beaten to a pulp, but that was probably because the rest of us would pull him out of the battle. What happened when he was on his own, however, I wouldn't like to say.

This particular night, at Maryann and Rusty's house, he was on his own.

Rusty was a big guy, a truck driver I think, and he did not approve of drugs.

"He found the quaaludes and flushed them down the john," Johnny explained once I picked him up. "I tried to stop him, but . . ." He gave me a sheepish grin and motioned at his battered face.

With Jerry's warnings in my ear, I wasn't sure how much of this to believe. It was just as likely that Johnny had downed the whole lot, and the Rusty story was a complete fabrication. But clearly Johnny had been in the wars and, besides, he said I'd still get my money. All I had to do was take a quick detour by his mother's house as we drove into the city.

We arrived there, and Johnny didn't introduce me. He didn't get the chance. Mrs. Genzale took one look at the state of Johnny's face—bruised, battered, bloodied, his eyes barely open, his lips thick and split—looked at me with an expression of absolute abject terror, and then hustled her son into another room. I was left standing there alone.

A few minutes later, Johnny came out and handed me fifty bucks.

"I told her you were a big local drug dealer, and you were going to have me killed if I didn't get the hundred dollars I owed you."

A hundred?

"Yeah, but I kept fifty so I can score later on," Johnny replied.

He didn't allow the state of his face to derail the photo session, either. Of course he'd gotten high before we reached the place, but still he rearranged that fabulous mop of hair so that it hung down over the worst of his facial bruises, and though you could barely even see his eyes for the battering they'd taken, he still looked good.

Roberta worked the lighting, too, to cast just enough shadow that none of that mattered, posed us in our black suits, and perched the new boy on a convenient stool, and I have to say, she did a great job with that session.

You couldn't even see how bewildered I was. Although I'd certainly been around junkies in the past, I knew it would take me a while to truly accustom myself to life in this band.

I had certainly never met anyone quite like Johnny. His appetite for drugs was astounding—he could, and would, take anything he was offered, mixing cocktails that would have felled any normal human being, but it effectively made no difference to him at all.

Even the chaos of the last twenty-four hours . . . for him it was just the way things were, the normal operating procedure. I remember how he used to walk up and down the line of people waiting to get into gigs and ask them for drugs. The idiots would hand him whatever they had, just drop a few pills into his hand, and whatever it was . . . he neither knew nor cared . . . Johnny took them. That's why he'd wind up unconscious before so many shows.

But my induction into life with the Heartbreakers had only just begun.

We had a routine—or, rather, the others did, and I became a part of it. First we'd meet up with Dee Dee, Willy DeVille, and various other friends, and then we'd head off to score.

It was a whole new world for me. Back then, one always tended to think that the "big" drug scene of the day was whichever one you, or your friends, were involved in—and, for the most part, it was relatively civilized. Acid, pot, even coke, somebody you knew always seemed to have some, or at least know where they could score some, and it was no big deal.

Yes, there was the occasional shady character who might shake you down, and there were the chancers selling who-knows-what in the guise of what you wanted—the rip-off merchants and the out-and-out crooks.

But word got around, and they were quickly exposed.

But dope . . . smack . . . heroin. Where did you get that from? And, just as importantly, from whom? How did you know it was good stuff? How could you tell if it had been cut with something? I worked for the FDA—I spent five days a week analyzing drugs to make certain that they were safe for the general public to take. If the big pharmaceutical companies were constantly trying to slip something "extra" into their legitimate drugs, God alone knew what some scuzzball smack dealer was slipping into his brew.

Into the Village, on East 11th Street. When it opened in 1966, the Psychedelicatessen was Manhattan's first-ever head shop, and though it only lasted a couple of years, the memory remained.

The building was empty now, abandoned long ago, but the street outside was awash with kids, some as young as eleven or twelve, all of them runners for the heroin dealers who lurked unseen around corners and doorways.

You'd hand the kid a few dollars, and he'd scamper off and return a couple of minutes later and palm you a small, sealed glassine envelope. According to Hell, the dealers used kids because, as juveniles, they couldn't be sent to jail.

Or deeper into Alphabet City. The Lower East Side. Row upon row of tenement buildings, dilapidated and derelict, crumbling relics of New York's first major slum-housing boom back at the turn of the century, and untouched and unpainted since then.

It was a ghetto, once home to mostly Hispanics and eastern Europeans, crammed into spaces that you could no longer even describe as rooms. A few of them still clung on there, and you'd see little old ladies walking down the street, carrying their shopping or walking tiny dogs, apparently oblivious to their surroundings.

Johnny had lived round there too, at one point, *before* he got into smack, and he pointed out the tenement, set a couple of brownstones back from Avenue A. He told us how he came home one day and found someone had broken in and stolen his guitar. He'd been furious, but now he seemed almost proud. It proved he belonged.

My first visit, I shuddered at the very sight of the place. I'd never been there, but of course I'd heard all about it—how it was an absolute world of its own, a no-go area for anyone who wasn't the kind of person who made it a no-go area in the first place. Even the muggers would get mugged after dark, and I seriously doubted any of us would get out of there alive.

But that's where we'd go, to whichever abandoned building that this grapevine or that one had pointed us toward . . . the best dealers, with the best stuff, constantly moved around, avoiding the attentions of both rival dealers and the occasional passing squad car.

Every so often, you'd hear a warning cry of *"bajando"*—"going down," although we always took it to mean "the man is coming"— from one of the lookouts who'd be posted on the street, and that was the signal for everyone to scatter, and wait until the threat, usually cops, had moved on.

No place was too sordid, too rundown, too devastated, for the trade. A building could burn down at night and be a dealership by morning. A roof collapse could open up a whole new parade of store fronts. It was still largely a Hispanic neighborhood, in as much as most of the dealers seemed to be Puerto Rican, but between my stumbling Spanish and their fractured English, it was easy to make yourself understood. Besides, most of the time, you didn't even need to speak. A handful of cash through a crack in the wall, or slipped under a locked door, a glassine in return, and then out as quick as you could.

Occasionally the police *would* swoop down, make a few busts, crack a few heads, hustle away a few hapless addicts. They might even rope off a doorway or two. The law never made any difference, though. It didn't matter how many dealers they busted or doorways they blocked off. The action would just move to the next available space.

On July 23, 1975, the Heartbreakers made our debut at Max's Kansas City. Of course Johnny and Jerry were no strangers there—despite the death of the Dolls, they were still something approaching royalty so far as the faithful were concerned.

It was the Dolls who had put the venue back on the map once its original association with Warhol and the Velvets had faded, and while there had been a change of ownership in the months since then—founder Mickie Ruskin closed the place in December 1974; Tommy and Laura Dean reopened it the following year—in many ways, it was the same old place.

A lot of that was down to the booker, Peter Crowley. Tommy's original idea for Max's was to reopen it as a disco, with occasional live entertainment—the opening night was headlined by a disco cover band, of all things. It swiftly became apparent, however, that this new regime was not going to work, which is when Jayne County recommended Tommy talk to Peter, who was booking bands at Mother's at the time.

We were among the first bands he called upon, and that was the night I made my celluloid debut, too. Ivan Kral, the guitarist with the Patti Smith Group, was also an aspiring filmmaker, touring the New York scene with his camera, capturing every band he could for the movie *Blank Generation.*

The Heartbreakers, however, would not be the easiest subject to capture. As Ivan put it: "Richard Hell wanted to be on camera, but the way he sometimes acted, I wasn't too sure. He would throw me out of a dressing room or spit at me during the show. It was as if he wanted to be seen as a confrontational artist, who is rebellious at whatever the cost."

Filming us at Max's was especially nerve-wracking. "I was afraid Johnny Thunders would jump on me for sure, and the anger from Richard Hell was frightening. I was in no position to defend myself since the band was a few feet above me."

Max's would become our most regular gig, to the point where the Heartbreakers' name remains synonymous with the place even today. It retains its old glamor, as well, and the memory of the days when the back room was somewhere worthy of preservation in song.

The thing that people forget, however, is that Max's Kansas City really wasn't much better than CBGB, at least in terms of the musicians' personal comfort.

It was nice on the ground floor where the bar and the restaurant were, and the free food in the afternoon was great. You'd go during happy hour and eat chicken wings for as long as you could. And that would be our meal for the day. Our money was being saved for dope.

The second floor was where the bands played and that was decent, too—a big bar, the stage at the back, the seating area for watching the bands, and the windows that looked out over Park Avenue. The third floor was where Tommy and Peter had their offices, and in the middle there were the dressing rooms, with stickers and shit on the walls.

But the bathrooms were CBGB's revisited. Everyone would shoot up in there, so there was blood all over the walls. You'd be lucky if the toilets worked, and I don't think there was a separate room for women. And the place stunk. It was horrible.

The Max's gig went well, and a run of shows at CBGB too. Three nights at the end of July, three more in the middle of August, three more in September.

Looking back, though, we really didn't play that many shows, and when we did, they tended to come either in bursts of two or three in a row—a few more stints at CBGB, with people like the Shirts, Talking Heads, and Blondie opening for us, three nights at the Village Gate, three nights at Mother's—or there'd be special events, a great Halloween party at Club 82 and a riotous New Year's Eve show at the Sea of Clouds (which was actually someone's loft), with the Ramones and a classic Jayne County DJ set.

I don't know why we weren't playing that much—it wasn't through any shortage of venues, and it certainly wasn't lack of demand. We could probably have played every night if we'd been willing.

But there was a disconnect . . . partly, perhaps, because we had no formal management at the time, so there was nobody answering the phone every time it rang, but also because we were already aware that we didn't *need* to be out there every night, that we *could* get away with rationing our appearances, so that when we did venture out, it would be an event.

It didn't help that there really was no press coverage to be had. The New York music papers would keep on top of things, of course, but beyond that, I think we received more coverage in the United Kingdom than we did in America.

The big British music papers—things like *New Musical Express*, *Sounds*, and *Melody Maker*—all had New York correspondents; in fact, it was a *Melody Maker* feature that broke the New York Dolls, after one of their writers splashed them across the paper in 1972, before anyone outside of Manhattan had even heard of them.

It was the same now. In November 1975, word went around that *NME* had just devoted several pages to the CBGB scene: the Ramones, Television, Blondie, Tuff Darts, Talking Heads, the Shirts, the Dollettes—and us.

We couldn't wait to see it, but of course we had to—it was probably Christmas or beyond before a copy finally made its way into our orbit, and there we were, in newsprint. "The Heartbreakers, the first (tadaaaaaa!) NY punk supergroup."

It went downhill from there. "They are dreadful. Brother, are they dreadful."

Hell read it first, I think, and he got at least one good laugh from it, the bit where I was described as "a morose-looking lead guitarist who looks as if his name ought to be Gary, but is more likely to be Albert." For an awful moment, I thought the others might suggest (or, more likely, insist) that I henceforth be known by one of those names, but the moment passed.

The writer slagged off the band, he slagged off our music, he even slagged off our instruments—Johnny's "huge, unwieldy" Gretsch White Falcon, my "anonymous looking" Les Paul, Hell's "Felix Pappalardi-style Gibson violin bass."

He complained about the volume, he complained about our fans . . . he even complained that Johnny was allegedly one of the few musicians in town who could enter CBGB through the back door so he didn't have to walk through the audience to get on stage. It was true, too, but only because Hilly knew that Johnny would probably never even reach the stage if he had to first greet, and then accept gifts from, everybody he met if he entered the place through the front door.

Charles Shaar Murray's "1975: A Scuzz Odyssey" was my first ever exposure to the British music press. So different to its American counterpart, which felt positively reverential by comparison, its bite-the-hand attitude toward the people it was writing about, and its self-appointed status as the ultimate arbiter of musical taste in the land, amazed me. But I would soon grow accustomed to it.

Murray did get one thing right, though. After a fashion.

"The basic trouble with the Heartbreakers," he declared, was that neither Johnny nor Hell "has the personality . . . to lead or co-lead a band."

Time would prove him wrong in both instances, of course. But there was a sense, and even I was aware of it, that in many ways, our two frontmen cancelled one another out.

They were very different performers, after all—while Johnny posed and preened and looked oh so cool, Hell jerked and jumped and messed around. Which, in some bands, could work in an attraction-of-opposites kind of way. But only if the two musicians had already settled their respective roles within the band, and that was something this pair was never going to do.

In his book, Hell says, "Most of the year I spent with the Heartbreakers was the best I would have in a band, in terms of good times." At the time, however, the tensions were both palpable and poisonous.

From the very beginning, I was aware that Hell and Johnny were not necessarily the most natural musical partnership. They worked well together; there were nights, both onstage and in rehearsal, when they locked together with perfect synchronicity. But there were nights, too, when the Heartbreakers felt less like a band than a clash of two very disparate, monstrous egos.

In Johnny's mind, he was the star of the band—he had the experience, he had the track record, and when we played live, he had the gaggle of acolytes clustered around his side of the stage, hanging on to every gesture he made. To this day, he remains the only person I've ever met who could get a round of applause simply from messing with his own hair, and when he chose to remove his shirt, even the guys would swoon.

Hell, on the other hand, saw himself as something more than a rock 'n' roll star. His lyrics, his music, his attitude—they all owed as much to an adolescence spent devouring poetry and art as they did to his need to cater to his audience. More, in fact. The rest of us, in his eyes, were musicians. He alone was an artist, a genius even, and maybe he was.

But genius has its downside too, and a big part of that is a refusal to admit that other people's ideas and thoughts might, in their own way, be as valid as your own.

Hell knew, at that particular point in his career, that he needed a band to get his poetry out to the public. What he didn't need were band*mates*. There was a reason why Patti Smith named her own band after herself—and why Hell, once he left the Heartbreakers, would do the same with his next project.

He couldn't do that in the Heartbreakers because he was up against an ego just as vast as his own and a team of songwriters just as strong as him—and, if anything, even stronger. Richard Hell wrote songs that were good for Richard Hell. The rest of us—Johnny in the main, but Jerry and I as well—wrote songs that were good for the Heartbreakers.

But would anyone get to hear them?

My early misgivings about the band's dynamic snowballed. Slowly at first, but with gathering pace as 1975 passed through the hourglass.

Little things to begin with: snarky comments or dismissive gestures, Johnny rolling his eyes when Hell took the microphone, Hell losing interest when Johnny started to sing.

There may or may not also have been some awkwardness surrounding Hell's latest girlfriend—Sable Starr had been with Johnny back in the Dolls days; in fact, I think Johnny introduced her to Hell in the first place. Now they were together, and though nobody thought it would last, I don't think I was alone in detecting a certain atmosphere.

The biggest battles, however, took place in rehearsal.

The conflicts were mostly Johnny versus Richard, with Jerry sort of playing the middle but mostly staying on Johnny's side. Hell was sort of funny in the beginning because he had all these wacky lyrics that made everyone laugh—you know, they were all junkies so they all had the same sort of humor—but that changed as time went on.

It was a good combination. It was rock—the Hell songs were just sort of wimpy without a rock band behind him, and he added that sort of "Blank Generation" element to the Heartbreakers stuff.

A lot of people already had an idea of Johnny and Jerry since they had already been around in the Dolls. It's funny since there was only like a two- or three-year difference between their generation and whatever was now coming through, but there was a sort of a credibility gap. So the combination of Hell, who was sort of the newer wave, with Johnny and Jerry, who were more part of the tail end of glam, worked well.

But then it started to change.

Songwriting in the band was very much a democracy at first. In the beginning, Hell had his songs, Johnny had his. Then I joined, and we started playing one of mine, "Flight," and soon after that, Jerry and I came up with one together—"All by Myself" grew out of a drum beat he was toying with in the studio one day; I was listening to him play and started adding chords.

Jerry began extemporizing lyrics, putting together what became the chorus. I added verses, and there it was. The Lure-Nolan songwriting team was off and running, and soon Jerry was showing me other things he'd started writing, things like "Take a Chance on Me" and "Can't Keep My Eyes on You." They were both songs that Jerry wrote almost completely on his own; I added some verses, but everything else was his, and that happened a lot.

Sometimes he'd have chords and a chorus, but because he never enjoyed writing lyrics, he'd ask me to finish them off. Other times, we'd hatch them together. In fact, we were doing so well that we even set up our own little Lennon–McCartney-style agreement, whereby anything either of us wrote, even if the other one was nowhere in sight at the time, would be credited to Lure/Nolan.

That's what happened with "Get Off the Phone," which I wrote on my own, although it had a tangled birth all the same.

Hell saw that something had gelled between Jerry and me, and maybe that bothered him. In the beginning, he only had Johnny to compete with. Now he had us as well. He started throwing his weight around, and that's what happened with "One Track Mind"—I'd heard that chord progression years earlier, when lots of kids were playing it, so it was always in the back of my mind. So I brought it in one day and the others loved it—including Hell, who promptly announced that he was going to write a lyric for it.

Conscious that I was still "the new boy," I didn't see any alternative but to agree. I think we played "Love Comes in Spurts" live once or twice, but when Hell left the band, I came up with a new lyric. I actually finished "One Track Mind" while we were in England, sitting around the studio one day.

A lot of people think "One Track Mind" is a drug song, probably because it's full of drug imagery and double entendres—what's strange is that I wasn't even aware that I'd done that. It was only when somebody pointed them all out to me years later that I finally understood why everybody had arrived at that particular conclusion.

All in all, then, I was willing to let Hell have his moment. If he wanted to sing my songs, he could. But then he started moving in on Johnny's territory, and before we knew where we were, he was vying to establish himself firmly as our lead vocalist, with Johnny relegated to just a couple of songs during the show.

It was a step too far.

Chapter Seven

I'M NOT THE NEW KID ANYMORE

None of this happened overnight. The events and disagreements that culminated in Hell's departure started in the early fall of 1975, and it was the following May before the split finally took shape.

Sadly, I couldn't say the same thing about my breakup with Diane. We'd been together through the Demons and these earliest days of the Heartbreakers; she'd seen—but certainly did not approve of—my descent into drug use, but the relationship felt as though it had run its course. The last night together that I remember was in the late summer of 1975, when I took her to see the Jackson 5 in concert.

Diane and I made more or less a clean break. The Heartbreakers were considerably less decisive, despite the growing tensions. We simply continued on as before, two or three gigs a month. During this time we also made our first trips out of town, and a big piece appeared in the debut issue of Alan Betrock's magazine, *New York Rocker*, a new publication that had dedicated itself to the new wave of bands. Amusingly, the article was written by Hell, utilizing the pseudonym with which he'd been fooling the New York poetry world for a couple of years now, Theresa Stern.

The story was that she was a twenty-something poet who lived across the river in Hoboken and who got into poetry because, "she" said, "I saw all this writing being praised and I knew I could do better with a splitting headache on the subway at rush hour."

Hell "discovered" her and set about bringing her name to prominence, and he did so with such conviction that he regularly received letters from poets and publishers hoping to meet up with her.

According to the article that the *Rocker* published, she liked us a lot, and she liked Hell even more. He was, she wrote, "a master rock conceptualist."

We did another photo session with Roberta, with Hell hatching an image straight out of a fifties horror movie for the occasion. It showed the four of us lurching zombiefied around in blood (actually chocolate syrup)-spattered t-shirts beneath the caption "Catch 'em while they're still alive."

We used it the first time when we played the Sea of Clouds with the Ramones on New Year's Eve, and I'm still not sure whether Hell intended the caption specifically to accompany the photographs, or if he was also riffing on our growing reputation as the most hard-core junkies (and, therefore, the most likely ODs) on the scene.

We also spent three days in SBS Studios, out in Yonkers, recording our first set of demos, which was basically our live set minus things like "(I'm Not Your) Stepping Stone" and the other covers we occasionally favored.

For all the drama that was unfolding behind the scenes, that tape captures much of what made the original Heartbreakers seem so special, and not only because the ten songs we chose to record offered up the perfect cross-section of material—three songs apiece by Johnny and Hell; a fourth, "Hurt Me," that they came up with together; "Flight"; "Can't Keep My Eyes on You"; and the song that would ultimately become regarded as our anthem, "Chinese Rocks."

Had we maintained that same equanimity, the future might well have been very different. As it was, we played our last full show together on a trip up to Boston to headline the local Rat on May 14, and the next time we convened—at what is now the Hammerstein Ballroom at the Manhattan Center on May 30—we couldn't even pretend to be a band.

Although we didn't know it when we first agreed to perform, the New York Rock Party would be our first gig without Hell.

We were at the SoHo loft where we were rehearsing; in fact, I was in the rehearsal area already, doing something or other. Hell and Jerry were sitting around in the other room, and when Johnny walked in, Hell started in on him.

Jerry told me what happened next, as Hell announced: "From now on, I'm singing the set. Johnny sings two of the songs, and Walter shuts up."

There might have been more, but Johnny wasn't listening. He didn't even bother to reply. He just walked out of the room, leaving Hell staring into an empty space.

Jerry stood up too, came into the back room where I was obliviously tinkering on, and gave me the gist of what happened. Two minutes later, we followed Johnny out of the door. Again, we didn't even need to debate the matter. We knew where our loyalties lay.

If the Rock Party had just been another gig, we'd have cancelled. But it wasn't. It was a benefit for Jayne County to raise funds for what was surely the most bizarre lawsuit of the age—best summed up, in Jayne's own words, as "Mad Drag Queen attacks Poor Defenseless Wrestler."

A short time before, Jayne was on stage at CBGB when Dick Manitoba, frontman with the Dictators, began haranguing her.

Some background, and this is important because it shows how the New York scene was splintering . . . *had* splintered. The Dictators were one of those bands that sprang up in the shadow of the Dolls, around 1972–1973, played the same circuit, made the same friends, and maybe made some better ones, too, because around the same time as the Dolls broke up and the Heartbreakers got started, the Dictators signed with Columbia and went into the studio with Sandy Pearlman—the ears behind Blue Oyster Cult, among others.

It should have been the start of something big. I was never a massive fan—the Dictators always sounded like a hard rock band to me. But they covered Iggy and they snarled in the right places and, during that long pause while everyone was waiting for the Next Big Thing to come out of post-Dolls New York, the Dictators must have thought they had it made.

But they didn't. Unbeknownst to the Dictators, the city had already moved on to other fascinations . . . CBGB, Max's, Mother's, wherever . . . and the Dictators were left completely out in the cold.

They should have knuckled down, gone back to basics, thrown themselves into the club scene, and proved their worth again. Instead, like the jilted bridegrooms that they were, they turned vicious. Or, at least, their singer did.

The night before the Jayne County incident, Manitoba was heckling Blondie at CBGB. A few nights before that, apparently, he was yelling abuse at somebody else.

Other people simply shrugged him off. Jayne didn't. Unaware at the time of who was responsible, she simply invited the heckler to "come up here and say that."

An ex-pro wrestler, Manitoba obliged. He had a beer glass in his hand, and Jayne was not the only person who feared the worst. As she writes in her book, *Man Enough to Be a Woman*: "I picked up my microphone stand and I just hit him with it, right on the collar bone. His collar bone broke, I heard it crack. He flew off the stage, went head first into the corner of a table and busted his head open."

Manitoba was dragged away, hauled into an ambulance, and rushed to a hospital. Then he sued Jayne for assault. If he had any friends on the scene before that, he certainly lost them now.

Tommy Dean and Max's were behind the benefit, booking the venue and putting the call out for guests to appear. The city opened up in response. Ian Hunter and Mick Ronson, Suicide, Willy DeVille and his band Mink DeVille, Divine, Cherry Vanilla, the Planets, Jackie Curtis, Holly Woodlawn, Tuff Darts, the Dollettes, a Joey-less Ramones, and more.

There was an auction—one of Iggy's stage costumes, some of Bowie's old boots, a signed Lou Reed poster. Andy Warhol donated some artwork. And we played, too—Johnny and myself, with Phil Marcade from the Senders and this guy named Octavio, who used to bring dope over from France, playing bass. Hell was there as well, but not with us. In fact, I don't think we even spoke to one another.

There was never any doubt that we would continue on without Hell, or that it was we who would remain the Heartbreakers. Besides, Jerry and Johnny were by now inseparable, bound by a relationship that Leee Black Childers, soon to become our manager, later described as akin to "an unrequited love affair."

Personally, I saw it more as a father-son type of thing. Johnny looked up to Jerry not only because he was a few years older, a lot more experienced, and possessed a fabulous knowledge of pre-Beatles rock 'n' roll, but also because Jerry could beat the shit out of him in a fight, and often did.

Today, Jerry would probably be diagnosed as bipolar. His attitudes were certainly a little schizophrenic.

On the one hand, he was utterly besotted by the wholesome values of the American 1950s—the whole *Leave It to Beaver*, white picket fence, "Pleasant Valley Sunday" way of living; the ideals of a one man–one woman romance; and so on. But on the other hand, there was his addictive side, and his inability to conquer what even he knew were bad habits . . . drugs, of course, but a host of other personal issues and distorted principles.

He had a mercurial disposition; he'd be your best friend one day, and the next, he'd refuse to speak to you. You never knew why—after a time, in fact, you just accepted it as who he was and stopped wondering what imagined slight or misplaced glance he had taken exception to.

He could find trouble wherever he went, no matter what he did. Even something so innocuous and ordinary as going to the bar at Max's.

Jerry, Johnny, and I, and maybe Philippe, were sitting at one of the tables at Max's, simply enjoying a night out after rehearsal.

We were probably talking about the band, and Jerry went up to the bar to get another drink.

We heard some sort of commotion, but we didn't pay attention—fights were common at most clubs, so this was probably just another. But then somebody came over to tell us that Jerry had been hurt.

We got up and went to the bar—there was blood all over the floor.

Slowly we pieced together what had happened. Or what people thought had happened. Jerry went up to the bar and somebody's drink got knocked over. It wasn't clear to me whether it was Jerry's or that of this other guy who was sitting at the bar. Either way, the glass was on the ground; the guy started cursing and screaming, and Jerry punched him a few times, knocking him to the floor. At this point, the guy picked up a shard of the broken glass and jammed it into Jerry's inner thigh, slicing an artery.

Somebody patched him up as best they could, and Jerry was bundled into a cab to take him to St. Vincent's hospital; we followed behind in another cab. We couldn't see him immediately, but we could hear him screaming and yelling in the room where they'd taken him, probably as he they tried to insert a catheter.

There was a back story that started to circulate, that the guy who stabbed Jerry was somehow mob-connected, and Max's owner Tommy Dean knew this, so he "took care" of things . . . whatever those things might have been. The police were never involved, as far as I know, and we never heard any more about the guy, either. And Jerry, being Jerry, spent a few days tucked up on the welfare ward, got discharged when his leg healed up, and probably had another fight with someone that same evening.

That was Jerry the brawler. On the other side, there was Jerry the peacemaker.

Many nights we would wind up at the apartment Jerry shared with his girlfriend, Michelle, on the Upper East Side, to get something to eat. It was a chance to chill out, relax, have fun, and occasionally have a good laugh as well—such as the evening Johnny's girlfriend, Julie, asked Michelle for a spoon to stir her tea. Michelle went to get one and then came back empty-handed.

"It's so odd," she said. "I used to have so many spoons here, and they've all vanished." The junkies in the room exchanged knowing smirks.

Or the night when Johnny, halfway through eating a sandwich, started nodding out from whatever he'd taken earlier in the evening. He literally sat in the same position for twenty minutes with his eyes closed and the sandwich hanging out of his mouth until finally we couldn't stand looking at it any longer.

Jerry leaned over to try and extricate the sandwich from between Johnny's teeth, at which point Johnny awoke with a start and swung an arm in protest, convinced that he was being attacked. Jerry simply laughed.

That was the thing. Jerry loved Johnny, saw in him a young kid who could play rock 'n' roll and was spunky—he converted Johnny to a lot of his rock roots, as well. And he was great at keeping Johnny under control; in fact, he was the only person who truly could. Even back in the Dolls, if Johnny was acting too crazy—which was especially likely when he did speed—the rest of the band would tell Jerry to take him into another room and sort him out.

Jerry would give him two or three punches and Johnny would be good for the next few months. In the Heartbreakers, it didn't even come to that very often. All Jerry would have to do was ask, "Johnny? Do you want a punch in the head?" And Johnny would say, "No," and behave.

But they would also get into the most terrible fights and not speak to one another for days or even months at a time—and, at the end, for years. Again, father-son. Musically, however, they belonged together, and when they passed away, both in the span of nine months, they were buried within fifty yards of one another. Together again.

Chapter Eight

FAREWELL TO MANHATTAN

We had to find a replacement for Hell, but before we began the search, we decided that three songwriters in the band were enough. We needed someone who would just play, and we auditioned a few different bassists.

Keith "Keef" Paul, one of the Dolls' old sound guys, tried out, and so did Albert Sce, my old college friend and Bloodbath compatriot. An ex-boxer named Steve Shevlin, who'd later join the Senders but who looked like something out of *West Side Story*, tried out as well. But finally a guy who ran one of the clothing stores around St. Mark's Place suggested we look at a friend of his, Billy Rath, who had just returned to New York after living in Florida for a few years.

Billy clicked immediately. A year older than me, he wasn't the smartest guy we'd ever met—in fact, he often came across as a bit of a dimwit, albeit a good natured one. He had that slow Boston accent that can often disguise somebody's intellect, but he also had these big blue eyes that would stand out when he was looking at you, and if there had been a brain behind them, he could have been so magnetic. Unfortunately, there wasn't, and after Hell's constant scheming and thinking, that came as something of a relief.

He didn't want to write songs or sing; he didn't want to wave his ego in our faces. He just wanted to play bass. He didn't disappear in search of drugs, and he didn't turn up late for rehearsals— once the Heartbreakers were out on the road, I often used to share a room with him, and he was the ideal roommate. Even speeding . . . and he continued to take speed, even after he started on smack . . . he was a perfect fit, just reliable and always there.

You wouldn't want to be stuck in a jail cell with him, though. He'd put you to sleep, as I discovered when he and I got busted in my car while we were on a drug-buying expedition. We spent the night in the Tombs, and it was a long night. The following morning, they gave us a ticket to come back in a month or two, but the arresting officer never showed up for the hearing, so we got out with a fifty-dollar fine.

Billy was a great bass player, with terrific feel, and I could see him and Jerry just sparking off one another the moment we started to play together. We offered him the job that same day, I think, and he accepted on the spot. And it was with Billy that we became the band we had always known we could be. The band about whom British journalist Kris Needs would soon be writing: "If the spirit of the New York Dolls still exists, it's in this group, who display the same reckless energy and flash. The playing is much tighter, problems of the past are gone and the new songs are all catchy, rock 'n' roll killers. One of the best live acts around."

Billy joined the Heartbreakers on June 15, 1976, and for the next month or so, we rehearsed and wrote. Hell's departure had opened a floodgate of sorts, and by the time we were ready to play our first show with the new lineup—a couple of nights at Max's on July 23 and 24—new songs "Baby Talk," "Take a Chance," "It's Not Enough," and "Born to Lose" were all ready to go.

They were all strong songs. Johnny wrote "Born to Lose" on his own; he got the idea from the tattoo ("Born to Lose") that Richard Speck, the serial killer, had on his arm. I'm not sure how the title then shifted as it did, but somebody started calling the song "Born Too Loose," which in a way was very appropriate, so we started using it ourselves. The song's official title, however, remained "Born to Lose."

"Baby Talk" was our take on a Yardbirds lick. Johnny had heard it on one of the live Yardbirds albums and asked if I could figure it out so we could write a song around it. Years later, the Ramones would record a cover of "Baby Talk" for a Johnny tribute album.

"It's Not Enough" was our Stonesy ballad. Jerry was never keen on it—in his mind, the Heartbreakers should only be playing hard, driving rock 'n' roll, so this went completely against the grain. But it turned out to be one of our best-loved songs, and Johnny was still performing it years later. In fact, you could say it was the foundation of the entire acoustic side of his solo career. It's also the song that Nancy Spungeon singled out as a highlight in her review for the *New York Rocker*.

Nancy was a Philadelphia chick who had latched onto the Dolls when they played her hometown a couple of years before—from what I heard she simply jumped into the van with them as they were leaving, probably fucked them all as they drove back to the city, and never went home again.

She'd cottoned onto us early because she thought we were cool, so in a way she was one of the people we needed to impress with the new lineup—she had a loud, obnoxious mouth even by New York standards, and the last thing we wanted was her wandering around telling everyone that we were nothing without Richard Hell . . . who, incidentally, she was also sleeping with at one point.

I'd never especially warmed to Nancy—in fact, only Jerry seemed able to tolerate her in anything more than the smallest dose. But I did almost end up sleeping with her one night.

I dropped her off by her apartment, and she asked me if I wanted to come in. I don't know how tempted I was, but clearly not enough. "No, no," I said, and left, which I count as a narrow escape. Because Philippe, who I guess was a little less cautious around her, later told me just how disgusting the full Nancy Spungeon experience was.

But she remained a vital cheerleader. Her write-up in the *Rocker* described us as "the biggest draw in New York," dismissed Hell's departure with a shrug, and declared that we were "better than ever." That little write-up did a lot to calm any nerves we'd been feeling about how the new lineup might be received.

The downside was that it allowed Nancy to stick even closer to us than she had. I hate to speak ill of the dead, but she really was a pig. She was working at the time as a topless dancer in a variety of bars around town—nowhere even remotely classy, though. They were deserted holes-in-the-wall for the most part.

A couple of times, if we needed to borrow some money or score some dope, we'd go out looking for her at whichever bar she was in that afternoon, and there she'd be, dancing on a makeshift stage, with some drunken postman sleeping it off in a chair or on a stool with his head on the bar.

He was lucky to be asleep—she'd take off her top and you could see her arms were just covered in huge, ugly bruises from shooting up. Why anyone would pay money to see this monster dance, I could not imagine.

But she had money, and she was generous with it too, so that certainly appealed to Johnny and Jerry. She was always making them little gifts of stuff—drugs, cash, items of clothing, anything she thought they might like, so they were happy to keep her around. Because money was a problem.

I was okay. I was still working at the FDA, bringing home a decent wage. I was living in Brooklyn Heights, a nice basement apartment with a working fireplace. True, I was occasionally struck by the sheer dichotomy of my professional and personal lives—sneaking out of the office every Friday at lunchtime to drive to the Lower East Side to score and then heading back to work to get high in the bathroom. But I was happy.

I was the only band member who did have a job, though. Jerry never worked; his girlfriend Michelle at the time had a job, and that was enough. She supported him when the Dolls money ran out. He did have his license to be a hairdresser, but he certainly never used it while he was with us.

Billy never worked in his life, either. There were rumors that he appeared on the cover of a couple of gay magazines while he was living in Florida, and that might be true. He did look pretty good. But that was just the story we heard; I don't know if it happened.

Johnny effectively lived on what we were paid for gigs and on what he could get in the way of freebies. Tommy Dean at Max's was especially good to him, allowing him to run up a massive tab and supplying him with different things—mostly coke, there was always coke in the office—to keep him going. He would always offer the rest of us occasional lines, but whenever Johnny was in the office, there'd be as much as was required.

We were bringing in up to $1,000 per show at Max's, which would be about $5,000 today, and that sounds impressive. But expenses and drugs devoured a lot of it, so we'd probably only clear a hundred or so apiece.

At least, we should have. Unfortunately, there were a couple of occasions when, no sooner had we booked a show, Johnny would be at the promoter's door, asking for an advance. Then, a few days later, he'd be back for another one. And a few days after that, as well. By the time we got to the gig itself, all the money was gone because Johnny had got it all in advances.

Finally, Jerry, Billy, and I went to the various club managers and told them, "Listen, you can give Johnny an advance, but no more than 25 percent of what we booked for." And even that didn't always work.

The problem remained the same as it always had. We were wholly self-reliant. It was we who booked the gigs, we who arranged the transport, we who hired anything we needed. It was time to find a manager

Kentucky-born Leee Black Childers had been around the New York scene since the end of the 1960s. He was a key element of the crowd that orbited Warhol's inner circle and was the stage manager of *Pork*, the Warhol play that caused such a furor when it ran in London in 1971.

It was *Pork*, which also featured Jayne County and another Max's regular, Cherry Vanilla, that introduced Leee to David Bowie—at the same time as Bowie was introduced to much of the imagery he would deploy when he became Ziggy Stardust the following year.

When Bowie arrived in New York in the fall of 1972, it was Leee who met him off the boat (Bowie never flew in those days)

and took him almost directly down to the Mercer to catch the Dolls in concert. In return, Bowie hired both Leee and Cherry to his management company, Mainman, with Leee swiftly rising to a vice presidency.

He accompanied Bowie on tours around the world, and when Mainman signed Iggy and the Stooges, it was Leee who was sent to Los Angeles to take care of Iggy and guitarist James Williamson, living in a big old house on Cielo Drive but spending most of his time driving around the less attractive parts of the city trying to find where his charges had disappeared to.

On top of that, he was also a brilliant photographer. Some of the earliest, and best, New York Dolls shots were Leee's, while his work was forever turning up in the music magazines of the day. Indeed, the first time I met him was when he came to shoot us for some spread or another, and that was when he suggested he become our manager. Or maybe we suggested it.

It wasn't an easy decision—I don't mean about hiring Leee; I mean about having a manager to begin with. When Jerry wasn't blaming Johansen for all that went wrong with the New York Dolls, he was blaming their management, and there, Johnny agreed with him. Both had been seriously burned by what they portrayed as a never-ending sequence of missteps and bad deals, and they were understandably wary of ever allowing an outsider to have so much power again.

At the same time, however, Johnny at least knew and trusted Leee—Jerry would never warm to him—and Billy and I felt confident, too. For a start, he didn't act like a manager, not around us. But we only had to see him in action, once we took him on and he started handling the day-to-day grunt work for us, to know that he could be as hard as nails when he needed to.

Leee's original plan had been to recruit another of the *Pork/ Mainman* crew, Tony Zanetta, as our co-manager. That didn't pan out in the end—I don't think Tony was interested. But Leee did have connections. People knew him and liked him, even

Onstage at My Father's Place, Long Island, 1980. *(Photo by Russell De Gaeto)*

Left: Portrait of the old punk as a young one. *(Author's collection)*

Above: I've been trying to recapture that stare ever since. *(Author's collection)*

A career in country was never in the cards. *(Author's collection)*

Eight years old. *(Author's collection)*

The Lure boys *(left–right)* William, Walter, and Richie. *(Author's collection)*

My first band, Bloodbath, in 1970. *(Author's collection)*

Early into my career at the FDA. *(Author's collection)*

Circa 1973, playing Staten Island with the Stray Cats. *(Author's collection)*

Richie and I working up a song for our grandmother's ninetieth birthday party in 1976. *(Author's collection)*

A Heartbreakers' photo shoot, the morning after Johnny was beaten up by his brother-in-law. *(left–right)* Johnny, Richard, Jerry, and myself. *(Photo by Roberta Bayley)*

The Heartbreakers as zombies. *(Photo by Roberta Bayley)*

Rehearsals, and Jerry napping, 1977. *(Photo by Bob Gruen)*

Here we go! New York, 1977. *(Photo by Bob Gruen)*

Live at the Village Gate, 1977. *(Photo by Bob Gruen)*

Johnny and I at the Village Gate, 1977. *(Photo by Bob Gruen)*

Left: The spit flew everywhere, then dripped back down. Onstage at the Roxy, 1977. *(Photo by Ray Stevenson)*

Right: Johnny No-Pupils, London, 1976–77. *(Photo by Ray Stevenson)*

Looking for something, London, 1977. *(Photo by Ray Stevenson)*

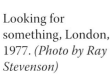

The Heartbreakers in full flight, 1977. *(Photo by Ray Stevenson)*

Back in New York with my family for a post-Christmas vacation. *(Author's collection)*

My parents and I, after the label flew them to England for one of our shows. *(Photo by Ray Stevenson)*

Carol and I. This was taken in New York a couple of years after we met. *(Author's collection)*

On the river, London, 1977. *(Photo by Ray Stevenson)*

Sid Vicious, Nancy
Spungeon, and I.
London, 1977.
(Photo by Anna Sui)

folks who might not have ordinarily looked at us for fear of that "reputation."

He was also very persuasive—our fees went up as soon as he took over, and when we went up to Boston for a run of four shows at the Rat at the end of September, 1976, he even made certain that we had a decent place to stay while we were there.

Not that it remained decent for long. We brought Philippe from the Senders along as our roadie, and as they seemed to do as often as they could, he and Johnny shared a room.

We played the first gig, and the following morning I walked into their room. Now, it was late fall, fucking cold, yet the windows were all wide open and Johnny was rolling around coughing and gagging, and Philippe was killing himself laughing. It turned out that Philippe had just taken his shoes off and the stench was absolutely disgusting. It smelled like he hadn't taken a shower in a month. Poor Johnny. He looked like he was going to throw up and never stop.

Those were the shows, incidentally, where Jerry played the entire set with one leg propped up on something while playing his bass drum with the other, as he continued to recover from the stabbing.

The only problem Leee couldn't seem to help us with was the one that almost every band in the city was facing—getting a decent record deal.

The Ramones had followed Patti Smith in getting an album out—their first LP was released during the summer of 1976. Now the race was on to follow them into the shops. But whereas Patti had gone to what you might call a major label, Clive Davis's Arista, and the Ramones had signed with Seymour Stein's Sire, so at least they had some muscle behind them, the other big labels of the day were paying no attention at all.

Columbia, I think, were already feeling as though they'd had their fingers burned by the Dictators, while Mercury, which was the Dolls' old label, were more interested in LA scenester Kim Fowley's latest project, an all-girl band called the Runaways, than anything that was happening in the real world. The others just didn't care.

So it was left to the smaller operators to court the New York scene, and honestly, we didn't fancy any of them. Bookstore owner Terry Ork had his eponymous label up and running, and both Television and Hell had singles out because of it.

Tommy Dean and Peter Crowley, over at Max's Kansas City, were preparing the first *Live at Max's* compilation, with people like Jayne and Cherry on board. They asked if we'd be interested in appearing on it, but we turned them down.

Hilly Kristal was planning to follow through with *Live at CBGB's*, with Mink DeVille, Tuff Darts, and the Shirts.

Doubtless there were others.

But they were all small fry, and besides that, the kind of deals being offered were laughable, sleazy fifty-fifty splits that the bands could never, ever hope to profit from.

So, when Richard Gottehrer—a co-founder (with Seymour Stein) of Sire Records way back when and the man who wrote "My Boyfriend's Back" (and a million others)—started showing an interest, we at least looked his way.

He was already looking after Hell's solo interests, which wasn't a point in his favor. He was also working with one of the Dolls' old management team, Marty Thau, and that immediately put Jerry's back up, and Johnny's too—although he, at least, remembered Thau as a fan as much as a manager. It was Thau who "discovered" the Dolls in the very beginning, and Thau who lost his own home when the group's career went pear-shaped.

At the same time, Gottehrer did know what he was doing, and he courted us very carefully.

His first approach came when he was looking for someone to back rockabilly singer Robert Gordon on a set of demos he was producing during the summer.

We agreed and cut a handful of old standards with him—I don't believe I ever heard the finished tape but, as Robert was singing, obviously it was some rockabilly Elvis type shit, and clearly, some people liked it.

In fact, there was even talk going around that maybe Robert should join the Heartbreakers—Jerry mentioned it a few times, but I was dead set against it, and the others weren't keen, either. It was just a rumor that was floating about, and of course it would have never worked.

For a start, Johnny had already been overshadowed once in his own band; it wasn't going to happen again. But there was also the fact that Robert never smiled. *Never*. It was still early in his career and, so far as we were concerned, he had a rotten personality. The only person in the band who might have entertained the idea was Jerry. He was into that kind of Elvis thing as well. But even he could see what a dumb notion it was.

Richard Gottehrer stayed in touch, and in October we met with him again, around the same time as we cut a new set of demos at what might have been Jay Nap Studios—"Born to Lose," "Do You Love Me," "Can't Keep My Eyes on You," "It's Not Enough," "I Love You," "Take a Chance," and a couple of backing tracks.

Gottehrer didn't have a label. His idea was to form a production company, making the records that he would then license on to others, and he was already in talks to place both Blondie and Robert Gordon onto Private Stock. It wasn't exactly Columbia or Warner Bros., but they did have singing actor David Soul, of *Starsky and Hutch* fame, on their books, so they knew how to push someone up to number one. It wasn't the worst thing that could happen.

But the deal that Gottehrer was offering to the Heartbreakers was as bad as every other one—a tiny advance, and even tinier royalties, and no room to negotiate either. It also turned out that he, too, was concerned about our reputation, and how it might prove problematic when he came to talk with labels.

As he, and various other people, reminded us, no matter how big the New York bands might be in our own city, and maybe

Boston and Philly, so far as the rest of the country was concerned, we might as well have been on Mars.

There was no "music scene" at that time, no vast clamoring of disaffected youth demanding new music played by new people. America was the land of Boston (the band), Peter Frampton, Fleetwood Mac, and the Eagles. Outside of our little toeholds in the Northeast, we weren't even big enough to be a cult. Even if a major label did bite, it wouldn't take much to make them spit us out again.

What did Leee think? The same as us. The deals we were being offered—and not only by Gottehrer; a few lesser entities, too, had shown an interest—were crap.

At the same time, however, if we at least had a record out, it would serve as a shop window of sorts, and that might bring some major label calling. Of course, they'd then have to extricate us from whichever contractual mantrap we'd originally climbed into bed with, but if they wanted us bad enough. . . .

Okay, we'd play nice with Gottehrer. In fact, we had more or less agreed among ourselves that we would sign with him, and Leee was about to pick up the phone to make the call when, completely out of the blue, he received another.

It was Malcolm McLaren, the Dolls' old manager. He had a new band that he was managing, called the Sex Pistols, and they were about to go out on their first UK tour. Would the Heartbreakers be interested in coming along as special guests?

That call to Gottehrer could wait. Of course we said yes.

Chapter Nine

AND HELLO TO LONDON

We didn't know what these Sex Pistols were . . . I'd seen their name in some local rag about six months earlier, with the insistence that they were part of "a scene," but what that scene might be, the journalist never let on.

McLaren's involvement left Johnny feeling a little unsure as well. Malcolm had only managed the Dolls for a matter of months at the very tail end of their career, and that had scarcely been a glowing (or even lightly illuminated) triumph. "He has great ideas," Johnny explained. "But I don't know whether he knows how to act upon them."

On the other hand, however, Johnny (and even Jerry) had to admit that Malcolm was open, entertaining, kindhearted, and, perhaps even more importantly, the co-owner of one of London's most adventurous boutiques, Sex. And again, Johnny had known him a long time—they first met when Sylvain was working in the rag trade himself, and ran into Malcolm at a fashion fair in New York back in 1971 or so. Johnny was one of the first people Syl called to come and check out the wares.

Since then, McLaren and his partner Vivienne Westwood had wholeheartedly supported the Dolls, both in word and deed— Westwood was constantly sending over samples of her designs, and she outfitted the entire band for that final Red Patent Leather Tour. If nothing else, Johnny reasoned, even if the entire tour was a bust, we'd probably get some decent clothing out of it.

In fact, later we discovered that Malcolm had only called us after the Dollettes had turned the same tour down, and there was maybe another band who said no, as well. So we were at least his second choice and possibly the third. But Leee knew Malcolm, too, and had always enjoyed his company. Besides, it was England!

Twenty-odd dates, all expenses paid, *and* we'd be home in time for Christmas.

Tickets were booked, bags were packed, and on December 1, we set off for the old world.

Except we didn't get there. We landed on Mars, instead.

I'd been there before, of course, and so had Johnny and Jerry, with the Dolls. But I went as a tourist, and they went as visiting superstars. We weren't even aware of the world outside the worlds that we wanted to see—a never-ending BBC historical drama for me; a lifelong rerun of *Beyond the Valley of the Dolls* for them. Why would we be?

Almost from the moment we landed at Heathrow on December 1, 1976, however, we knew there was something very strange going on.

Malcolm met us at the airport with his secretary, Sophie Richmond, a pretty, short-haired brunette whose boyfriend, Jamie, was Malcolm's graphic arts designer. We piled into the limo, and it was immediately clear that something was wrong because it was Sophie who did most of the talking, while Malcolm just sat there quietly, twitching and fidgeting.

At first, we thought he was on drugs because he was acting so weird. His eyeballs were twirling around in his head, and his mouth was working silently as he sat. But finally he spoke.

"I don't know what to do. The band just cursed on television."

Allow me to repeat that.

The.

Band.

Just.

Cursed.

On.

Television?

We looked at one another.

"Well, duh, they cursed? Everybody curses." Maybe not on television, not even in America. But so what? Even if they had, no way would people have been as upset as Malcolm seemed to think they would be.

We laughed him off, and his silly neuroses . . . according to Johnny, Malcolm had been a world-class worrier when he was managing the Dolls, and clearly nothing had changed in the interim. So we checked in at our hotel, and arranged for him to pick us up later, to go for a meal and meet his Sex Pistols. We didn't give Malcolm's fears another thought.

The phone rang. There were two gentlemen waiting for us in the lobby. We trouped down to see two nervous-looking kids standing there, all but staring wide-eyed at Johnny. They said hello, and we barely heard another word out of them. Paul Cook and Steve Jones, the Pistols' drummer and guitarist, were two of the biggest New York Dolls fans to walk this earth. We'd thought they were just quiet and shy. It turned out they were terrified at the prospect of meeting their hero, Johnny.

Johnny, on the other hand, basked in their obvious admiration. In New York, a lot of people regarded him as simply a part of the musical furniture. Now, he teased us, we would see how beloved he really was.

Johnny's attitude toward his past fame was interesting. He was the youngest member of the Heartbreakers, just twenty-four years old when we arrived in London, but he was by far the most experienced, both in rock 'n'roll terms and simply life.

But he rarely felt the need to lord it over us. He might offer us "the benefit of his experience" if we ever found ourselves in what he considered a familiar situation, or confronted with the kind of sharks he had met during the Dolls; he rarely sat around spouting off on former glories unless somebody asked him outright.

In some ways, he didn't need to—Jerry did that enough for both of them (although he tended to focus on the bad times, not the good), and the fans never tired of bringing the Dolls into the conversation.

But I also felt that Johnny viewed the Dolls as old news. The past was the past, and while they had been very special, that was where they belonged. As far as he was concerned, it was like talking about an old girlfriend. That's one of the big reasons why there were no Dolls songs in our live show, no matter how often audiences called for them.

Back into the limo, and off to meet with Malcolm again, still twitching, still fidgeting, at a place that prided itself in making American-style hamburgers. Except they weren't American-style, and I'm not sure they were even hamburgers. Instant flashback to my last visit and the horrors that awaited my digestive system.

We made it through the meal, though, and were deposited back at our hotel. And the next morning when we woke up, every fucking newspaper in the country had the Sex Pistols on the cover, with the story of how they'd cursed on television.

We were standing on the street, looking at the rows of papers on display outside a newspaper store, and it was wall-to-wall "the filth and the fury." How these foulmouthed punks had effed and blinded through the city's tea time; how one viewer was so outraged by their language that he put his foot through the television screen. In front of his children!

It was like something out of *The Twilight Zone*. We couldn't get our heads around it. "All of this, just because they said a few rude words?" How many people even watched that show? It was an early evening local magazine program that only went out in London. If it hadn't been for the papers taking it national, it would have been forgotten in five minutes.

One thing's for sure, though. Back home, you couldn't have bought this kind of publicity if you had all the money, or swear words, in the world!

Even Leee couldn't believe it, and he remembered all the fuss about Bowie being bisexual back in 1972 and how people were screaming blue murder about him. *Pork* as well, for that matter, although there they maybe had a point. Even today, there aren't many West End stage shows that feature, every night, a naked man lying on the stage while a co-star takes a dump on his face.

The outrage that arose around the Sex Pistols made those controversies sound like generous applause, however, and it didn't stop with that day's headlines, either. This was a major story. Questions in government, sackings on television—Bill Grundy, the presenter who'd been interviewing the Pistols, was placed on permanent leave. The little old ladies at the pressing plant where the Pistols' single was made went on strike, refusing to handle the record. Their label, EMI, was under pressure to drop them. All because they cursed on television.

Mars was getting stranger all the time.

From our point of view, of course, this was great. This was the Sex Pistols' first proper tour, built around promoting the single (well, that was out of the window, now) but also aiming to introduce the group to audiences outside of London.

The music papers had done their bit, suggesting some kind of London-based cult called punk rock, and Malcolm had booked two other bands on the tour—the Clash, whom very few people had heard of, and the Damned, who also had a single out, "New Rose." Add the Heartbreakers as special guests from the United States, and together, we were going to inculcate punk rock into the masses.

Except now, we didn't need to. A few minutes on television and the Sex Pistols had not simply coalesced what had hitherto been a few disparate pockets of punk awareness; they had transformed it into one giant pulsating pimple, set to burst across the face of English society. It was perfect. As we clambered onto the bus that was taking us to the first show in Norwich, up on that bulge on the country's east coast, all we were thinking of was how huge our audience was going to be.

Or how huge it already was. We suddenly realized that we were not traveling alone. It felt as though every press man in the world was coming with us, a swarm that was waiting on the street outside the Pistols' rehearsal space in Denmark Street, snapping photos and shouting questions as we got onto the bus, and then piling into cars and onto bikes and following us as we drove.

The Clash alone joined the Pistols and ourselves on the bus; the Damned, for whatever reason, were following behind in their own van, so right away, our companions started telling us what a bunch of assholes they were, what a bunch of wimps, and so on. And we took it all in because we never even met the Damned until we played the first show.

Which was not in Norwich that night, nor in Derby the following evening, nor even in Newcastle the night after that. Amid all the excitement that surrounded the tour, and the flood of publicity that now accompanied it, there was one thing that none of us expected to happen. We arrived at the first show to discover the local council had banned the Sex Pistols from even taking the stage. The same the next night, the same the night after.

The rest of us were okay; the Heartbreakers, the Clash, and the Damned were welcome to perform, we were told. The bans only extended to the Pistols. But of course we weren't going to break ranks—there'd have been a riot on the bus if we had, and besides, there's such a thing as solidarity. Ban one, ban us all. When the rumor went around that the Damned had said they'd be willing to consider playing alone, that only ostracized them even further.

As it turned out, once we did get to meet them and spend time with them, we got on fine. The first time we saw the Damned was a bit of a shock . . . "What the fuck's that guy dressed like a vampire for?" And musically, they were a bit too heavy metal for me. But they were nice enough guys, and later, after Jerry quit the Heartbreakers, we auditioned Damned drummer Rat Scabies for the job. He didn't get it.

So there we were, back and forth across the country in the bus, drawing up in town after town and booking into our hotel while we waited to discover whether or not the evening's gig would happen. Then going to the hotel bar when we learned that it wouldn't.

That's how I discovered Carlsburg Special Brew, by the way, an innocuous-looking lager that turned out to be the strongest beer I'd ever had in my life. And it was also where we realized just how different this punk scene was to anything we'd seen back home.

The clothes. Back in New York, the uniform was more-or-less your street clothes. Ripped t-shirts, jeans, leather jackets, and a few strategically placed tears were as out there as it got. We stood out a bit with our '50s suits and skinny ties, and a few other bands had their own peculiar looks . . . Jayne County, for example. But even Jayne (who Leee would also bring to London early the following year) in full drag would have to up the game if she wanted to compete with the locals.

They looked so cool, the Pistols in particular. Just like the Dolls before them, the Pistols had the run of Sex and were duly transformed into a walking billboard for Malcolm and Vivienne's wares, be they sleeveless raincoats or bondage trousers or mohair sweaters with one arm that stopped at the elbow and the other that hung to the knee.

Everything was in your face. One T-shirt—a pair of naked cowboys, facing one another and standing so close that their dicks were touching—was prosecuted for obscenity. Another, bearing the masked face of the Cambridge Rapist (a notorious nasty of the day), brought another barrage of press hatred down upon their heads. Yet another depicted a naked boy with the cowboy hat and his dick hanging out.

Garbage bags with holes torn into them, to be worn as T-shirts or even minidresses. Zippers, lots of zippers. Homemade haircuts, rendered with the bluntest pair of scissors in the room and died in various neon colors. Torn clothes held together by safety pins. Of course we'd seen that look before—Richard Hell used to sport it, and apparently that's where Malcolm got the idea from. But the English kids took it further . . . much further.

I realized that when we got to Leeds, where we were finally allowed to put on a show, the first of the entire tour. The gig was at the local college, in a big room with a large crowd, and considering punk rock had been unheard of a week ago, the kids had caught on quickly.

We watched a few walk past with safety pins in their cheeks, and we laughed because everyone had seen those novelty clip-ons, the ones you slipped around the side of your mouth, to make it look as though you'd mutilated yourself.

Then we saw the blood. And sometimes, the pus. I remember they'd get into fights and the safety pin would be the first thing their adversary would try to rip out. There'd be blood everywhere and then the kid would come to the front of the stage to impress us.

These weren't novelty clip-ons. These were the real thing, actually forced through the flesh; one hole in, one hole out, and then locked into place. I can't even imagine how much it must have hurt, both during and after the operation. But these kids were laughing, smiling, happy, and so proud of themselves. You'd see them coming out of the restrooms, still oozing blood and gloop but running over to us with beaming smiles. "Look what I just did!" And we'd be like, "What the fuck have you just done to yourself?"

That was one of the ways that the kids had of identifying with their newfound punk rock heroes. The other was by spitting at us.

Months before, at a London show, one of the music papers reported that Johnny Rotten, the Pistols' singer, had spat at the crowd. So now the crowd was spitting back, but not as a sign of distaste or abuse; it was a show of appreciation.

It was disgusting. I don't think any musician from that time has ever claimed to have enjoyed being gobbed on, or even understood why the fans insisted on doing it. But it was impossible to dissuade the kids—I know, because Johnny lost his temper more than once and started screaming at them to stop, and all they did was spit even more.

Unless they really liked you, in which case they might also throw pint mugs and beer cans and bottles. Usually full ones. Heavy fuckers. I don't remember ever getting hit in the head with a bottle, but I do recall Jerry's drums getting banged a few times. It was pretty close, and one of those bottles could have knocked you out and left you with a concussion.

But it was the spitting that we dreaded. You could dodge a beer can. The gob, you didn't even see until it was arcing towards you, glistening in the stage lights. So, gig after gig, it was always the same; standing on stage, under hot lights, with this tubercular green shit all over your clothes, all over your guitar.

You couldn't even get up the guitar neck because of these great blobs of mucus, and your fingers would be covered in it, too, so you couldn't hit the notes. It was all over the controls, and I had to change my strings every night. In the end, you'd be playing with your eyes closed, your mouth shut tight, and turning away when you had to breath, because the last thing you wanted was this stuff in your eyes or up your nose or . . . and this was where I dreaded the songs where I sang lead . . . down your throat. Which happened. A lot.

Afterward, you'd come offstage dripping in the stuff, your clothes stained, your hair sticky, and your jacket could stand up by itself because this stuff had dried and formed a thick, rigid crust. Every time you caught a cold or developed a rash, you'd wonder which diseased little punk at the front of the stage had passed it on with a well-aimed glob of phlegm—because that was the other thing about English kids. They all looked so sick.

Chapter Ten

ANARCHY ON TOUR
(OR NOT)

The tour stretched out before us. Every day we'd check out of the hotel and back on the bus, hoping against hope that tonight might allow us out of the cage. We'd talk, smoke, nap, and every so often we'd throw sandwiches at Joe Strummer, sitting with his nose buried in another political tract. "Put that shit down and read a fucking *Playboy*." It was pretty boring on that bus.

Then we'd check into another hotel, and off to the bar we'd go, watching the effortless ease with which Rotten could transform himself from just being one of the lads, cracking jokes and having fun, into the cruel and twisted hunchbacked hobgoblin that the media demanded he become, every time a stranger walked into the room.

We knew it was an act, and it was hilarious at first. It was only later, when it became second nature and he forgot to switch off the snide, that it grew boring, and later still that it became a parody. At the time, you just watched him in awed fascination, a one-man verbal wrecking crew. And soon, the switch broke altogether.

Watching Rotten was one of the few lasting distractions on the tour. The rest of the time, it was deathly dull. Some nights, the Clash's Paul Simonon and I would break the monotony by staging impromptu wrestling bouts in one of the hotel rooms. Other nights, we'd compete to see who could drink themselves into the deepest stupor. And, once in a while, we'd play a gig.

In Manchester, six nights (but just one show) into the tour, I caught my first ever glimpse of the Buzzcocks, a local band who replaced the Damned for that particular gig. We were still up in the dressing room when they came on, but the Pistols had seen them before, the last time they played that same city, and they told us we ought to watch.

We were up on the second floor, in a room that overlooked the stage, and it was hard to believe what we were seeing. Even harder to keep watching, too, because we were pissing ourselves with laughter.

They were a good band, four very serious young kids, playing away. But I couldn't tear my eyes away from Pete Shelley's guitar, a regular axe to which he had taken a hacksaw, and carved into something that resembled the bottom of a milk crate.

It looked ridiculous, more like a ukulele than a guitar, or something he'd built with an Erector Set. He had also jammed all the controls on ten to unleash such an earsplitting noise that the singer, Howard Devoto, had no choice but to scream every lyric. Add to that the fact that everything they did was at 100 mph, and you couldn't even tell what song they were playing. The music was awful (although it quickly got better), but it was so fucking funny.

Another unforgettable sight that first time in Manchester was a visit to Tommy Ducks, a pub in front of the Midland Hotel on East Street that was renowned for its unusual choice of decor. Hundreds of pairs of knickers hung from the walls and ceiling, all of them donated by female visitors over the years. There was a sand-filled toilet bowl in which there sat a skull, and a couple of glass-top coffins that were being used as tables. It was an astonishing place to visit and another reminder of just how far from home we were.

More bus journeys—Preston, Lancaster, Liverpool—more cancellations. I couldn't figure out why, if the shows were all being cancelled, we even bothered turning up. I suppose it could have been a contractual thing, or maybe Malcolm worried that, if we simply didn't show, there'd be another headline to nail us with— "Punk rock shockers scorn waiting fans."

We didn't make it to the Bristol show, though—while our tour mates wasted another evening sitting around, we were making our London debut at the Hope and Anchor pub in Islington. Or so I'm told.

To be honest, and I'm going to have to confess to this on a few occasions later, as well, the various history books and lists of our gigs include a lot that I have no memory of whatsoever and didn't note in my diary, either. Meaning, either I've always been forgetful or, and this is equally plausible, they're shows that perhaps were scheduled and announced but didn't ultimately take place for some reason.

I must admit, though, I especially enjoy reading about the shows we are supposed to have played around England when I know for a fact that we were elsewhere on that date.

Cardiff—cancelled. Caerphilly—ah, now that one we played, although our presence did not go unnoticed. In the car park across from the venue, a local priest had set up a soapbox and, before an audience of about two hundred placard-waving moms and dads, he preached on the evil that was taking place in the Castle Cinema over the road. "Don't let your children in to see the devil!"

They sang carols (it was ten days before Christmas) and hymns, the priest bellowed his prayers—it was like we'd stepped back four hundred years and were watching the village priest conduct an exorcism. All his congregation required were torches and pitchforks, and the image would have been complete.

It didn't scare off the audience, though. Johnny and I hung out of the window, watching every kid for miles around pour in through the doors, all come to see us devils incarnate. And that was perhaps the most amazing thing of all, the sheer shallowness of the protestors, unable to comprehend that the more they ranted and raved, the more people would want to find out what all the fuss was about. Particularly in the more rural areas, where local excitement was thin on the ground at the best of times.

But still, how could any adult truly fall so completely for so much self-righteousness, ignorance, and narrow-mindedness? The so-called backbone of the nation clearly wasn't very flexible.

Not that the knowledge did us any good. Both financially and physically, the tour was a disaster. We were even more broke now than we had been in New York City.

In terms of publicity, however, it continued to astonish. Two weeks on from that television appearance, we were still trying to wrap our heads around the manner in which the country reacted, *and continued to react*, to the simple word "fuck."

The more time that passes, too, the harder it becomes to convey how mortally and morally outraged people were—not just the tabloid newspapers, from whom you expect that kind of knee-jerk response (they have to sell copies somehow), but the general public.

It wasn't only the so-called grown-ups, either. Kids the Pistols' own age were often as disgusted as their parents, writing anti-punk diatribes to the music papers, screaming worse things than the Pistols had said as you passed them on the street.

I'd seen the generation gap in action in my teens, and been on the receiving end of its unreasoning, meaty fist, but that was the battle between old and young, the same old story playing out once again. I'd seen culture wars as well—Hell's Angels descending to stomp hippie heads. But this was different. The gap was not only between generations and cultures; it was within them as well.

But we were beginning to acclimate. We were still on Mars, and that would never change. But we were starting to understand it.

We knew that most adults were going to hate us on sight, and any kid with a denim jacket emblazoned with the names of Led Zeppelin or Uriah Heep would probably insult us as well.

We became accustomed to the freezing hotel rooms, where a tiny, ineffective heater was the sole concession to warmth; we got used to dressing rooms that were little more than crowded closets, and toilets down the hall, or even on another floor, that were basically a tiny room that you could smell from ten feet off, where a piss-filled ditch ran beneath a plastic wall, and the men would stand side by side and hope to avoid the splash back. We became accustomed (or at least resigned) to the food—or, at least, less repulsed by those soggy mounds and blackened blobs. I had never eaten so much starch in my life.

We even learned, from talking with the fans that we did meet, to accept that no matter how quaint England seemed, and how very, very English it was, it was also the most uncomfortable, inconvenient rat hole we'd ever seen.

Forget the food. (I wished I could.) Accommodation was atrocious—I couldn't believe how many kids I talked to, including people in bands, who lived in communal squats, which in turn were effectively abandoned buildings that they tried to transform into some kind of halfway decent living space. Or others who *did* have a conventional home but still might have looked at Alphabet City with a degree of envious longing.

Unemployment was soaring, strikes were crippling, and money was both hard to get and easy to lose.

I wondered how people kept going; wondered, too, how they managed to maintain some kind of high-spiritedness. I guess it's true what they say about the British "stiff upper lip," although maybe it was fatalism, too. No matter how bad things may get, you should always look on the bright side of life, because they'd be getting even worse soon enough.

 The people as a whole tended to be civilized even when we didn't agree with their outlook. Better-looking, as well, although the fact that there seemed to be a lot fewer fat people around than in America brings us back to the food. They were probably all undernourished.

What we couldn't understand was the drug culture. Back in New York, scoring was easy. The Lower East Side was effectively one vast open market; you'd go out, walk down the street, and join the line that snaked out from your favorite hole-in-the-wall. Then you'd put in your money, pull out your bag, and off you'd go. It was like a drive-through.

In England, it was completely different. For a start, while heroin was common among the "older" generation of rockers, it was not a part of the punk scene, which meant nobody we met had a clue where to get it.

There were no Psychedelicatessens in Lancaster, and none that we could find any place else. All there was, as we quickly discovered, was speed, acid, and hash, rolled up with plenty of tobacco—the Clash spent almost the whole of the tour in a thick pungent cloud of the stuff. That was it, though, which left Johnny, Jerry, and me looking around going, "Fuck, we haven't done those drugs in years."

There were even poppers drifting around, fragile capsules of amyl-nitrate, and that was something else that I'd done a few times in college, because there would always be some in the medicine cabinet. They just gave me a headache, though.

Someone did introduce us to Collis Brown, which was a cough medicine that had a ton of codeine in it, and which you could buy from any pharmacy. We drank it a few times, but it didn't really do too much beyond give you a bit of a buzz.

Billy was okay with this. He was using speed when we first met him, and he just went back to using it now. We had always done our best to keep him away from it—as I've said before, junkies and speed freaks aren't the best combination. But he would always sneak it in on the side, and he usually had some hidden somewhere. Plus, because he was so dimwitted, we could never tell when he was using it from studying his behavior. The only way you knew was if you looked into his eyeballs. They would be beaming.

It was no surprise when, later, Billy fell in with the guys from Motörhead, the biggest speed freaks of them all, and occasionally we'd join him in his amphetamine buzz just to wake ourselves up in the morning or perk ourselves up for a show. We didn't like it, though.

Coke was around, and that we didn't mind. Back in New York City, we used to mix it with heroin and make speedballs, because whenever you went to buy dope on the Lower East Side, they used to sell coke alongside the smack.

There wasn't that same association in London, and although it wasn't that widespread—musicians used it, but the kids really didn't—Johnny and I both started using coke more than we ever had. Although for him, there was an image aspect to it, as well—people expected him to be constantly high, constantly fucked up, constantly shooting up, so he did it to please them. It was an ego thing. Jerry, on the other hand, was simply a hypochondriac, and the worst kind. He had no will power at all. It was a lethal combination.

But what we really wanted was smack. And none of us had Keith Richard's phone number.

(We did see him once, though, sitting with John Phillips of the Mamas and the Papas, in an ice cream shop down the King's Road somewhere, looking as blissfully out of it as we wished we could be. It was Leee who pointed them out to us, and at first we thought they were two fucking rats or homeless bums. It was only when you looked closer that you saw who they really were.)

None of us, at that time, had what you would call a serious relationship with smack. It was our poison of preference, and life seemed smoother when we had it. But if we didn't, we could still function—even Jerry, who later complained that he'd been so fucked up by the lack of junk that he didn't sleep a wink throughout the whole tour. But he was exaggerating. I shared a room with him every night. I heard him snoring.

On the road, we got by. Once, Johnny got a lift back to London with one of the music press journalists who was along on the tour; he scored, then came back the next day to share his largesse. Apart from that, though (unless Johnny was holding out on the rest of us), we went through the entire tour without touching the stuff. I actually felt good about that.

Which was when Johnny and Jerry suggested, I believe in all seriousness, that we should change the band's name to the Junkies. I wasn't at all sure—it was too obvious, to begin with. But it was Leee who finally shot the idea down. It would only work, he explained, if you weren't junkies. Otherwise, it would be an invitation for every cop in the country, if not the world, to come down on us at every opportunity they were given.

Finally they dropped the idea.

Chapter Eleven

CHRISTMAS

Back on the bus. The tour ground on, and the buzz from the Caerphilly concert didn't last long. Three nights later, we were watching *King Kong* on TV with Sophie Richmond, and tapping her up to lend us a fiver. Maybe that's how we could afford to spend the next couple of nights shivering our asses off in a freezing-cold hippie hotel somewhere.

But a few more shows did materialize, a triumphant return to Manchester, and another chance to admire Pete Shelley's hysterical guitar; Cleethorpes on December 20, and two successive nights in Plymouth (after another show, in nearby Torquay, was canned). We came off the road, though, wondering—what was that all about?

Audiences loved us and so, it seemed, did the critics. "The Heartbreakers . . . present speedy if traditional rock and roll," wrote Caroline Coon in *Melody Maker*. "Johnny, moving like a pneumatic steer, slides through a slick battery of moody poses. Numbers like 'Chinese Rocks,' 'Let Go' and 'Born to Lose' are delivered with raunchy, gut-level grind, and are free of the sound problems that plagued the Clash. They are explosively well-received."

Another early supporter was Paul Morley at the *New Musical Express*.

"Johnny Thunders and the Heartbreakers . . . [are] a band for twisting to—more New York Dolls than the New York Dolls, whispers a voice in my ear. Which can only be a good thing. Their music is a mishmash of all the New York bands you've ever heard, not just the Dolls. Regular rock 'n' roll, lyrics about love and going steady, a lotta beat, no glitter, no choir, no synthesizers, no shit.

"They move like they oughta, casual, play simple, hard and driving. . . . Buy their singles. And dance."

Of course, we knew we'd been good, and not just because we were better musicians, and more experienced performers, than the other bands on the bill. That didn't count for anything in what already felt like a new musical era. We were good because, once we got out on stage, we let everything go.

The other bands, and I mean no disrespect, were still honing their craft, but more than that, they were still at that point where a degree of self-consciousness cannot help but creep in, and self-awareness as well. They knew they were playing a part, trying to live up to a reputation that grew more fearsome every time they opened a newspaper, and sometimes the responsibility got the better of them.

We, on the other hand, had passed that point long before. If we had what others called "attitude," it was because that's who we already were. We'd already made our name and didn't care about making another one. If the Brits wanted to call us a punk band, that was fine. But we would be punks on our own terms, not theirs.

We arrived back in London on, I think, December 23. Despite all the controversy that surrounded the tour, record company interest was percolating—not only in us, but in every band that had been roped into the so-called punk phenomenon. Venues that had previously fought shy of booking punk bands were changing their policies overnight, and a new venue—the Roxy, which was dedicated wholly to punk rock—had sprung up as well.

The problem was that they had already booked their next few weeks' worth of live shows; and, worse than that, this was a country where not only the music industry, but almost every other sign of life, effectively takes two weeks off for Christmas.

(There is some confusion about our first gig at the Roxy. A lot of websites claim we played there during the Anarchy Tour, on December 15. But again, I don't remember it, and my diary doesn't mention it. So I'm guessing that's another one that history misremembers. Because, believe me, when we did finally play the Roxy, it was a night we would all remember.)

The sensible option at this juncture would have been to fly home. But the failure of the Anarchy Tour meant we couldn't afford to do that. Plus, we wanted to take advantage of the one legacy with which the tour had gifted us, and that was a ton of publicity.

There was just one solution. We should resign ourselves to be stuck in London and patiently twiddle our thumbs until the industry finished its holiday. And then we would rise up and strike.

It would not be easy. While we were certainly aware of the lucrative possibilities that were ranged before us, the reality was the here and now. Money was running out, and we were growing more and more depressed.

Even the possibility of scraping together at least a couple of gigs was no real solution—they didn't pay that well to begin with, but on top of that, we would also face the expense of renting a back line, monitors, and so on. We had literally flown over with nothing more than our guitars and a few changes of clothes. If we needed anything else on the tour, we borrowed it from one of the other bands. Going out on our own, however, we'd be expected to supply all our equipment ourselves.

To make matters even worse, our sound guy, Keith Paul, had just learned that his wife was in the hospital. He was returning home to be with her. So we'd need to hire someone to replace him for any shows we did—at a time when we didn't even have the money to book ourselves into a cheap hotel.

Tempers frayed. We were fighting constantly. Nothing important, nothing I can even remember today. Just a constant drip-drip-drip of petty disagreements, aggravations, discontent, and uncertainty. Homesickness. Every day, the decision loomed—should we stick it out in England for a while longer to see what the new year might bring? Or should we follow Keith home? And even if we did return to New York, what then?

There was nothing there—yes, Richard Gottehrer would still want to sign us; yes, Tommy and Hilly would still want to book us. But was that it? This band was too good to simply drop unprotestingly back into the New York scene, grinding around the same old venues with the same old support bands and the same roomful of fans.

"Just passed through the worst week in our stay here yet," I wrote in my diary on December 30. "No money, no places to stay, everyone wants to go home." I sympathized with Keith's reasons for leaving, but I knew "it was probably just as much from being fed up with us and London."

As far as I could see, we were confronted with just two options. Either the Heartbreakers would break out of that mold, or we would break up, and the only way to find out was to stick it out in London.

Strangely, and completely unexpectedly, Billy took our enforced exile the worst. I don't know what his problem was—maybe homesickness, maybe England, maybe he was just sick of hanging around with the rest of us. But he was becoming ever more negative. No matter what position he took one day, it would change the next, and it was impossible to agree with him on anything because his attitude changed so much, so often.

Jerry, Johnny, and I were even considering sending him home alone and asking Keith (who was actually a guitar player) if he'd come back to replace him on bass. I wasn't sure if he'd work out; even as a soundman, he was too conscious of trying to be a rock star to slip into the comparative anonymity of playing bass.

But then again, Johnny and Jerry weren't much better.

Johnny hated inactivity. He always wanted to be doing something and to know there was a point to whatever was happening at that moment. It might be playing; it might be scoring; it didn't matter. If there was not an end in sight, he didn't want to know. To him, London felt like a black hole full of nothingness. We weren't playing. He wasn't scoring. He was simply waiting. I had never seen him so restless.

I tried to keep a cheerful outlook—past experience had taught me, as the old cliché goes, that the darkest hour is before the dawn. Leee, too, was convinced that "something would turn up."

I took to exploring London, revisiting some of the sites I knew from my last trip, riding the underground, being a tourist. I spent a day at the Victoria & Albert Museum—museums and art galleries did not charge an admission fee, so they were popular destinations.

I went to the theater—tickets were absurdly cheap compared to New York; in fact, if you went to an afternoon matinee performance, it was cheap compared to a lot of things. I remember thoroughly enjoying *The Mousetrap*, at that time the longest-running play in the West End.

I walked around the parks, and I revisited the King's Road and marveled at how quickly fashions had changed since the last time I was there. In 1973, it was all flared trousers and wide-collared shirts, tank tops with stars on them and platform boots. Now, it was as though every boutique on the street was gearing up for the punk explosion, spilling out of Sex to infect them all.

Yes, the darkest hour is just before dawn.

Or is it? I'd recently read Yukio Mishima's novel *Spring Snow*, which preached a very different doctrine about fate. Sometimes when things get bad, it's merely a prelude to them becoming worse.

In many ways, my current predicament reminded me of the end of my basketball aspirations. I kept rising in the business, but would it last? Or was it just an interesting hobby?

True professionalism, as in actually making a comfortable living from music, was a plateau that I hadn't reached yet. If and when I did, I'd be able to rethink my options. But I also couldn't help but wonder whether I was going against fate, digging a grave for myself and blocking out the sun with a guitar. Or was this struggle and uncertainty necessary as a trial by fire? My brain just wouldn't shut up. Round and round I went, but right now, all I could do was wait and see.

Thankfully, we had friends in London. Most evenings, somebody or other would invite us to a gig, or there'd be a party thrown for us by one band or another. I already knew that Cook and Jones were big Johnny fans, and some of the Clash and the Damned as well. But it sometimes felt as though every musician on the punk scene had their soft spot for him, even if they'd not been especially impressed by the Dolls—although I don't think we met many people who fell into that camp.

More likely, we'd sit for what felt like hours, being regaled about how they saw the Dolls when they played Biba's in 1974, or supported Kevin Ayers in 1972, or turned up on the *Old Grey Whistle Test* and were written off as "mock rock" by the hippie who hosted it. It was touching but also weird—the sheer reverence with which Johnny was regarded—and of course, he had no problem whatsoever lapping up the accolades, no matter who was dispensing them.

A couple of nights, Leee took us to Louise's, a gay club on Poland Street in the West End, that the punk cognoscenti had adopted. Johnny could have scored with *any* guy in the place, and he knew it. Made certain that the rest of us knew it, too. I think that was where we ran into Freddie Mercury, as well, and that was hilarious. He was such a flaming queen that it was almost like a parody, as though he was doing it on purpose just to shock people. And from what I've heard about him, that probably was the case. It was Freddie who greeted Sid Vicious, for example, with the words, "Ah, Mr. Horrible."

Every day, we'd be out all night. We'd start out at the Ship, watching while it filled up not only with kids (and musicians) waiting for whatever was playing at the Marquee that night, but other faces, too—Keith Moon and Joe Cocker sitting at a table, roaring drunk, screaming at the top of their lungs, and throwing those big pint glasses around.

From there, we'd invariably move on to the Marquee, where we met Marianne Faithfull and Ian Hunter one night. Marianne was still recording AOR country albums at the time, but punk fascinated her, and she was absorbing everything she saw, until it all came pouring out a couple of years later on her *Broken English* album.

And finally, the Speakeasy, a tiny after-hours club that was crammed with journalists and industry people. It was a good place to hang out, though, because you wouldn't be harassed by punks (just by idiot writers), and later, when we played there, it was nice to play a show and not get gobbed on.

Of course, without a permanent base to call our own, it really did feel sometimes as though we were homeless. But again, people took pity on us. Sophie Richmond, Malcolm's assistant, allowed Billy and me to crash at her apartment for a couple of nights while Leee tried to make longer-term arrangements; and it was when we moved on from Sophie's place that Billy and I were permitted a peek inside another of this peculiar country's most bizarre predilections—the ruling class's penchant for being given a damned good whacking.

Jordan and Linda were two more of Malcolm's (and, therefore, the Pistols') circle, with Jordan in particular a much photographed and much fetishized figure. Unmistakable with her sharp features, jagged hair, brutal makeup, and large bosom, she exuded power and punishment—appropriately so, because she also happened to be one of the most popular dominatrixes in London.

The two women lived in a beautiful apartment overlooking Green Park, just round the corner from Buckingham Palace; later, Jerry told me that was where he first got one of the Pistols off on smack, but I wasn't there at the time, so I don't know.

I did run into Adam Ant there a couple of times, though. He was still a nobody at the time, not like he became, but he struck me as being very standoffish. Somebody later told me that he hated American bands—us included, I presume—because he didn't they think belonged in England.

Another person I remember was Chrissie Hynde, yet another of Malcolm's acolytes, who was still a long way from forming the Pretenders but with musical aspirations of her own all the same.

She was accompanied by two other American girls, Judy Nylon and Patti Paladin, and maybe that's what affected my mood.

Although all three of them had been living in London for a lot longer than me, the last thing I wanted to hear in England was an American accent.

Gritting my teeth, I put up with them until I had to leave the room for a moment, and then I walked back in to find Chrissie had picked up my guitar and was playing it.

No "May I?" No "Would it be okay?" None of the standard etiquette with which musicians, even punk musicians, regard one another's instruments. She just picked it up and I went nuts, screaming "How dare you?" and "Who do you think you are?" until she sheepishly put it back down, apologizing profusely. Then we made up and were good friends thereafter—and I admit, I was probably the more obnoxious of us both. But that was how I met her.

Jerry and I only stayed with Jordan and Linda for a few nights, but even in that short time, we grew more than accustomed to the sight of well-turned-out older men nervously filing into the (suitably soundproofed) back room and then filing out again, looking suitably chastened and beaming. And also red-faced and sweating.

Who were these men? I don't remember most of the names. (TV presenter David Frost is one of those that I do.) But barely a night went by that we couldn't watch the evening news, or some other current affairs program, and recognize another politician or television celebrity who we'd seen pay a visit to Jordan.

Christmas itself we spent with journalist Caroline Coon, who cooked at least two turkeys and a mountain of other food and then invited the Heartbreakers, the Clash, the Pistols, and sundry friends and hangers-on to her place for dinner, which, hardly surprisingly, became a party and just went downhill from there.

I later heard that most of the people in attendance would blame us for whatever shenanigans took place—things about us throwing up and shooting up and generally playing the obnoxious, ugly Americans. In fact, we were too busy either going to the bathroom or sitting on Caroline's phone, running up a massive bill.

Finally, Leee came up with the goods—a Belgravia townhouse whose owners were abroad for the holidays but whose son, Sebastian Conran (a roadie for the Clash), was willing to let us stay.

His father, Terence, was the founder of Habitat, one of the era's more up-market "lifestyle" retailers, which sold furniture, lighting, nicknacks, all mod cons for the well-to-do classes. The flat reflected his style; the place was enormous, five floors, eight bedrooms, and everything furnished with exquisite taste and care. It was beautiful—so much so that I know Sebastian was positively shitting himself at the thought of us moving in and destroying the place.

In fact, we were actually very well behaved, not only by punk rock standards, but by anybody's. Part of that, of course, was because we really liked Sebastian. In fact, it was Sebastian who took me on my first ever motorcycle ride, down to McDonalds in Piccadilly.

The other thing was that we didn't have enough cash to bring in lots of drugs and booze and start vomiting over everything. Even when we had visitors—the Clash would stop by regularly, usually with a few friends and food for the starving Americans— we all behaved ourselves.

It was during one of those visits that Johnny sold Strummer the Gretsch White Falcon guitar he used to have. It was a piece of shit and *always* out of tune, but Strummer liked the way it looked in pictures. He even paid cash for it, which I'm sure Johnny immediately spent on drugs. (I don't recall whether or not he shared them with the rest of us.) There was also talk that Strummer wanted to take Jerry away with him as well and install him as drummer for the Clash. That would have been interesting!

Leee's presence alongside us in the house also encouraged us to keep a lid on things, not because he was at all hard-assed, but because he was such a charming, calming presence. His time spent nursemaiding Iggy in LA obviously taught him some valuable lessons. He knew if he gave us large sums we'd spend it on dope, so he'd give us fivers to see us through a meal or two.

It was my first (and only!) experience of having a manager, and he probably still ranks as the best I ever had. He took care of everything that needed to be taken care of, and he would always be there when we needed him.

It was certainly different to what Johnny and Jerry had experienced with the Dolls' management, where even asking for their weekly wage could turn into a battle of wills— going up to the office on the appointed day to discover either that nobody had turned up to work that day, or they wanted to argue that you'd already been paid. I heard a lot of stories like that.

We were not in receipt of a weekly wage. But if Leee had the cash, he'd share it around, and he was always very hands-on when it came to our needs.

For example, back in New York, Jerry had started conducting an on-off relationship with methadone in an attempt to shake his heroin addiction. As it turned out, it became more of a supplement than a substitute, but when he found a program that would accept him in London, out in Harrow, in the north of the city, it was Leee who made certain that he got there. At one point, Jerry even had his own driver, Dibbs Preston, who would soon be playing with an up-and-coming rockabilly band called Levi (Dexter) and the Rockats.

It was Leee who introduced us to the Rockats, and the discovery surprised us. So far as we were concerned, there were just two music scenes in England—the punks, and the last dying embers of the "old guard," the progressive rock bands that punk was supposedly dedicated to destroying.

We didn't know because nobody told us (and the music press certainly wasn't writing about them) that there were other scenes also percolating away—electronics freaks in their bedrooms playing Kraftwerk and Can; teenaged heavy metal bands still listening to *Deep Purple in Rock*; and a huge reggae scene, which would begin to make its presence felt as the months passed. I'd heard the Wailers and Toots because the music was just starting to break out among the Jamaican population in NY, but what we discovered in London was astonishing.

And there were the rockabilly bands, living and sounding as though the past twenty years had never happened.

Eddie Cochran, Gene Vincent, Elvis—at last, Jerry and Leee had found something in common because Leee loved the music as much as Jerry did, and he loved the look as well.

All we knew about so-called Teddy Boys was what we learned from the punk rockers who were beginning to get beaten up by them. We'd never even heard of them in the States—we saw the Elvis freaks, but Teddy Boys, Teds, were new to us.

Personally, I loved their shoes, those Brothel Creepers were great. What I didn't love were the gangs who apparently roamed late-night London's subways and alleyways looking for punks to kick several shades of shit out of.

Leee, however, found other uses for their nocturnal energies, as we would soon discover.

Chapter Twelve

DRUGS

Our other great revelation was that London was not quite as devoid of dope as we had been led to believe. You just needed to know the right people, and now that we had a place that we could call our home, at least for the moment, that's who we started meeting. The right people. A journalist here, a musician there, a friend of a friend someplace else.

Although heroin had never been openly available in the United Kingdom (at least, not since the Edwardian era), it was only within the last ten years that the law truly clamped down on it. Prior to that, an obliging doctor could always write prescriptions for the stuff, and I would soon be hearing tales of the long queues that used to form outside the all-night pharmacy at Piccadilly Circus—people waiting for the dispensary to open, I think, at midnight.

That ended in 1967, which is sort of ironic—the same year that homosexuality was decriminalized, heroin addiction became a crime. Beginning in February 1968, doctors were forced to notify the government of any addicted patients they were seeing, and the police were actively rounding up, and busting, junkies.

Inevitably, whatever benefits the new system was supposed to engender were quickly swamped by the pitfalls. With no legal supply of heroin, users turned to the black market, and the crime rate soared. The purity, and even the safety, of the drug nosedived as dealers began cutting the smack with whatever was on hand.

In ten years, the number of known addicts soared from a relatively small and generally regulated coterie of around six hundred to several thousand, at least. In fact, according to recent statistics, the eighteen months or so that the Heartbreakers spent in the United Kingdom, 1976–1978, coincides almost exactly with a threefold increase in the number of heroin addicts!

It's funny to remember how the first time we played Leeds, during the Anarchy Tour, an almost baffled silence fell over the audience when Johnny asked, "Ain't there any junkies in Leeds?" The next time we were there, kids were lined up to share their stash with us.

It still makes no sense. In New York, buying drugs is a simple transaction. You go in, you pay your money, you leave. It's Lou Reed's "Waiting for the Man," pure and simple.

In London, there wasn't any street market; or, if there was, you had more chance of being severely ripped off than you did of getting high. So you'd have to make connections, and it could take an hour of fucking about, chatting with the people, making "friends," before they'd finally get out the goods. Different people, different flats, you could spend your entire life just trying to score.

The other thing was that British addicts didn't seem to like needles very much. Most people either smoked smack or they snorted it, which is probably healthier, but we weren't interested. We were thoroughly enmeshed in the needle culture in New York, where you weren't cool if you didn't stick a needle in your arm—which just added to the glamor, in a way, because it was really hard to source needles in New York. You'd have to buy them from someone who'd probably stolen them, and you never knew (if you even cared) whether or not they were clean.

In London, it was the complete opposite. You could buy the needles over the counter. You just couldn't get anything to put in them.

Slowly, however, we figured it out. And as Christmas gave way to the New Year, and 1977 finally picked up speed, we started making our way out into the world.

According to my diary, we had a gig in Derby, in the Midlands, on December 30, and one in nearby Birmingham on January 1. There was a hop across to the Netherlands with the Pistols during the first week in January, and it was refreshing to be able to play a couple of shows without all the baggage that had surrounded the Anarchy Tour gigs.

Plus, I was in Amsterdam. Again!

The last time, I'd been deported but that had no impact on my return. There was no paperwork that I was aware of, and the only thing I was told was, "Don't come back for six months." That was three years ago.

At last, an open drug market, right past the red light district. It was largely a Surinamese operation, and the first time we went there we got ripped off; what we thought was dope turned out to be chalk or something. But we scored in the end, and besides, it was great to be somewhere that didn't close down at 10:30 every night—where you could buy pot in the bars and see whores in the windows. After the long dark night of English buttoned-up repression, Amsterdam felt like a whole new day.

Of course, a few English journalists followed us, just in case the Pistols decided to do something wicked—and they did. According to the papers, when we returned, they swore and spat at fellow passengers when they arrived at Heathrow Airport, and one of them apparently threw up. We missed that. But we did see the group's reaction when Malcom broke the news, once we'd arrived in Amsterdam, that they'd been dropped by EMI.

I don't think anybody was surprised about that. Both the media and the company's shareholders had been pushing for the label to sack them ever since the TV show. But it was still a blow, and there were genuine concerns as to whether they would even find another label. As it transpired, of course, there was, and history now looks at the swath that the Pistols carved through the UK music industry—signed and sacked first by EMI, and then by A&M, before finally finding a happy home at Virgin—and describes it as some kind of magnificent master plan.

The expression on Malcolm's face as he broke the news, on the other hand, was as despairing as the one we'd seen when he picked us up from the airport six weeks earlier. This wasn't a master plan, and it certainly wasn't a great rock 'n' roll swindle. It was a succession of disasters, as the Pistols' roadie (and, later, the Banshees' manager) Nils Stevenson pointed out years later.

"There was no plan," Stevenson said. "That's why the punk era was so wonderful, and that's why it was so different to what happens now, because everybody has a plan and a computer and . . . it's all done by numbers. Malcolm didn't know what was going on. Most of the things he set up as publicity stunts fell completely flat." It was the things he didn't contrive that worked.

The dates themselves—two nights at the Paradiso and one in Rotterdam—passed off trouble free for the Pistols, while we were just thankful to be playing back-to-back gigs for the first time since we left New York—the night before we left for Amsterdam, we played a late night show at Dingwalls, inside the Camden Market.

That was the night I started putting Band-Aids ("sticking plasters," as the Brits called them) all over my shirt. It was just an odd look I devised, and I was surprised later to see how much it caught on. Mismatched shoes was another of my fashion statements, although that one didn't travel as far—in fact, I remember how confused I was when somebody asked why I always wore "odd shoes"—meaning, in British terms, a different one on each foot. Whereas I was looking down at them thinking "odd . . . peculiar . . . no, they're quite ordinary!"

We went down well at Dingwalls and again in Amsterdam. The Dutch had loved the Dolls, so of course we got a hero's welcome. Great crowds, great venues—we played the Paradiso, then moved on to an after-hours club that might have been the Melkweg, and got off in the bathroom.

We returned to London with a whole new attitude, to find Leee had finalized an actual plan of action for us.

A few weeks earlier, we were sitting in the Ship—a pub on Wardour Street, just down from the Marquee—when Leee spotted someone he knew, a gent named Andy Czezowski. Andy joined us and we chatted about the Anarchy Tour for a while, how

Malcolm had stopped paying us even the meager stipend he had originally promised, and how miserable we were.

Quick as a flash, he offered us a gig at the Roxy, the club he'd opened on Dean Street, in Covent Garden.

Of course we were interested, but the money was not good. Leee asked for a hundred pounds; Andy offered thirty. Leee went down to seventy-five; Andy still offered us thirty.

Finally, we agreed, on the condition that he give us half of it upfront. He was happy with that, and we had our showcase concert, the gig to which Leee would be inviting the assorted great and good of the UK music industry to check us out.

And the day after the showcase, which was on January 11, we'd return to New York City.

Leee's thinking was flawless. While the A&R guys absorbed our performance and waved about their check books, we could relax in familiar surroundings, spend time with our families, rehearse, and write songs. We could do anything we wanted. Hadn't we earned a break?

The other thing was that our work permits were about to expire, and it would be pointless renewing them if we didn't at least have some concrete interest from a record label—in fact, it would be difficult to renew them if we didn't. After all, if you're being given a work permit, the expectation is that you'll be working—not hanging around a succession of other people's apartments, hoping to play a gig or two.

We filled in the next few days in much the same way as we'd spent the last few weeks, sitting around Sebastian's place, waiting for the pubs and clubs to open, and then going to whichever gig we'd been told we were on the guest list for.

The punk scene seemed to be growing by the day, with new bands playing their first-ever show every night. Some, like the Pistols, had already found their voice, could play their instruments, and knew their sound. Others were still learning their way, and some—a lot, in fact—were still learning to play, treating the stage like the rehearsal room, in front of audiences that not only welcomed their amateurism but encouraged it.

It was the most egalitarian musical movement I've ever seen because even the most hopelessly hapless bunch of kids served a purpose by letting onlookers know, or at least believe, that given a couple of guitars, some amps, and a drum kit, they could be up on the stage as well.

I won't pretend there weren't some nights when we'd get back to Sebastian's place, still unable to believe precisely how bad the band we'd just seen had been. But there were others when the performers' enthusiasm so outweighed their abilities that we couldn't help but love them. After all, we'd all been there ourselves.

At last, the showcase.

Outside of the Speakeasy, the Roxy was probably our favorite club at the time, even though it had only hosted a handful of gigs so far. The place was an absolute firetrap, however, with many people confined to a tiny basement space with just a single, narrow staircase leading to the outside world. But it was also a self-contained universe in which anything went—or would if somebody thought of doing it. And the center of that universe was—you guessed it—the bathrooms.

That was where punk rock came of age, physically, socially, sexually, and chemically. More cherries were popped, more drugs were imbibed, more deals were confirmed, and more were (fill in your own blank—it probably happened) in the bathrooms at the Roxy than at any other place in England. Ever.

By the standards of any civilized society, or even the uncivilized corners that we'd experienced in New York City, the bathrooms were disgusting—rarely cleaned, seldom flushed, and caked with the kind of filth that the wall-to-wall graffiti could only begin to camouflage; you needed a strong constitution to even contemplate entering those barely lit barracks. There were people who'd rather leave the gig early and pee in the street than even think about entering the smallest room.

But those hardy souls who did venture in, who pushed through the once-green doors at the back of the dance floor and sloshed across the perma-puddle that pretended to be the floor, were in for an experience they might never forget.

Jayne County once admitted: "One of my strongest memories of the Roxy was going into the men's room, and being told by a cute young man that I was in the wrong toilet."

She wasn't, of course. Long before unisex bathrooms became even a fringe concession to modern political correctness, somebody had either stolen or obscured the signs on both doors, and besides, nobody ever paid attention to them anyway.

But surreptitious dope-dealing and undercover fellatio were merely the opening attractions, the first things you'd see when you entered the throne room. Graduate past them and the toilets were the catalyst for a mind-blowing variety of weird and wonderful experiments, some involving drugs and sex, a lot involving both, and a few adding some good old fashioned business dealings to the brew.

How many future punk superstars agreed to their first record deal in the Roxy bogs? Nobody knows. But at least one received his first advance on royalties in there, with his future A&R man on his knees in the puddles.

Rubber wear squelched and fishnets were torn. Fluids were spilled, exchanged, and imbibed. Body parts were pierced and disinfected with Colt 45—the only alcohol that the Roxy sold. Broken mirrors filled the washbasin with bloodied glass, and passing punks would take turns slashing their own flesh with the shards, to prove their allegiance to a cult that the tabloid press insisted was dedicated to self-mutilation.

In fact it wasn't; that was just something that the papers made up in the hope of selling more copies. But as punk's tentacles reached ever further out into the suburbs, a lot of kids who believed every word came calling. And if the bathrooms were Bacchanalian before the part-timers arrived, they were halfway to Sodom and Gomorrah now.

Sid Vicious, the live fast/die young epitome of punk fame and fortune, wondered aloud whether he might be gay, cornering both Jayne and Leee on the subject, and according to legend, the Roxy bathroom was the place where he first learned the reality behind his private ponderings. Only they wouldn't have been so private. Someone had long since removed the doors from the stalls.

Not every tryst was consummated so successfully. A lot of the kids were on that fucking awful cheap speed, amphetamine sulphate, and as Jayne, laughing, used to say: "That stuff would knock your head off, and give you the shits to boot! I remember overhearing a conversation between some punks about how much they loved sulfate, but it was impossible to get a hard on with it."

But sulphate merged perfectly with the mood of the music, aggressive and speeding, bellicose and brash, and more than one passing critic seemed to notice that the better the quality of the drugs sold in the bathroom, the worse the standard of the band onstage. Worse, of course, being a subjective term, dependent upon whether you wanted your music played at 200 mph by musicians struggling to keep pace with their frontman's speed-singing, while he hoped the high would keep going long enough to get him through the set. Because the sulphate comedown was horrible.

Like the sulphate high, and like the Roxy itself, the Roxy bathrooms' reign was short. Andy Czezowski threw in the towel in April, unable to keep up with the landlords' constant rent increases, and the old place was never the same after that. But not because Czezowski had some magical influence on the quality of the music—there were probably more great bands at the Roxy after he departed than he had ever allowed on the stage during his tenure. The Roxy went downhill because the new owners decided to tidy it up.

The bathrooms were repainted, and signs and doors replaced. The light bulbs seemed brighter, and the drug dealers moved on. So did the leather boys, the drag queens, and the rest. And so did the record companies—officially because they reckoned that they'd already signed up the best bands around, but unofficially because the Roxy wasn't fun anymore. And it wasn't fun because its bathrooms were just like those in every other place.

That was certainly true for us. The Roxy showcase was destined to be remembered as one of the greatest gigs we ever played—there's a terrific photo of me that was taken that night, with blood on my shirt and my eyeballs up in the air.

Not every concert the Heartbreakers played went off according to plan—there was always something that happened to make you cringe, and that, in a way, became a part of our appeal. Eschewing even the dubious subtlety of Hell's old "Catch 'em while they're still alive" slogan, the word on the street now seemed to be "Come and see the Heartbreakers! Johnny might OD tonight!" That was his reputation. A spectacle! And the last-ever Heartbreakers gig, as well. Who could resist?

The showcase, on the other hand, was perfect.

We sounded okay and the sound system was pretty good. The place was seething, too. It was completely sold out—three hundred people, maybe more, and all of them, it seemed, were shouting Johnny's name. We tore through our set and would probably have torn through it again had there been time. It was one of those nights when you just don't want to leave the stage, and the audience would keep you there all night if it could.

That was the night, I think, that Giovanni Dadomo, writing in *Sounds*, gave us another of those reviews that bands can only dream of: "Thunders is cranking away at his axe and leaning forward towards the mike and singing and pouting and popping his eyes and defining rock 'n' roll like no mere scribbler could ever get down on paper.

"He's not alone of course. Over on his left there's this skinny fair-haired guy in a black suit and he's got a guitar too and his fallen angel face is adorned with two enormous sticking plasters. His name's Walter Lure and, damn, if he ain't defining rock 'n' roll too." And so on.

It was an unbelievable show. Johnny was buzzing for hours after; we all were. I've heard it said that, later in life, Johnny would be so out of it on drugs that he often didn't know (or care) whether he'd played the best or the worst, or even if he'd actually played a gig to begin with. Maybe that's true, although I also know that it suited him to play up that side of things, simply to keep the image alive.

Right now, though, he was like a kid at Christmas. "If that doesn't bring them running," he announced as we sat, drenched in sweat, in that tiny little box that the Roxy referred to as a dressing room, "nothing will."

But we had little time in which to savor the triumph. Less than twenty-four hours later, we were on a plane back home.

I've seen it written that we played one final show in London, at the Red Cow pub in Hammersmith on January 13, before flying home. We didn't. We left the morning after the showcase, leaving Leee behind to get the negotiating underway, with the assistance of Peter Gerber, a lawyer he knew from the Bowie days. As he said goodbye, he was adamant that, by the time we returned, we'd have a deal in the bag. And so it turned out.

But still, climbing into the cab for the ride back to the airport, with London shrouded in a mid-January snowstorm, we really didn't feel like a band of musicians returning home from a tour abroad. We felt like a team of astronauts on our way home from Mars.

Chapter Thirteen

TRACK MARKS

Back in New York City, my first port of call was the FDA, to hand in my notice—or, more accurately, to announce that I was leaving on the spot. I wouldn't even have time to work out the statutory two weeks' notice.

My boss understood, but he was still surprised. He gestured around the room, all those test tubes and microscopes, jars and bottles, mysterious substances and peculiar odors, and said, "You're going to give up all this for a bunch of guitars?"

I nodded. "Yes sir, that's exactly what I'm going to do."

I surprised myself—I was actually sad to leave. I'd made some good friends there over the years, and the work was fascinating, even if it could also be boring.

It was one of those situations where you spend years dreaming of leaving the nine-to-five, to turn your dreams into reality, but when the situation actually arrives, it's not as joyful as you expected. But I wasn't going to change my mind. Besides, a little more than a week later, we were back in England, and according to some accounts, we were immediately loaded into a van for the drive up to Middlesbrough to play a show. Welcome back.

To be honest, however, I'm fairly certain this was another of those phantom gigs that never happened—we may have been scheduled to play there, but I'm sure I'd remember fighting jet lag through a four- or five-hour drive to the far northeast of England. Or maybe we did play it, and I was simply too jet-lagged to remember.

Leee was at Heathrow Airport to meet us when we landed and fill us in on the latest developments. We already knew that we had a record deal, with Track Records—it was they who sorted out our work permits; and at least a slice of the label's largesse had already been put to good use, as Leee introduced us to our newly recruited full-time road manager, Gail Higgins.

In fact, Billy was the only one of us who didn't know Gail. I'd met her a few times during the last days of the Dolls, but she also happened to be one of Johnny's oldest friends. They'd known one another even before the Dolls got started; she'd housed him during one of his spells of homelessness; and he'd dated her cousin Janice for a time. Even Jerry couldn't object to her presence.

Leee and Gail were old friends, as well; in fact, the two of them were now sharing a house—a big, beautiful three-story place in Islington—where the pair of them lived like vampires. Every night when we weren't gigging, they'd go out on the London club circuit looking for pretty boys to take home, and that's how they got into the whole rockabilly scene that was coming up. They'd go out and they'd meet kids at the concerts, and they'd bring them back home.

Leee would have first pick, but if he wasn't able to get the kid into bed, then Gail would have him. That didn't happen too often, though. Once Leee set his mind to something, he usually succeeded, and I cannot even imagine how many young straight kids he ended up deflowering in that house. Most of them musicians, some punks. But the majority of them were rockabilly, just a horde of the pretty little things.

It was like Babylon on Thames. You'd go over there in the morning and there'd be some kid getting dressed and you'd ask him, "Who fucked you last night?"

And, occasionally, the answer would come back, "You did."

I'm not sure this has any relevance to either the music or the era, but I had never identified as either straight or gay. I've been bisexual all my life, although when I joined the Heartbreakers, I wasn't really advertising my male liaisons and had no reason to. I wanted the band to accept me as a musician, so I didn't need any distractions.

Jerry was probably the most homophobic, but even he didn't really hate gays and neither did Johnny. He would, occasionally, make remarks that modern sensibilities would not tolerate even as jokes, but I don't believe they were ever intended with malice. It was simply his mouth running faster than his mind. Besides, Leee was a flaming queen of the first order, and of course, there were those rumors about Billy in the years before he joined the band. You can add to that the fact that most people on the scene totally accepted gays, and there were plenty of them about, performing or just hanging out. So, because it really wasn't an issue for me, I felt no need to make any proclamations.

Later on I got spotted in a few one-off situations, both in the United Kingdom and later in New York City, but it made no difference to either the band or me, especially as I would also show up with girls on my arm. There would be a few passing jokes in later years, but I would hit back just as hard with their foibles, and believe me, Johnny and Jerry both had them.

Back to Babylon on Thames. We'd been to a party south of the river, in Deptford, and Leee, as usual, had scored. Sitting in the cab on the way back to Islington, however, I noticed that the boy he'd picked up seemed far more interested in me than he did in Leee. So, while Leee had one arm around the kid's shoulders, I had one around his waist, and when we got back to the house, it was my room he ended up in.

Leee didn't mind. It was probably good for him to have a night off. But after the same thing happened for a second time, he did start calling me Spiderwoman. And the nickname caught on. One morning I was in one of the spare bedrooms with a boy, and we were going at it when suddenly Jerry opened the door. He walked in, looked silently at the pair of us, and then walked out again. A few minutes later, I heard him downstairs saying, "Hey Leee, I guess the Spiderwoman struck again last night."

Back to business. I don't know how many of the labels that were invited to the Roxy showcase actually put in bids for us or what their offers were like. I did hear later that Johnny's reputation, at least, had caused some trepidation among the bigger labels—punk was still a headline horror in the tabloid press, and one can only imagine what kind of fuss *The Sun* would have made when they got wind of a junkie punk.

EMI did show an interest, though, or at least, one of their producers did. Mike Thorne was something of a punk trailblazer—he would soon be at work producing the *Live at the Roxy* album, showcasing a bunch of the bands that played the club, and he was already encouraging his paymasters to launch a dedicated punk subsidiary. His first three signings, he dreamed, would be Siouxsie and the Banshees, Wire, and us. In the end, he didn't get his label, and only Wire joined him at EMI. We didn't even get a look in.

Track Records—perhaps appropriately, given one definition of their name —were not so squeamish. Or, rather, they were, but Leee was able to convince them that it was only Johnny and Jerry who were using, and that they could both be kept under control. There was nothing to worry about with me or Billy. As it happened, I managed to completely demolish that image later, but more about that further on.

So we ended up signing with Track, which apparently offered the best deal, although I was never a part of the actual negotiations and to my knowledge neither were Johnny, Jerry, or Billy. Neither did I ever have the chance to discuss things with Leee in later years, although it wouldn't have changed things. We were just pleased to have a label and happy it was such a hip one.

Track Records had been around since 1967, when Kit Lambert and Chris Stamp, managers of the Who, set it up for a clutch of bands that also included the newly arrived Jimi Hendrix, the upcoming Crazy World of Arthur Brown, and Marc Bolan's first electric band, John's Children. The Who were at their pre-*Tommy* peak and firing off hits like "Pictures of Lily" and "I Can See for Miles." Hendrix was the hottest thing in London, and Arthur Brown would soon have a worldwide number one. Not a bad start for any label.

Neither did it end there. Track had a huge hit with Thunder-clap Newman; they launched Marsha Hunt; and later in life, they picked up Golden Earring. Then, around 1974, a major bust-up with the Who, regarding unpaid royalties, pushed the label into something approaching hibernation.

The last album they'd released was Golden Earring's *Switch*, back in 1975, but managing director Mafalda Hall, A&R head Danny Secunda, and label head Chris Stamp were intent on re-launching. We were the band they chose to make it happen.

In truth, it probably wasn't quite that straightforward. I don't know the exact story, but I believe it had something to do with needing to prove, for legal reasons, that Track was still a going concern in order to get whatever cash they believed they were due.

Certainly we weren't the only band on their radar. Nils Steven-son was being paid a retainer by Track to keep them informed of worthwhile bands, and the label was also courting rock 'n' roll re-vivalists Shakin' Stevens and the Sunsets (several years before any-body had heard of Stevens himself) and Siouxsie and the Banshees.

Indeed, Nils was already the Banshees' *de facto* manager, and he soon confided to us that he had no intention whatsoever of signing the group to the label. He was happy to let Track pay for the Banshees' rehearsal space and finance their first studio demos as well. But Lambert and Stamp, he said, were too crazy.

Kit Lambert certainly was. A total drunken queen, he was com-pletely out of it, and whether he still had any business smarts, I don't know. My only memories are of him laughing and giggling all the time, so infectiously that the rest of us couldn't help but join in.

Chris Stamp, on the other hand, was very businesslike, and there was another guy who ran their books, Mike Shaw—I liked him a lot. He was one of Stamp's old school friends and was prob-ably the Who's first roadie. He also did their lights and drove the van until a traffic accident left him critically injured. He would be in a wheelchair for the rest of his life. Of all the people in the Track office, he was probably the most stable and down to earth.

Then again, so were most people compared to Kit, although he was hilarious to be around.

It turns out that there was a lot going on behind the scenes that we didn't know about—the ongoing dispute with the Who was common knowledge, but the fact that our contract was with a company called Chris Stamp Band Ltd., as opposed to Track itself, would have set alarm bells ringing if we'd been aware of it. In fact, we didn't even sign it until we had more or less finished recording (but not mixing) the album.

I was cautious, and Johnny raised the occasional question as well. But Leee was smart. Included in the contract was a provision that, should Chris Stamp Band Ltd. ever go under, ownership of all the tapes would revert immediately to the company that Leee and Peter Gerber had established, Heartbreakers Ltd. In the end, when this did happen, Leee was forced to break into the Track offices under cover of darkness and pick up the tapes himself, but it did give us a certain security.

Track was good to us, but it was a strange label—very friendly, but there was always an undercurrent, the sense that they could also be very treacherous.

The A&R man Danny Secunda—a cousin, I believe, of the more renowned Tony Secunda—definitely had something of a reputation around the music industry as a sharp operator; in fact, we had barely signed with the label when Secunda, aided and abetted by Jerry, tried to oust Leee in a management coup. The rest of us quickly put a stop to that.

There was also a dispute over percentages, but Leee and Peter took care of that.

So there was room for misgivings, but we shrugged them off. Most of them, after all, were born more of the rumors and whispering we heard from other people than from anything we saw with our own eyes. Plus, look at all that the label was doing for us!

Having cleared us for new work permits, paid for our flights back to London, and arranged to keep up the rent payments on my apartment back in New York City, Track then set us up in a basement flat on Denbigh Street in Pimlico. They arranged for us to receive a weekly salary and paid for almost anything we needed. The restaurant tab alone must have been astronomical—we just signed Track's name to every bill.

We even learned that we'd been shortlisted for parts in the Who's then-gestating *Quadrophenia* movie, and when my parents came over to visit in June, Track put them in a car and took them to one of our gigs in St. Albans. There was a picture in one of the music papers of me standing there with my mother in her seventies pants suit and my dad in his polyester jacket. I always thought that was kind of cool.

What did my parents think of punk rock? Well, I remember dad standing there with a pint glass of beer when some kid ran into him. The beer went all over the kid, and my parents were both apologizing profusely. But the kid didn't care. He just ran off laughing.

I also introduced them to one of the secretaries at Track, an Irish girl named Eileen, who seemed to have taken a liking to me. A few years later, when she was visiting New York, she called me up and I invited her to dinner with mom and dad. In a strange way, I think they liked her even more than I did!

Track allowed us to amass an impressive pile of equipment, although nothing replaced the Les Paul Deluxe I'd had since the Demons, which I still own (and which I still get asked about today). But we all got new instruments, and amps, too, fit for every occasion. Depending upon the size of the venue we were playing in, we usually used Fender Twins (or Pros in the smaller clubs) or Marshalls.

Johnny and I liked Fenders for the reverb, but Marshalls were terrific for bottom end and distortion. In fact we often used a Fender Twin and a Marshall in tandem because the sound was so much brighter and heavier. And that made a difference. A lot of other bands had only the one set of amps, no matter how big or small the club was.

Where Track fell down was in the publicity department. I don't know if it was economics or what, but while we didn't go short on actual advertising, it was very unimaginative—a straightforward name, rank, and number page in the papers, and that was it. I remember thinking at the time, if we could have garnered half the column inches that the Pistols received, we'd have been as big as the Rolling Stones.

There again, Track could have said the same thing about us. The Heartbreakers had an image, that was for sure. But it was scarcely one that could be broadcast in the media as a role model for the kids—"Follow the Heartbreakers and you too can become a New York junkie." One time, a kid came up and asked if it was true that the only reason we wore ties was so we'd always have a tourniquet handy.

I agreed that it was problematic. We needed *something* to set us aside from the rest of the punk pack—something that the audience might not be able to simply identify with, but become swept up by. Role models, lifestyle models. People have to want to see a band for more than the music and the possibility that the singer was going to OD on stage. They want to identify and fantasize so when they hear your new record, they're also hearing their dreams.

That was the magic that the Dolls had woven; that was the trick that the Pistols had mastered. And Johnny still had it, if only he wanted to use it. After all, to the fans, he was already the main man, but beyond that, his guitar playing was unique, even with half the punk scene desperately trying to emulate it.

Johnny had the gift of presence too—he could walk into the most crowded room, and all eyes would turn to look at him. But though he could never turn those things off, he never turned them *up*, either, and I seriously doubted whether he ever would. Even this early in his career, I could see him remaining much the same person, playing much the same songs, in much the same way, for the rest of his life, and so it transpired. He would never change.

To make matters worse, I think I was the only member of the band who actually thought that way, who looked toward marketing the band as opposed to simply playing in one.

 For Johnny, Jerry, and Billy, it was enough that they were in a band and making money. They didn't look to the future; they were content in the here and now, except of course on those occasions when they didn't have any drugs, in which case they were as miserable as sin. In fact, I don't think they actually had any ambitions beyond getting high. They expected more, but they didn't do anything to help get it.

I'm not criticizing them for that. I knew the score when I joined the band, and nothing had changed to alter that beyond the fact that I knew how good we were and that I saw the looks on people's faces when we played live.

I also saw the lines of interviewers who wanted to talk to Johnny, and if he had only been able to put aside his reality and take on some other kind of role—meaning, talk about something other than New York, drugs, and the death of the Dolls —maybe that could have made a difference.

He was a smart guy. He knew a lot about music; he had sharp opinions on a lot of bands, and though he wasn't especially well-read, he had the kind of second-sense intuition about the "human condition" that most people rely on the great philosophers to explain.

For example, he knew at a glance whether somebody was worth his time or not. Which isn't to say he was never surrounded, or taken advantage of, by conmen. Just that he usually knew they were conmen the moment he met them, and he tolerated their tricks because he knew he could also get something out of the relationship. If he got ripped off, or taken advantage of, that was simply the price of doing business with that person, and Johnny was willing to pay it.

On the other hand, if he genuinely liked somebody, then his mind was made up. He might never tell them how he felt; the most effusive greeting they might ever hear from his lips would be a quick "hi man." But the fact he said that much let you know you were "okay."

The only person he didn't seem to trust was himself—the voice inside him that could have elevated his public profile so much higher than it was ever raised. *He* was kept tightly under wraps.

Jerry was the same, and it was a shame because he was a great storyteller in a bewildering free-association kind of way. We'd be sitting in the van going to or coming from a gig, and Jerry would just start talking, laughing as the tale picked up speed, and within minutes, the whole van would be laughing with him.

It could be anything—a Deep Purple song, something he saw on the news, someone he knew back in New York City. Terrible heavy metal bands. It didn't matter. Jerry used to tell detailed stories about how those groups came up with their most horrible (as in best-loved, most played) songs while sitting on the toilet, and maybe they did. It didn't matter, though. Whatever he said, it would kill us all.

Occasionally, and this was true of Johnny as well, something would get his interest, and for as long as it lasted, his enthusiasm would be boundless, as contagious as it was all-consuming. But then he'd drop it and never mention it again.

When we first started the band, for example, Johnny was obsessed with fifties clothes, skinny suits and skinny ties, completely out of context with the time, but it worked.

In terms of outfits, in fact, his fascinations knew few boundaries. He was a great one for barter and always had been. In the early days of the Dolls, and even before that, he was constantly trading clothes with people.

For example, the very first pair of snakeskin boots Johnny ever owned was the result of a trade with Stiv Bators of the Dead Boys—Stiv got Johnny's vest; Johnny got Stiv's boots.

He was the same with fans. If someone—a musician, a fan, a groupie, whoever—was wearing something that Johnny liked, he'd trade something for it. The fans loved it because they would have a piece of Johnny, and Johnny loved it because now he'd have all these weird-ass outfits to wear, simply from going through other people's closets and offering them his jacket for something he liked. And he'd wear it for a while, convince everybody that it was the greatest piece of clothing ever made, and then it would vanish back into the closet, never to be seen again.

There would be certain songs that he'd become obsessed with for a time and that he would play and talk about constantly, and then you'd never hear him mention them again. One day he heard "Green Onions," by Booker T and the MGs, somewhere, and he came into the studio, insisted that we add it to the set, and was armed with lyrics as well. (The original, of course, is an instrumental.) We played the ensuing "Who Needs Girls" a few times, and then he tired of it.

Another passing fancy was the Stones' "Under Assistant West Coast Promotion Man," only this time, he stripped away the lyrics and used it as a vehicle to get into a version of "Bright Lights, Big City"—another song that was important for a while before it fell away. The songs he actually wrote would stick around, but the ones that he just came up with on the spot, or after hearing something else on the radio, would soon be out of the way.

Old TV shows would obsess him for a few days. Ideas for the band. Adding a girl singer to the lineup, for instance. You never knew what his next fascination would be; the only constant was that you knew it wouldn't last.

The moment would pass, the enthusiasm would fade, and he'd turn back into Mr. Get-the-fuck-away-from-me.

Chapter Fourteen

OH CAROL

Ensconced in our new flat, we continued the party. Different people remember different things, and I'm no exception, so forgive me if I don't reiterate every "stoned Heartbreakers" story that you might have heard or read elsewhere.

I do, however, recall the night when Nils, as he put it, "save[d] Thunders from drowning when he nod[ded] out in a plate of spaghetti Bolognese." Johnny had volunteered to cook a meal for all of us—the band, Nils, Cook and Jones from the Pistols—and it was pretty good. Only he never really got to taste it. Instead he passed out face-first onto a heaped plate.

I also remember the times when certain visitors—Steve Jones and Sid Vicious among them—would be left banging on the locked door because we knew they'd come to cop, and we didn't want to share.

Nils and his brother Ray, who was a great photographer, were the exception to that rule—in fact, Nils had all but moved in with us, and Johnny celebrated by shooting him up for the first time. Apparently, Johnny also confided that he was still considering getting rid of Billy, and he sounded Nils out as a replacement.

Nils turned him down. "Playing bass is very boring. I think I'll stick to managing the Banshees."

Nils and I got along really well. A couple of times he shared my room because I had two beds in there, and Johnny used to make jokes about us moving the furniture around at night. But he was funny, he had some great stories, and we remained close until his death in 2002.

Another regular visitor, although his presence made us squirm, was a journalist who used to be around a lot and was writing for one of the weekly music papers, and we tolerated him almost solely because he always had dope.

He did make us suffer in return, though. A great writer he might have been, but his biggest dream was to become a rock star. No, I'll correct that—his greatest ambition was to become one specific rock star, or at least be mistaken for him. I'll never forget sitting on the sofa one evening, watching as our visitor preened in front of a mirror, saying: "I look a lot like Keith Richards, don't I? Don't you think so? I've always thought I look like him."

He didn't look anything like him, the fucking idiot.

There were several writers who supported us. Jane Suck and Jon Savage both used to come to the shows a lot. Giovanni Dadomo, too. Caroline Coon was often around, and so was Nick Kent, although he wasn't the most reliable friend we could have had.

One night at the Speakeasy, I got up onstage and sang a couple of songs with Cook and Jones, only for Kent to write the following week, "Walter should never get on stage without a guitar." What the fuck was that all about? But that was Nick Kent for you.

Paula Yates was another visitor before she hooked up with Bob Geldof; I believe Nils met her at the Speakeasy, where she worked as a cleaner. And a girl named Viv Albertine, who would soon be playing guitar for a girl band with the incredible name the Slits but who was currently in the Flowers of Romance with Sid Vicious.

She'd been at Caroline Coon's Christmas dinner, and in her book she tells a really sweet story about coming to see us at the Roxy, and Johnny changing the words to "Can't Keep My Eyes on You" to "Can't Keep My Eyes *off* You," all the while staring into her eyes.

But she also tells how a lot of Johnny's interest in her served as a conduit to her flatmate, Keith Levene—yet another junkie who had fallen into our orbit. In fact, after the long night of Anarchy Tour abstinence, it was beginning to feel as though we'd landed bang in the heart of Smack Central. Every place we turned, the junkies were crawling out of the walls.

Or maybe, as less approving heads have suggested since then, we drew them out.

I really don't know whether we were responsible for introducing smack to the London club scene. Jayne County is adamant that it was already circulating long before we got there, and returning to what I was saying about the Heartbreakers being role models for our fans, we were scarcely poster children for smack.

Lou Reed, Iggy, and people like that gave junk a far more glamorous sheen that we ever could, and "Waiting for the Man" is a far more alluring advertisement than "Chinese Rocks." (The title rhymes with "all my best things are in hock." Need I say more?)

So no, I don't believe we were responsible for introducing the punk scene to heroin. It was bad enough that we introduced it to Nancy Spungeon.

I never really understood what happened, but this is my best shot. Back in New York City, either before the Anarchy Tour or while we were there in January, Jerry pawned this guitar he owned in order to buy drugs. He gave the ticket to Nancy, and she came up with the money for an airline ticket. Then, once we settled on Denbigh Street, he called her up and asked her to bring it over.

The rest of us knew nothing of this. But we were sitting around one day when there was a knock on the door. Somebody, maybe Nils, got up to answer it, and in she sauntered.

We almost fell over. Johnny, Billy, and I were just staring at her in horror, thinking, "Oh God, not her!" But Jerry's all, "Hey, Nance, thank you," and because I was sharing a room with Jerry at the time, all I could think of was, "Oh fuck, am I going to have to listen to them screwing all night?"

In fact, she was only there for about thirty minutes before Jerry threw her out. I don't know what it was, or why she did it, but there was something about Nancy that made you want to treat her like shit. And it was impossible to resist.

She encouraged it, she welcomed it, and as far as she was concerned, it was water off a duck's back. You could say the most terrible things to her one day, and the next she'd be back as though nothing had ever happened. It was like living in a time loop—"If it's three o'clock, it must be time to tell Nancy she looks and smells like shit."

Because she did. I don't know where she was living at the time, or if she even had a place; the best we could figure was that she was crashing with whomever she could persuade to sleep with her that night and was whoring to make whatever money she had. Which was fine by Johnny—he didn't care where the cash came from so long as she would lend him enough to score, and he, Jerry, and Billy availed themselves of her other services on occasion, as well. As Johnny, I think it was, used to say, "Even groupie pigs have their uses."

Not that Johnny was ever going to go short of female company. Smack is not the male libido's best friend, and Viv's book tells another story to illustrate that—how, the first time he kissed her, he was so pleased to feel his body react that he actually shouted across to Jerry, "I felt something."

But the girls lining up for Johnny's attention weren't to know that, and a lot of them didn't seem to care even once they found out. Indeed, barely had we signed with Track than Johnny was moving out of our Denbigh Street flat and into the considerably more luxurious Mayfair home of another of the secretaries at Track, a girl named Janet.

Not that that was going to slow him down, and neither was the news that, back in New York, his girlfriend (and soon to be wife), Julie, was pregnant with Vito, a brother for Julie's own son, John. Even when Julie and little Johnny came over to visit in May, their arrival didn't check either the groupies' or Johnny's glances in their direction.

As it transpired, Nancy would not be around for too long—although it felt like an eternity at the time. I remember her developing a fake British accent; she'd be sitting there rabbiting on in her slutty American English, and then a word or an expression would pop out and you'd be like, "Where did that come from?"

But then she ran into Sid Vicious, and we didn't see so much of her after that. She'd come to the occasional show, but most of what we knew about her arrived secondhand. I really don't know whether it's true that Sid only liked her because she was so disgusting and it made him look even more punk, but the rest of the Pistols hated her—even tried to kidnap her and deport her back to New York. But Sid found out and saved the day, so they were stuck with her.

Viv was still around, though, getting drawn deeper and deeper into Johnny's web. Of course it was he who shot her up for the first time in her life—on the same day that Sid Vicious intended throwing her out of the band they'd formed together. The way she tells it, that was when Johnny asked her if she wanted to join the Heartbreakers.

The rest of us knew nothing about it, but I doubt whether it was ever a serious offer. Johnny liked her—we all did, although we didn't know her very well—and he felt bad about her being kicked out of the Flowers of Romance, even though we all knew that the group was going nowhere. But he invited her down to the rehearsal studio where we were and suggested we try "These Boots Are Made for Walking." Another of the songs we used to throw into the set on occasion back in New York City.

None of us were especially enthusiastic, but we went along with it, while a clearly nervous Viv talked her way through as many of the lyrics as she knew. Johnny remained enthusiastic, though, and led us all through it a couple more times; then, with Viv sleeping off that first-ever fix in one of the chairs, we got back to our own stuff.

We never heard another word about her joining the band, and of course she joined the Slits soon after. But Johnny had always loved that sixties girl singer sound, and it was never far away from his songwriting, particularly after the Heartbreakers broke up, and he'd be working with Patti Paladin soon enough.

With Johnny spending his nights in Mayfair and Jerry devoting his to Steve Dior's sister Esther, Billy and I had Denbigh Street to ourselves, which suited us fine. It wasn't a big place—two bedrooms and a living room with a pull-out couch. Initially, Billy and Johnny shared one bedroom, and Jerry and I were in the other, so once they moved out, we both had our rooms to ourselves.

It was a great flat in a terrific location. We even found a local connection, and that's how we got stuff, from Teddy, who was a Turkish guy who used to hang out around there. His father was part of the Turkish Embassy staff, so this kid was able to travel back and forth between Turkey and London and carry all the shit he wanted without being searched. He actually stayed in our flat with us a few times, sleeping in Johnny's room, and I remember Jerry waking me up one night to announce he'd discovered where Teddy hid his stash—under the carpet in the bathroom.

It was like we had discovered hidden treasure, and we partook generously of the bounty. Then we put it back where Jerry had found it, and we never heard a peep about it from Teddy. Maybe he didn't notice, but more likely he was too embarrassed. Of all the places to hide junk in a house full of junkies!

We were also walking distance from the tube, which was very useful, although I would have to brace myself when I stepped outside. There was a fruit and veg market that set up close by, and even in the early morning, as the traders set up for the day, the smell of . . . not rotten, but certainly bruised and battered . . . vegetables hung thick in the air. Then, once the market cleared out for the day, the sidewalks would be slippery with discarded produce.

It was disgusting, and of course it only added to my already confirmed antipathy toward English food. The only times we had decent meals were when we ate at French and Chinese restaurants, and occasionally, fish and chips. Or we would go to the McDonalds in Piccadilly although that wasn't the most delectable thing, either.

There were a few pizza shops around, as well; we had that a few times, and it was probably better than the Wimpys, but the worst was when we were out on the road and stopped for kippers and bangers—or, as we used to put it, cardboard and cardboard—at those rest stops on the motorways.

You could get decent food in the pubs—I loved Scotch eggs, but I could never handle fried tomatoes for breakfast, and that was a staple. I even tried haggis once when we were in Scotland, and it wasn't as bad as people make it out to be. At least, I didn't jump out of the window screaming, but then you go to Scandinavia and they eat rotten fish all the time, so I guess it's just a matter of getting used to things.

We were getting by. Our presence in the city, and our renown as well, were both still novelty enough that we were forever being asked to parties, or taken out for drinks, and of course you'd meet people who'd then invite you back to their place for the night.

One evening, I ended up staying over at Nora Forster's house—this was before she started dating her future husband, Johnny Rotten. The following morning, I went down to the kitchen to make coffee. Nora was still sleeping, but her daughter Ariana—Ari Up of the Slits—was already up, rehearsing with the band in the living room. She walked into the kitchen, took one look at me coming sleepily through the door, and shouted, at the top of her lungs, "Hey mum? Did you have a good fuck last night?"

Another time, just a couple of weeks after we arrived back in London—it was February 4, 1977, to be precise—Track invited us to a party being thrown for John Fenton, one of Golden Earring's songwriters, at someone's apartment. Somewhere around Knightsbridge.

I was thoroughly drunk that night, and I think mandies and maybe speed had found their way into the equation as well, so I have very little memory of the party itself. But the following morning, I awoke in bed alongside one of the most beautiful women I have ever seen, maybe half-Egyptian, half-Irish, and so stunning that I wasn't sure, at first, if I was still dreaming. I also realized that I didn't even know her name.

I climbed out of bed as quietly as I could, pulled on my pants, and crept out into the hallway. The morning post arrived early in those days—I'd take a peek at her mail and get her name that way.

All of a sudden, another door burst open and out stepped this little blonde boy. Then another opened, and out came a little black boy. Still a little tired, perhaps a little hungover, I wondered for a moment whether I'd spent the night in an orphanage. How many more of these kids were going to appear before I got to the mail slot?

Thankfully Carol—that was her name, Carol—appeared a moment later to make the introductions; both were hers, by different fathers, of course—in fact, it turned out that the blonde lad's father was none other than Jim Price, who'd been the Rolling Stones' horn player for a few years in the early seventies and was still one of the most in-demand session men around.

That's where he was now, in America working, and I suppose I always knew that at some point, he'd be back. But that didn't stop me from falling head over heels in love with Carol or from being absolutely devastated when we parted.

In a word, she was wonderful. Beautiful, mysterious, and very intelligent, but naturally so—she didn't have any intellectual pretensions whatsoever, thank God. She was twenty-nine, a year older than me, with exquisite taste, a great sense of self, and as I got to know her, it became more and more incredible that she'd even looked at me, let alone taken me home that night.

It was hard to believe, too, that she was a junkie. You would never have known it to look at her, and you would certainly never have believed that she used the stuff as often as she did. The flat was beautiful—a large second floor just off Kensington High Street with three or four bedrooms and a fabulous old wrought iron elevator. The kids were clean and healthy; there was none of the squalor or dirt that you normally associate with junkies or empty spots on the mantelpiece where she'd sold off the family silver.

She was also a dealer, in that gentle, relaxed, English way; she had a coterie of customers, who were also counted among her friends, and so I grew accustomed to seeing the likes of Jack Bruce or Arthur Lee when he was in town, stop by for a few hours of conversation, before disappearing once they'd secured whatever they'd come round for.

She had class, she had style, she had money, she had looks, and she had a habit, and they were all mutually compatible, bound up in this languid, beautiful, lazy, carefree existence. Even today, if I had to picture the physical manifestation of the symbol—the goddess, if you like—of heroin, it would be Carol.

Unfortunately, that isn't as romantic as it sounds. Like heroin, she was physically addicting, but—again like heroin—the more I needed her, the worse she treated me. She was beautiful and promised endless pleasure if you could win her heart. But love was unknown to her, and that is why nobody has ever beaten heroin, and nobody ever will. You can only avoid it.

As for why we broke up, I never knew. Jim Price, who was still paying the rent on the apartment, I believe, was coming back to see Carol and their son, and he'd be staying with her as well. Of course I couldn't stay. What I didn't understand was why we never got back together again after he left. Or, rather, I did understand because I've probably done the same thing myself over the years.

Carol and I had a great time together—five, maybe six weeks that, in my memory, became six or more months. In fact, until I looked back at an old diary while writing this, I would have sworn we were together through most of 1977. But no, we met on February 4, and for the first month or so, we were together almost every night.

By the beginning of April, however, we'd spent just two nights together in the past three weeks. We still hung out together, but the thrill, at least for her, had gone.

I, on the other hand, never lost my fascination for her. I was hurt when the phone calls dried up; I was shattered when she didn't turn up when we'd arranged an evening out; and I was devastated when she didn't call on my birthday despite swearing she would.

In other words, she behaved in the same way as every other junkie I knew, but this time, I was surprised.

Chapter Fifteen

BANDS

In the midst of all this, we finally went into the studio. Track wanted a single as soon as possible—that, we'd already agreed, would be "Chinese Rocks"—and an album for the end-of-year schedule.

We started out at Essex Studios on Poland Street—a few demos at the end of February sandwiched between what was fast shaping up to be the most concerted series of gigs we'd ever played, which, given our New York schedule and the fate of the Anarchy Tour, really wasn't too many.

One of the best was back at the Roxy, with Eater and Chelsea opening for us. We didn't get paid for appearing—the show was effectively a benefit for the Roxy after it was hit first by a couple of robberies and then by a doubling of its rent. But Andy had helped us out when we were broke, so we were happy to return the favor.

We were rewarded for our generosity by the first support band. Little more than a bunch of high school kids, Eater was the funniest group we ever saw, so much so that we actually made a point of going to their shows whenever we could.

It wasn't the music. It was the lack of music. They couldn't play their instruments, and you couldn't understand a word they were singing. They'd just get up there and scream and yell for fifteen minutes. There was one night they brought a pig's head onstage and jumped up and down on it for a while, still screaming and yelling. They really were fantastic.

They also brought home to me why punk was so important. There was a lot of debate in the music papers at that time surrounding the musical abilities of so many of the bands; I remember reading a review of the Adverts and the critic complaining that their bass player, Gaye Advert, was, let's say, less competent than Jack Bruce. What did the writer expect? She'd only been playing the instrument for six months, and I doubt whether Jack Bruce was as competent as he would become after that short a time. The fact was that her playing was perfect for the songs that the band was playing, which themselves were some of the best of the entire punk movement.

Or Steve Jones, who I thought had the greatest guitar sound of them all, being told he wasn't yet Eric Clapton because he'd only been playing a year. He didn't want to be Eric Clapton. Gaye Advert didn't want to be Jack Bruce.

(But Rat Scabies, I think, would have loved to be Ginger Baker. Later in the year, when we auditioned him for the Heartbreakers, we were halfway through a number when he launched into Cream's "Toad" drum solo.)

For me, punk was almost like an extension of modern art— Yoko when she was screaming alongside John, or Steve Reich recording harpsichords that sounded like knitting machines. Punk should never have been a musical term; it was a cultural umbrella that allowed people to dress, say, and do whatever they wanted, and the only caveat was not to do it with too much slickness or professionalism. And even that didn't stop some people.

Where we fell into this equation, I don't know. Our music fit the demands of the day, and whatever image we had did as well. But we'd also been around the block. We were competent musicians, and we didn't care who knew it; we were serious about music, and we didn't disguise that, either, and we were older than a lot of our so-called contemporaries, as well.

Not all of them—Jerry turned thirty about six months before we even arrived in the United Kingdom for the Anarchy Tour, but compared to, say, Knox from the Vibrators, or Jet Black of the Stranglers (he was staring forty in the face), Jerry was a positive babe-in-arms.

I was getting on a bit in punk terms too—my twenty-eighth birthday was just around the corner, and Track were throwing a party for me at the Zanzibar, a members-only club in Covent Garden. Mick Jagger's brother Chris and Sandy Denny were playing shitty blues on this tiny little stage in the corner, and Julie Christie was in the audience—it was a very exclusive place.

My advancing years meant absolutely nothing to me—my diary mockingly declares: "It's like saying I'm twenty-eight eggs or seventy-four pages or nine chairs old. It's a just a number. I still feel eighteen or nineteen years old and mentally, and maybe in ten years, I've lost some energy. But I still feel I can do anything I want."

Twenty-eight? Who's counting?

So far as the invited press folk were concerned, however, I was celebrating my twenty-third. That's what it said on the invites. I'm not convinced that anybody believed us, but Track thought the deception was important. It reinforced our youthful "punk" credentials. Even if one of the published reports did add a question mark, in brackets, alongside my purported age.

It was a healthy scene as well in that there really didn't seem to be that same snide rivalry that sometimes disfigured the New York bands. Of course the media was always inventing little clashes and combats, and yes, some groups couldn't stand the sight of others.

But I don't remember us having problems with any of the bands we ran into in the United Kingdom, and some of them did become friends—the Pistols and the Clash, of course, the Banshees, the Models, with Marco Pirroni before he was an Ant. The Adverts were pretty cool, and we used to hang out with them. They were fun to watch, and I liked their guitar player, Howard Pickup.

The Slits—musically, they didn't have too much going for them, although I enjoyed Palmolive on drums. Viv and Tess were still learning as they went, though, and Ari was less a force of nature than a box full of every kind of natural disaster you can think of, tipped out onto the stage and unleashed to do whatever it wanted. The Slits are still one of the most exciting bands I've ever witnessed.

There were other groups that I appreciated without ever really liking. The Stranglers were a decent band; they didn't do much for me, but they had some good songs, and they were good musicians. I also remember going to see Elvis Costello at the Hope and Anchor.

Gail and Leee would always go to see him, so I tagged along, and I have to confess I never really liked his stuff that much, although a lot of people did. He came out of nowhere, and in a few years, he was huge. But a lot of his songs were so fucking awful, and he looked weird too. The last time I saw him was right after Joe Strummer died. Joe's wife was throwing a memorial, and I was chatting with Mick Jones when Costello came in, looking all fat and bloated and wearing, I swear, the same black suit he had on when I saw him thirty-some years before.

The Banshees were probably the people we spent the most time with, both socially through our friendship with Nils, and also on the road. We played our first gig with them, I think, in Croydon at the end of February, and long after they broke with Track Records, they remained our support band of choice. We did so many tours with them, often with the Models on the bill as well, and Nils's brother Ray would often be around too, taking photographs.

I say we got on with the Banshees, although Siouxsie herself was a little harder to get to know than her bandmates. The press used to call her the Ice Queen, and she did live up to that billing. I remember backstage at one of the gigs, she made some remark to Johnny about his sound, telling him, "You should have played with your knobs some more." He shot straight back, "I'd like to play with your knobs," and Siouxsie just froze. She was *so* insulted.

Those tours were so good, though, even if they have so blurred in my mind that even when I look at the itinerary, it doesn't help me remember. Although I do recall the night in Liverpool when I almost knocked myself out onstage. We were playing the Cavern— not, sadly, the original basement of Beatles fame, just its latter-day replacement—and I was leaping up and down as I always did when we were playing. I'd forgotten, or maybe not even noticed, that the venue had a somewhat lower ceiling than others. And it was a hard one.

I also remember a journey, from somewhere to somewhere else, with Johnny seated beside me, sleeping with his head against the window, and Jerry opposite. Suddenly Johnny let out the most enormous fart. "I guess Johnny's thinking again," I said, and Jerry burst out laughing. Slowly, Johnny awoke with a sly smirk on his face, and looked at us. "Sticks and stones may hurt my bones . . ."

We also found ourselves spending time—understandably, I suppose—with any visiting Americans. Cherry Vanilla and Jayne County had both relocated to London now, on their old friend Leee's recommendation, and though neither were ever to become a part of our immediate circle, it was good to know that we were no longer the only New Yorkers in town.

In fact, it was through County that we first learned of possible troubles ahead with Track Records. They were showing an interest in signing her, and part of the initial deal stipulated that Track would continue to pay the rent on the New York apartment that Jayne and Leee were sharing.

One day, Jayne came steaming over to announce that the rent had gone into arrears and the landlord had thrown all of their possessions out onto the street. Of course they were long gone, now. Needless to say, any hope Track had of signing Jayne and her band, the Electric Chairs, promptly went out of the window. They went with Safari instead.

We spent time with Television and Blondie when they toured Britain together in the spring, and we even had a reunion with Hell when he and his new band, the Voidoids, toured with the Clash. We went to see them at the Music Machine and there was a party backstage— there are some pictures floating around of him talking to Johnny and Jerry in the dressing room.

It was a good gig. That was the thing with Hell—if you weren't actually working with him, he was exactly the kind of person you'd *want* to work with; he was funny, he used to come up with some great lyrics, and he looked like a spaceman on stage. Not until you'd been seduced into his orbit would you learn the reality of being in a band with him. Hell was hell.

The group we couldn't get away from was the Ramones.

For many UK journalists, they were the key to the whole New York scene, probably because, apart from Patti, they were the first of the CBGB generation that anyone in England got to hear.

They'd first visited the previous summer, and already the show was being talked about as some kind of golden catalyst for everything that took place in the United Kingdom afterward, even if they were only opening for the Flaming Groovies at the time.

The strange thing is that all the while I lived in London, I very rarely heard one good thing about the Ramones from any of the bands. It was only later on that people started competing with one another as to who was influenced the most by them, and the audience at that first ever show swelled to include pretty much everyone who even thought of themselves as "punk rock."

Also, I couldn't help but feel that the Ramones looked down on the audience, almost as if the band agreed with the critics who complained their music was dumb. Maybe it was. But how much dumber did someone have to be to enjoy it? And when the spitting started, they got so offended. The Heartbreakers, on the other hand, were rarely offended by anything.

Nevertheless, many journalists saw the Ramones as the benchmark for New York punk success, and it soon became difficult for us to make it through any interview whatsoever without being asked, at some point, what we thought about the Ramones. The truth is, we didn't think about them very often.

But that's not an answer, so we'd come up with other responses. Such as the time I was asked the inevitable question, and being a little drunk and forgetting the Ramones were in the country at the time, so they had a good chance of reading my answer in the paper, I just shrugged and said, "Ah, they've reached their peak."

Johnny and I. *(Photo by Ray Stevenson)*

With the aptly-named (and sadly late) Magenta DeVine, London, 1977. *(Photo by Ray Stevenson)*

Backstage with Billy and two European fans. Charlotte is the laughing girl in my lap; I don't recall her friend's name. *(Photo by Ray Stevenson)*

The Heartbreakers. I'm not sure why I chose that moment to eat an apple. LAMF cover out-take. *(Photo by Roberta Bayley)*

Another LAMF out-take.
(Photo by Roberta Bayley)

And up I go! *(Photo by Ray Stevenson)*

Linda Danielli *(left)*, Anna Sui *(right)*, promoting Anna's pirate line. *(Photo by Anna Sui)*

En garde! Anna Sui looks on as Linda Danielli and I fence to the death. *(Photo by Anna Sui)*

Anna Sui *(left)* and Linda Danielli *(right)* prepare to kill me. *(Photo by Anna Sui)*

Joey Ramone joins our fencing bout, as Anna Sui looks on. *(Photo by Anna Sui)*

Just me. *(Photo by Anna Sui)*

Doing my Hindu dance routine!
(Photo by Marcia Resnick)

Max's, with Ty Styx on drums. *(Photo by Bob Gruen)*

Backstage at Max's, December 1979, at a Voodoo Shoes show. *(Photo by Doug DeGaeto)*

The Heartbreakers at Max's, June, 1979. *(Photo by Russell De Gaeto)*

Onstage with the Heartbreakers at our spiritual home, Max's, June, 1979. *(Photo by Russell De Gaeto)*

Johnny and I onstage at Max's, 1979. *(Photo by Russell De Gaeto)*

The June 1979 Max's reunion show. Who knew we would still be playing similar shows a decade later? *(Photo by Russell De Gaeto)*

Live at My Father's Place, Long Island, April, 1980. *(Photo by Russell De Gaeto)*

With Johnny at My Father's Place, April, 1989. *(Photo by Russell De Gaeto)*

My Father's Place, April, 1980. I think a fan gave me the medal, but I don't remember what it was. "Best NY Junkie Guitar Player of the Year," perhaps? *(Photo by Russell De Gaeto)*

My son Damien and I. *(Author's collection)*

Working on Wall Street. *(Photo by John Nicolai)*

The author, today. *(Photo by Leland Bobbé)*

Like I said before, I'd seen them far too often and I'd become so bored with them playing the same song all the time. I still don't know how they got away with it for so long, and now I hear them in the fucking supermarket.

The day the quote came out was the day we were supposed to be attending a party that the Ramones' label was throwing for them at some place on the Kings Road. Immediately, they spread the word that I wasn't welcome, and eventually, the word reached Leee. But I thought, "Fuck it, I'll go anyway."

I walked in and, of course, they were all throwing me the filthiest looks that said, "What are you doing here?" So, bold as brass, I walked up and told them I never said that, that I was misquoted, that the guy turned my words around.

Joey and Dee Dee were fine after that. Johnny not so much, but they warmed up after a while. Besides, they gave as good as they got, of course. Johnny Ramone and Dee Dee both raged about us in the *New Musical Express*, and when our Johnny got into the party, he complained: "I got a better reception from da Talking Heads [the opening band on the Ramones' tour]. The Ramones just told me they're gonna sue us."

They didn't, but it created a rift. Particularly when Johnny, responding to the Ramones' insistence that singing about heroin just wasn't cool, hit back, "But of course it's okay to sing about glue an' all that shit."

Which isn't to say we never spoke again. In fact, a few years later, they asked me along to the sessions for the *Subterranean Jungle* album, and I was on board for *Too Tough to Die* and *Animal Boy* as well. *Jungle* was the one that I spent the most time on, rehearsing in the studio twice a week for something like six months, getting there straight from my job on Wall Street and learning the songs in my suit and tie.

That's when I realized that Dee Dee was the main songwriter and creative force. Johnny never came up with anything, and Joey was more interested in covers. It was not a happy band, either.

Dee Dee was still doing smack; Marky, the drummer, was drinking; and if one of them discovered where the other was hiding his stuff, they'd rat one another out to Johnny.

It was the same in the van. We'd be sitting there, riding out to Long Island for the *Subterranean Jungle* sessions, and there was this whole weirdness about who sat where, how this one hates that one, and how that one hates this one—it was a difficult situation to be in, although it was that tension, I think, that made the band tick.

The other thing was that Joey suffered from OCD, which meant nothing could happen unless he'd done everything he needed to. Walking across the street, for instance, he'd have to tap his foot on the curb five or six times before he could bring the rest of his body along, and the same with stairwells. Cracks in the sidewalk scared him.

He came home from a tour once, got all the way back to his apartment, and then took another cab back to the airport because he realized he'd forgotten to tap something.

He was also very sickly. Every time he got a new pair of sneakers and a blister on the back of his foot, he'd end up in the hospital for a week with a severe infection. His body had no way of fighting it.

All of that was still to come, of course. We went to their party, and a few nights later, we went to see the Ramones at the Roundhouse, which was (and still is) a gorgeous old Victorian railway turntable building that had been converted into a theater and concert venue. They were headlining this time, although the thing I remember best was meeting Marc Bolan backstage.

He and Jerry were off talking somewhere, and when Jerry came back, he was white as a sheet. Apparently, Marc had asked him if he wanted to join T. Rex and, all the while, had been squeezing his ass!

Jerry was losing his mind because he didn't want to piss off Marc. At the same time, though, Jerry rejoined us once the conversation ended, doing that famous Jerry giggle, barely able to get the story out. If only he'd listened to Nils! A few years before, Nils was having an affair with Bolan's wife, June, and he told us how he'd go over to the apartment and Marc would be chasing Nils around the room, and Nils would be chasing June. . . .

Chapter Sixteen

CHINESE ROCKS

I don't think the two things were at all related, but my birthday, on April 22, coincided with a brief period of sobriety. The Sunday before, Jerry woke me up at 6 a.m. with a handful of Chinese rocks and coke—it was like something one dreams about. And I'd not touched a drop of stuff since then.

No great resolution, nothing like that, I just stopped taking it. Not for long, a couple of weeks maybe, but I couldn't help but feel pleased with myself.

Drugs were becoming far too easy to do—I'd be feeling bored or restless, and just reach for the closest thing at hand. More than that, though, with both Jerry and Johnny about to start on methadone programs, suddenly there was a lot less paranoia and madness around—and I'd realized that that was as much an incentive for me to get high as anything else. The old "if you can't beat them, join them" mentality kicking in.

The methadone was a necessity. Heroin was still hard to source; there were a few people who could supply it, but it was so much harder to cope—just that endless routine of socializing and hanging out, waiting, or the times you'd track over to someone's house and they'd be out, so you'd end up sitting on their doorstep for hours.

Plus we didn't have money. However, we discovered that so long as you could find a doctor who would recommend the treatment, you could get onto a methadone program through the National Health Service, meaning it was free of charge.

We already had a doctor, a gentleman known as Dr. Diamond, with an office somewhere around Kensington. A lot of other bands were also among his patients, so that's probably how we first heard of him. They'd go to him and say, "I've got to go on tour, can you give me some Mandrax to help me relax?" Then they'd hand him ten pounds, and he'd give them the necessary prescription.

I didn't follow the methadone route myself, so I don't know how Johnny and Jerry got into the program—I imagine, however, the obliging Dr. Diamond was involved in some way. And, as I said, it didn't last. Johnny never got sick on smack—he knew his dosage, and no matter how fucked up he was, he never exceeded it. Methadone and more or less any other drugs, on the other hand, were less predictable. Particularly the way Johnny consumed them.

Methadone he drank like it was soda, saving his doses for one great blowout and then having the most appalling withdrawal while he saved up for the next one. Even Jerry could restrain himself, but not Johnny.

He couldn't help himself. When we toured, he would always save up enough dope to see him through at least the first few days. Invariably, it would all be gone by the end of day one.

Johnny did OD on methadone once. We were in Pimlico, screaming down the phone for Gail and Leee to come over because Johnny was turning blue. They were in Islington, frantically trying to gather up sufficient small change to pay for a cab, and by the time they arrived, Johnny was awake again. He was stumbling about, but he was functioning.

He went back to junk after that, and a few weeks later, I was bitching Johnny out for selling me some of the shittiest smack I'd ever had. While it lasted, though. . . .

Boredom was a problem. In fact, a lot of different things were the problem. I was still mourning the loss of Carol, of course, and would have given anything for the opportunity to simply curl up in a ball, in the dark, on my own, and feel sorry for myself.

Unfortunately, the basement flat on Denbigh Street wasn't designed for that kind of solitude. Too many people, not enough quiet. Even on the rare occasions when it was just us band members sitting around, there would always be squabbling, chattering, inane observations, and pointless pronouncements until somebody suggested we go out for the night.

So we'd go, but even that loses its appeal after a while—sometimes you do just want to wrap up in front of the television and watch something mindless on your own. Or sit and read a book.

No chance of that here. There was always something going on, someone having a meltdown, someone knocking at the door, and if I did manage to get the place to myself for an evening, it was only to be reminded precisely how little there was to watch on TV before it shut down for the night.

Boredom was a relatively new sensation for me, and it was ugly. Powerful, too, in a sinister way. It drives people to the most extreme lengths in an attempt to avoid it. I know "boredom" was very much a part of the punk ethic, and it was incredibly hip to claim you were bored—but actually *being* bored, as opposed to affecting weariness with the world, is a very different emotion.

In New York, it was never a problem. There was always something to be interested in, something to be fascinated by. London didn't offer such diversions. How could it, with its shops that closed on Sundays and Wednesday afternoons, its pubs that kicked out at 10:30, and cinemas that shut down even earlier?

The handful of clubs that did cater to a late-night crowd also catered to much the same crowd every evening—it was like being trapped in a time loop, the same thing with the same people, day after day after day.

Occasionally I'd bring someone home, be it a visiting Sable Starr, who poured cognac over my cock before giving me a blowjob (if you haven't tried it, you really should sometime), or some pretty boy I'd run into in some club or other, and those were diversions. Before the Heartbreakers, my sex life had been . . . okay. Since then, well, I'd never say I got too much. But there were evenings when I wished my companion would just turn over and go to sleep. Or, better still, go home.

Even the things that used to excite me—writing songs or playing guitar—went by the board. Again, how can you concentrate when there are always people around? I couldn't even keep my diary up to date in peace. One entry actually ends, "Nils just came in, See ya later." I was growing lazier and lazier. I went for days without practicing or even thinking about reaching for ideas.

At the same time, the Heartbreakers' career was actually picking up speed. The Essex Studio demo sessions had gone really well. We knew the songs in our sleep, after all, and the gigs we were playing allowed us to fine tune them.

Plus, it was a nice studio. It was a small space, a basement, but it felt good. We did most of the songs, and I thought they came out sounding excellent. But Track seemed less happy with them, so they moved us on.

They booked us into Ramport Studios in Battersea, just across the river from Denbigh Street. It was the Who's own studio, and I remember Roger Daltrey turning up one day to watch us.

We barely recognized him. He was dressed as a punk, green and yellow hair, a safety pin in his cheek, a chain from his lip to his ear . . . it was hilarious.

Speedy Keen was to be our producer. He was another name from Track's glorious past, one third of Thunderclap Newman, whose "Something in the Air" was such a huge hit for the label back in 1969. He'd also released a couple of solo albums, and he wrote "Armenia, City in the Sky" for the Who. He was a nice guy.

But was he a producer? To the best of my knowledge, all he'd really handled in the past were his own recordings—although around the same time as he was working with us, he also took Motorhead into the studio to cut their first single, and we went to a few of their sessions. It sounded okay.

Still the doubts—or, more accurately, uncertainty—remained. For sure, I know we were never given a say in the matter; at most, they may have convinced Leee that Speedy was the man for us. They certainly never asked the rest of us.

But what the hell? We went along with it, and he was pretty good. He knew how to operate the boards, and he wasn't an idiot. I don't know whether he actually understood punk rock, or whatever we were supposed to be playing, but he came to a few of our shows, and he seemed receptive to our ideas.

Of course, once we got into the studio, we suffered through the usual trials and tribulations—waiting for Johnny to turn up was the main one. Time-keeping had never been one of his strongest points, and I think his record for arriving late was five hours, which was the amount of time it took him to score that day.

We just got on with things while we waited; we even took to snorting coke when it made its appearance, because it was quicker than shooting up. We didn't want to waste studio time!

It also helped that neither Billy nor I were especially strung out at that time, and Jerry was on an even keel thanks to the methadone program. Of course, if we'd known that he would then continue the treatment for the rest of his life, we might not have welcomed it so warmly. For now, though, all was well.

Speedy never lost his temper, even when Johnny was late. He would give us time if we fucked up or couldn't get a solo out, and there would always be heaps of amphetamine, Rémy Martin, and coke in the studio. In fact, we quickly discovered that Speedy was a lot like Johnny in many ways. He was a wild guy. I don't think he was ever out of it, but sometimes by the end of the night, he'd have a little bit of a loop on.

The fact that Leee had expressly demanded that they keep the studio drug-free was completely overlooked. There was never any shortage of it in there, and it was only later that we discovered that Track were adding the cost to our studio bill, not only by keeping us supplied, but by also charging us for however much Speedy and any other visitors were taking.

Ramport itself was a terrific place to work, much larger than Essex and better equipped as well, so we started recording all over again. Not that it made much difference to the finished thing.

Playback time arrived and, to my mind, we performed equally well in both studios. I never had a chance to actually compare the takes from the different studios to see if either was genuinely superior; they both sounded good to me.

We recorded the single first, "Chinese Rocks" backed with "Born to Lose," plus half a dozen others for the album. Even unmixed, they sounded fine. We had always prided ourselves on the fact that we could play anywhere, and as we gigged between the studio sessions, we proved that.

Compared to the United States, touring the United Kingdom was easy—few of the venues we were playing were more than an hour or so from the next, and a lot of them were in easy reach of London as well. We had a few nights bunked up in barely habitable hotels, devouring barely edible food, but we got by.

Our reputation had usually preceded us, as well; at some point in the evening, somebody would emerge from a darkened corner to offer us drugs, while Johnny in particular had the most incredible ability to take a quick walk down the street and bump into exactly "the right person." Everyone's heard about that strange sixth sense that allows junkies to recognize one another from across a crowded room, but Johnny took it to a whole new level.

Or maybe they were already out, looking for him.

If the nuts and bolts of touring didn't faze us, local traditions and practices could. All four of us quickly got over the shock of hearing cigarettes referred to as "fags," and an especially inedible-looking meat dish being a "faggot." We'd never heard such terms before, but we got used to them. We probably started using them ourselves. Only Johnny adhered to the American definition. Every time someone asked him if he had a fag, he'd reply, "Yeah, take my manager."

But had we ever heard of a canteen that eschewed the usual "first come, first served" routine that any normal place adhered to, and went out of its way to make things as complicated as it could? No, not until we got to Winchester, where the sheer madness of whatever system the student canteen was operating reduced us to impotent fury. I've been told my parting words to the serving lady were "you fucking whore."

There were also problems with the payment we received for gigs, as Gail declared that we were a cash-only business—no checks. More than one venue tried to insist on adhering to their interpretation of the contract, but Gail belied her peroxide beauty queen looks with a mouth, and a temper, that could quell the most determined objections.

What we didn't have was trouble with the law, which—considering what people said about us—was fortunate. Not once during our time in England did we even receive a funny look from the police, not even when Johnny's wife all but bared his track marks for an officer.

I'll get to that story later, but considering everything we'd heard about the British police's attitude toward both "punk rockers" *and* "drug addicts"—remembering back to the sixties when all they seemed to do was bust sundry Beatles and Stones—so far as we were concerned, the law couldn't give a damn.

Later it was different. I remember Johnny getting busted in San Diego sometime in the 1980s, and some newspaper had a picture of Johnny's arms on the front page, with circles drawn around the track marks. But he was only in jail for a day or two, I think, and I don't know if they found stuff on him. More likely, he got picked up because of the track marks, or maybe the cops knew his reputation and wanted an easy bust.

What happened to us in Leeds at the beginning of June, though, was weird.

We were at the hotel—Johnny, Gail, and Leee were in one room; I was upstairs in mine; Billy and Jerry were in theirs. I was about to go out, so I called down to Leee to ask for some money. He told me to come on down, so I made my way to the room, walked in, and there was a young blonde guy sitting there, wearing a suit and brandishing a gun.

Now, what he said, and what was really going on, might well be two very different things. Or they might not. We never really found out. But his story was that he was with Special Forces, and he was acting on a tip-off that somebody was planning to kill us.

Apparently, and again we only had his word for it, there were more officers in the hallways, and even more outside, surrounding the hotel. If the hit squad turned up, they were going to blast it into oblivion.

I looked at the others. Jerry and Billy had arrived by now, and they were as confused as I was. But I sat down, and we waited.

This dragged on for what felt like hours. Every so often, the guy would get up, go to the phone or look out of the window, and then return to his seat. Nothing was said—some desultory small talk, maybe, and the occasional "I wonder who's after us?"

Odd notions crept through my head, and I'd imagine everyone else's. Had Johnny stiffed some dealer, who had more firepower behind him than we ever could have guessed? If we were in New York City, maybe. But Leeds? No way.

A jealous boy, or even girlfriend? Again, plausible, but unlikely. England, unlike America, was scarcely awash in firearms—in fact they were largely illegal—and I'd never heard of a crime of passion being committed over a one-night stand with a rock musician.

Finally, our Special Forces man stood up and left the room. He walked down the hallway and then returned five minutes later to inform us that the threat was over. We could leave any time we wanted to. "Just keep your eyes open," he cautioned.

We were completely baffled. If somebody was gunning for us, we wanted to know who. And if they weren't, then what the fuck was that all about? Finally, Leee suggested we head round to the local police station and see if they knew what was going on.

They didn't. They'd not heard of any threat against us. There was no mobilization of Special Forces that they were aware of and nobody staking out the hotel. What they did do was promise to investigate, beginning with a visit to our hotel room, to pick up the guy's fingerprints from the phone.

Of course, this meant they had to take our prints as well so we could be eliminated from the investigation—what they intended to do about the hundreds of other people who must have touched that phone since the last time it was thoroughly wiped down, I can't imagine.

Years later, probably on the Internet, I read that our self-appointed bodyguard was arrested three weeks later while trying to steal a car with a plastic replica gun in his pocket. At the time, however, we never heard a thing; never had the events of that bizarre afternoon explained to us.

We did, however, get copies of the sheets on which we'd placed our fingerprints, and when our album came out later in the year, those were indeed our genuine dabs that adorn the back cover. Except maybe not Johnny's. According to Gail, Johnny's prints arrived too late to be included in the artwork, so they used hers instead.

Ah yes, the album.

"Chinese Rocks," our first single, was out by now, and nudging the UK chart as well. It shifted twenty thousand copies in that first week, topped the independent chart, and entered the national listings at number fifty-six. Yes, it was small change compared to the Pistols crashing in at number one, but it was a start. The problem was that it didn't go any higher.

There was only one television program worth appearing on at that time, *Top of the Pops*, every Thursday night, and unlike a lot of radio DJs, the show had no qualms whatsoever about featuring punk bands.

If you climbed high enough up the chart, or your record label put enough muscle behind you, any performer had a good chance of making it on, which is how one June evening's viewing could swing from a novelty song about farming to the soul of Gladys Knight and the Pips, from the Stranglers bellowing "Go Buddy

Go" to Greek balladeer Demis Roussos, without anyone pausing to consider the sheer dichotomy of it all.

We, however, did not come within sniffing distance of the show. Radio was a little more accommodating—I think John Peel played us a couple of times, but that wasn't really much help, either. If there's only one DJ playing punk, and playing a lot of it too, it meant that every night listeners were bombarded with new releases and bands. Nobody could ever afford to buy every record they heard him play.

They could get it for free, though, if they arrived early enough at the Music Machine when we played there at the end of May. I don't know quite what the idea was—maybe Track had over-pressed the single, or maybe they thought that if they gave a few copies away, jealousy would force everyone else to buy one.

Or maybe it was the only way they thought they could entice people into coming to see us.

Johnny wasn't impressed either way. "Hope you liked your free single. You probably wouldn't buy it anyway."

I know we let ourselves down, as well. In Manchester, again at the beginning of June, I found myself in front of the microphone, giving a live radio interview.

It was awful. Even as I talked, I knew I was failing. I'd never done live radio before, and although the theory—just be yourself, speak normally, be witty and engaging and all that—is easy to say when you're miles from the mic, it's a very different proposition when you're actually sitting there. Projection is key, and I didn't project.

It's strange, I had a really bizarre relationship with Manchester-based broadcasters—or, at least, my hair did.

One time, it was Billy and I, and maybe Johnny, and I was smoking as usual, my cigarette in my hand, and my head resting on that same hand. Somehow the cigarette got turned around, or went up at an angle, because all of a sudden, the room filled with the awful smell of singed hair, and I was sizzling away. I had to smack myself around the head a couple of times to put the fire out.

Worse, though, was the day I set out for the studio with a newly colored haircut, only to run into a typical Mancunian deluge. It all began the evening before when I decided I needed to have my highlights touched up. Leee was drunk at the time, and I should have known better, but I asked if he could just touch up the ends. Instead, he did the entire thing, and I came out looking like a platinum blonde.

It was awful! "I can't go on television looking like this," I said—we were due to appear on Granada TV's *So It Goes* the following evening. Leee agreed. So he sent one of the road crew out to a local market to pick up a few bottles of food coloring and proceeded to pour them onto my hair to create an at least tolerable multicolored look. And then the rain started. By the time I got to the studio, I had dye running down my face, onto my clothes, everywhere. Never again.

That TV appearance was one of the highlights of the "Chinese Rocks" period, and not only because I survived the dye disaster. That was the night when the host, Tony Wilson, asked Johnny if he "missed looking like a lesbian." He was referring to the old Dolls look, of course, but Johnny looked completely baffled. "My mother doesn't think I do," was the best reply he could manage.

Otherwise, promotion was poor. Even the print ads for the single were disappointing. We had no ideas to offer, so that's what Track went with—a page of next to nothing. A better-sounding recording would have been nice, as well, but in their haste to get the single out, Track didn't worry so much about such niceties.

It wasn't so bad if you picked up the 12-inch single version—that, at least, was everything we'd hoped for. But the 7-inch sounded cramped and cranky, and it didn't make us feel any better when the two Dolls albums were reissued around the same time, to remind us just how dreadful *they* had sounded. In fact, all it did was set Jerry off on another of his increasingly common rages.

Unlike Johnny, who would explode and get it over with, Jerry's fury simmered. He wouldn't scream and rage, but he could remain pissed off for days, being nasty to everyone and never missing an opportunity to gripe about whatever it was that set him off in the first place.

The other thing he would do: if there were bridges to burn, he'd burn them. He was great at making the grand exit and slamming the door behind him, both literally and figuratively.

I don't recall how many days this particular rage lasted for. But I do remember how Jerry's sole topic of conversation, for however long it was, was how it was a complete waste of time rereleasing the Dolls records. They should have remixed them both as well.

How quickly that comment came back to bite us.

We'd started mixing the album at Olympic in May, moved on to Trident, back to Ramport. And every time . . . . no. It just wasn't right.

It was the strangest thing. No matter how terrific something sounded in the studio—and as the process went on, we listened back on every size speaker and every piece of equipment we could lay our hands on—the moment it got to the test pressing, it fell apart.

We toured the pressing plants, trying to find one—just one—that didn't translate the tapes to a murky mush. And every time it was the same. The music sounded great when they were pressing it, but the test pressing would come back and it had transmuted into shit.

We were at our wits' end, not only with the process but with one another, too. I'd long since grown accustomed to wondering how long this band could hope to survive, but now I was beginning to doubt whether we'd even make it until the record was finished, let alone into the future.

It felt as though we were breaking apart, and we hadn't even got started yet. Johnny was going through one of those phases where he was negative about absolutely everything, to the point where he didn't even want to have another go at the tapes. "It won't make any difference. They're still going to sound like shit."

It was a trait that he never relinquished. A few years later, I was reading an interview he gave with the *New Musical Express*, and there it was again. "[It] don't bother me what people think [about me]," he complained. "People gonna write what they want to anyway. Journalists don't unnerstan' anything of what I'm about, so kids that read what people write about me don't get the true . . . meaning . . . of what I'm about. I jus' do what I do, it's all different every night. I don't have to live up to what anybody thinks, you know, I just do what I do."

In other words, what's the point in trying to explain anything? People have already made up their minds. When, in fact, it seemed to me as though he was always trying to live up to what people thought about him, until the moment arrived when there was no difference between the person he was and the person the public expected him to be.

The single never made it past its first-week high of number fifty-six, which gave Johnny something else to complain about, and Jerry had all but vanished, burying himself in his relationship with Esther and surfacing only to complain about how appalling the latest mixes sounded and threatening to leave the group.

It made no sense—all his life, he said, he'd wanted to play in a great rock 'n' roll band. Now he was, and it wasn't enough.

None of us were happy, but Jerry was as mad as I had ever seen him. Back to the studio, Advision this time, once more, but now with Jerry at the controls. Track did not stint on time; they gave him a week, which we all agreed was more than enough to rework every song on the album. Billy and I had already proved that when we remixed four songs in one all-night session.

Jerry, on the other hand, devoted that entire week to no more than four or five, and three of them turned out even worse than the mixes he'd started with. "All he did was bring the drums up in the mix," Johnny reported back after he listened through Jerry's handiwork. "The drums are now the loudest thing on the tape."

Chapter Seventeen

DEPORTEES

We were still gigging in between the mixing sessions, all over the country now. We played the opening night of a new club on Wardour Street in central London, the Vortex—we were the only non-Manchester act on the bill, for some reason, and there was another diversion when a new band of Heartbreakers turned up, opening for Nils Lofgren on his latest British tour and fronted by a skinny guy with stringy hair named Tom Petty.

If something like that happened today, the lawyers would have a field day. Our band had already been around for close to a year by the time Petty formed his group in Florida, so there was no question as to who had the rights to the name.

At the time, though, you only had to look at the bands, let alone listen to them, to know that there was no way on earth someone could confuse them. Besides, they also had Petty's name plastered in front of the band's. Our feeling was that if someone was stupid enough to mistake one for the other, they deserved what they got.

There again, it was beginning to look like we wouldn't even be around long enough for anyone to get confused. At the end of July, midway through the tour, midway through the mixing, a grim-faced Leee delivered some bad news. Track, for whatever reason—be it incompetence, forgetfulness, or bloody-minded spite—had neglected to renew our work permits.

We were being deported.

We flew home on July 13, 1977, and landed in New York City to find the place in total darkness. Not just the airport. The whole metropolis. Earlier that evening, a lightning strike fifty miles away in Buchanan set off a chain of events that led to the entire city being blacked out.

No lights, no signals, no subway . . . no air conditioning. What there was was rioting, looting, and, nine months later, a massive surge in births. It was also desperately hot—104 degrees Fahrenheit, with not a breath of fresh air to be found. A thousand fires, 1,600 stores damaged, more than 3,000 people arrested. It would take more than twenty-four hours for power to be fully restored. But hey, New York is New York. We just go on with things.

Luckily for me, my father picked me up at the airport, and we made our way out to Nassau County, where I was staying with my parents, and they still had power, one of the handful of places whose lights stayed on. I went to bed early, though. None of the television stations were operating.

Although there were hopes that we'd only be gone for a couple of weeks (that's what Track kept saying, anyway), we would ultimately remain in New York until the beginning of September. And it was great because it meant we could cop as much dope as we wanted without all the messing around that it entailed back in London. But any hopes that a change of scenery might bring about a change in Jerry's attitude toward the band were swiftly shattered.

He was still going on about the mixes, only now he wasn't just blaming the studios, the producer, the label, and everyone else he could think of. He was turning on the rest of us as well, and each of us, in turn, would eventually feel his wrath—"If you hadn't done *that*, and you hadn't insisted on *this*, everything would be fine."

A lot of his objections were ones that we agreed with. The sound was muffled, it didn't have any presence, and so many mixes had sucked all the fun out of the music. What Jerry didn't understand was that there was nothing else we could do.

Yes, we could have put our collective foot down and refused to allow the record to be released, but there was no guarantee that Track would even listen to us. They had already told Leee that if the album wasn't released on schedule, they would have no hesitation in dropping us, and they'd probably make sure no other label in the country would touch us after that.

There was also the question of how much money they had devoted to us—not just our recording and living expenses but the hours that had been devoted to remixing the tapes. They'd been supporting us for a year and had sunk an enormous amount of money into us. We never looked into the legalities of the situation, but what if they suddenly demanded we repay all of that? No matter how you looked at the situation, it was just too huge for us to ignore.

Except for Jerry. He'd threatened to leave the Heartbreakers in the past—maybe not as often as our publicist Alan Edwards said ("Jerry quits the group every week") but a lot more frequently than the rest of us.

That's just part of *being* in a band, though. Everyone gets sick of it every so often. This time, however, he seemed more convincing, particularly after we rolled up at Max's for a show, and Jerry was nowhere in sight.

We wound up borrowing Lee Crystal from the Boyfriends (he later played with Joan Jett), and the show passed off well. Musically, at least, Jerry's threats carried a little less weight after that.

We played a handful of other shows around the city while we were there, but the biggest were three nights at the Village Gate, with both Sylvain Sylvain and Robert Gordon joining us onstage for a few numbers. Full page ads in the papers ensured we had a packed hall each night, and it was the weekend after Elvis Presley died, which also added to the vibe.

I wasn't especially touched by the passing of the pelvis—I know it's considered a big deal when any rock star dies, but you could also say that it goes with the territory. Eddie Cochran, Gene Vincent, Jim Morrison, Jimi Hendrix, Janis Joplin, Duane Allman, Billy Murcia, Mama Cass, Keith Relf, Tommy Bolin . . . at least Elvis was allowed to grow old (forty-two . . . that seemed old at the time) before he went. And he hadn't made a decent record in—how long?

The audience was in two minds, too. Robert Gordon fans, like Robert himself, were heartbroken. But there was a new wave of nihilism lurching onto the scene now, a post-Iggy self-destructive-ness that, we quickly discovered, was exemplified by a new band called the Dead Boys, whose best live numbers included a song—"Ain't It Fun"—written by another of rock's fallen, Peter Laughner.

We were already aware of them. Back when Hell was still in the band, we played a show in Cleveland, where we ran into a local band called Frankenstein. We were playing in the ballroom of a hotel, and that's where they met us, Cheetah Chrome with his long frizzy red hair, Stiv Bators with his wiry, Iggy-like frame.

Of course, all we wanted to know was where we could score, so they put us in touch with these old-school black drug dealers, heavyweight gangster types who looked like B. B. King, chunky frames and bedecked in diamond rings. We scored, we played, we went home. Now Frankenstein were the Dead Boys, and the new kings of CBGB.

Those Village Gate shows were truly the peak of the Heart-breakers—particularly the second and third nights. For some reason, none of us had scored before the first show, so we loaded up on Billy's speed beforehand. We also blew out the P.A. on the first night. We learned our lesson and doubled our efforts to pick up some junk the next day.

Periodically, or so I've heard, different elements of the Village Gate audience would break into their own bellowed response to Presley's passing, but I can't say it affected us. We just enjoyed playing for a huge hometown crowd . . . they must have been edu-cated during the six months we went away. They even danced to us there! Pogo dancing! We looked out and there they all were, jumping up and down. There's a live album out that was recorded at the Gate, and it's really one of our better shows.

Despite the emergence of the Dead Boys, we quickly realized that very little had happened on the local scene during the months we'd been away. As I told a writer once we returned to London: "The music scene is shit, there's no new groups or anything; aah, there's one group, they're like the New York equivalent of X-Ray Spex, which is interesting, but that's about it. It's the same old scene, [and] there's still only two places to play . . . CBGB's and Max's."

I was being a little disingenuous. There may have been few new bands, but the ones we'd left behind had grown remarkably in stature.

The music industry had finally come to terms with what had been happening on the streets—a far cry from what we had left behind just nine months before. Now, everybody had a record deal, it seemed, with Sire sweeping up the majority of them: the Ramones had been joined by Hell, Talking Heads, and the Dead Boys themselves.

Blondie had switched from Private Stock to Chrysalis, David Johansen was about to go to Columbia, Television were with Elektra . . . even my old band, the Demons, were now with Mercury.

It was incredible and, maybe, disheartening. When we left New York at the end of 1976—in fact, the main reason why we left New York at the end of 1976—it was because we could not see any way out of the same old CBGB/Max's, Gottehrer/Ork/Marty Thau grind that had been there all along.

We could never have foreseen that, just a few months down the road, there would be punk rock boutiques springing up all over Manhattan; big punk parties being hosted by major fashion designers; and all the stores flaunting pictures of Johnny Rotten on everything. Nothing else, just Johnny, but at least they were becoming aware.

Could never have imagined the major label feeding frenzy that had since descended upon Manhattan. Could never have dreamed that the bands that the Heartbreakers had literally grown up alongside would be undertaking their own tours of the United Kingdom and continental Europe, and doing it without *any* of the shit that we'd been subjected to for the past six months.

Most of them even had albums out, whereas we . . . what did we have? A heap of tapes that half of us admitted were barely usable, and the other half weren't even that kind.

No wonder Jerry was pissed.

At the same time, did I have regrets? No. If you want to play the big fish, small pond game, in New York we'd have been just another band fighting for space in the national music mags, or fighting with one another in the back of a tour van as it drove three days across Kansas on its way to the next show.

In Britain, despite all its faults, and our flaws as well, we were *someone*. We didn't have much money, it was true, but Track hadn't yet allowed us to starve, and they were as desperate for a hit as we were. And when we toured, we were rarely less than a few hours away from whatever venue we were booked into.

Even Europe was just a short hop away; and when we got to the show, we knew the audience would be our own. Not a bunch of bored locals who, in best American fashion, just turned up because they wanted to hear some rawwwwk and rolllllll.

Plus, when we did come back to the United States, we were the conquering heroes, the returning legends, *the little junkies that could*. NBC television had just aired a punk rock special, dripping with drama and sensationalism, and when anybody heard that we'd just come back from England, that's all they wanted to talk about. "Is it really that heavy in England? Do people really get killed at the shows and get beat up and stuff?" Of course I said yes.

We were far better off where we were. We just had to get back there. Especially when it became apparent that Track's promise to send the album tapes over to New York so we could work on them there was not going to materialize.

Our New York vacation wasn't all work and waiting. I hooked up with a couple of friends, Judy and Guillemette, and we ran around together for a while. One night, I banged them both at the same time. On another occasion, Judy and I had gone back to her apartment in the West Village when her ex-boyfriend, Richard Lloyd of Television, turned up, banging on the front door until she finally let him in. And what did he do? He jumped into bed with us.

Another night, Judy and Eric from the Marbles came back to Brooklyn Heights with me. I ended up in bed with Eric for a while, while Judy went to sleep in another room. She awoke to discover that we'd emptied a can of whipped cream down her body, from her mouth down to her twat, and Eric was licking it off.

There were orgies.

They were never planned or pre-arranged. But they seemed to follow a similar pattern regardless. Every night, hanging out at different clubs or bars, there'd be different people around—photographers, fashion designers, musicians, whoever. You'd meet, you'd chat, and at some point, someone would say, "Let's go over to my house; I have some coke or dope or whatever." So we'd go there, three or four girls, four or five guys, all sitting around getting stoned, and suddenly clothes would be coming off and everyone would be boning on the bed.

And suddenly there'd be fingers going up your ass, cocks and cunts everywhere, arms and legs—it was like you were in a snake pit or a barrel full of eels. The lights are low and you'd have no idea who or what was there, just this weird sensation of bodies everywhere. You'd look in the wrong direction and there'd be someone's ass in your face.

It was sheer lust, everybody rolling around, crawling around, kissing anything you found, sticking fingers and toes wherever they'd fit. You'd be pretty out of it, but not so much you didn't know what you were doing. It was just who you were doing it with.

It's not really like a sexual encounter; it's more like giving yourself over to this sheer lust and looseness—you can't even call it an orgy, really. It was just something that happened, and never with exactly the same people, either.

That was one side of life. But there were more sedate evenings, too—nights when I'd get together with Guillemette as well as Eric and his girlfriend, Susan, and we'd play pinochle for hours. It was a totally different scene from anything that happened with the

Heartbreakers, a bunch of junkies falling asleep at the table—we'd have late-night card games, a few drinks, a little coke, just kicking back and having fun.

I spent time at the beach; I hung out with my brother. And I took way too many drugs—it was just so easy. Reading my diary from that time, even my handwriting deteriorated.

And then, of course, there was Johnny's wedding.

It was a couple of days before the first of the Village Gate shows, and it remains the cheesiest, sleaziest ceremony of its kind that I have ever attended.

I wasn't invited to the actual wedding ceremony. I joined the party at the reception, which was staged at a run-down church hall in Queens. I think it was also used as a gymnasium, which should give some idea of the decor (and the smell), and I was waiting outside with everybody else when the limo arrived from the church. There were Johnny and Julie, Steve from the Senders, who was the best man, and Babette, the bridesmaid, who was Phillipe's (also from the Senders) girlfriend.

Of course they were already stoned; in fact, they'd been throwing up all over the limo, but they tumbled out of the doors, stumbled into the hall, and Johnny was being his best obnoxious self, swearing loudly as he staggered into the building.

I followed and I couldn't help notice a woman sitting in the little vestibule area, wearing a dazzling neon-colored, exotic-looking Eastern dress with chiffon and clutching a basket.

For a moment I thought she was begging, and I will forever be thankful that I didn't reach into my pocket and hand her some change. It was Julie's mother, a devout Muslim who refused to enter either the church or its hall. She remained sitting outside in the vestibule for the entire reception, keeping her distance from the evil demons she was convinced were lurking inside.

Inside, it was like a bring-and-buy sale. There was no formal seating, just a line of fold-away tables piled high with paper plates and tin foil trays of food—catering courtesy of the cheapest local deli they could find. Guests would then pile this not-altogether-edible muck onto a paper plate and then take one of the plastic seats that were arranged around the walls.

There was no band to serenade the happy couple, just a tinny little record player in the corner. A few people did get up to dance but not the wedding party. They were now too stoned to move.

This went on for I don't know how long, but finally people started to leave, so I took that as my cue to exit as well. As rock 'n' roll weddings go . . . this wasn't one. It was simply poverty-stricken.

Chapter Eighteen

BACK TO LONDON

At last our visas came through.

Jerry flew back to London first to be with Esther. Johnny, Billy, and I remained behind in New York for another few days. We returned to the United Kingdom on September 14.

Just like New York City, little had changed during our absence. A few more bands had scored hits—the Adverts, with "Gary Gilmore's Eyes," was one of the best. A handful of new groups had broken through, but aside from the Boomtown Rats from Ireland, none of them struck me as being particularly remarkable. It was the old story, the first bands through were the talented ones—those that followed were the makeweights.

But it was good to be back.

The lease on the Denbigh Street basement had lapsed while we were away; now, Track were putting us up in an apartment on Oakley Street in Chelsea. It was a vast improvement: three stories, two bedrooms, and a fully converted live-in attic. That's where I went; below me, Billy took the front bedroom, Johnny the rear one. The place was laid out in such a way that, if we were so minded, the only time we'd have to see one another was if we happened to be in the kitchen at the same time.

It was also just up the road from where David Bowie had lived. There are a few photographs around of Johnny, Billy, and I messing about in the doorway, while Leee and Angie Bowie, separated from David and still living in London, told us endless stories of the things that had occurred behind that door. The now-famous tale about the time she apparently discovered Bowie and Mick Jagger naked in bed together, for example. She said Bowie told her to go and make breakfast for them.

Angie had been around us for a while; of course she knew Leee from way back, so she was always a familiar presence, but now that she was banging our soundman, Keith Paul, we started to see a lot more of her.

She was there the night we played the Vortex, with another great band, the Boys, opening up for us. I'd decided I wanted to go onstage got up like a minstrel musician, with Al Jolson-style black face and a red hat, and Angie loved it—in fact, she probably egged me on to the point where I couldn't change my mind.

Unfortunately, what neither of us noticed was that I'd forgotten to do my ears. With the possibility of a coal miner's strike in the air—every other industry in the country had downed tools at that time, it seemed, why not the miners as well?— people ended up thinking I was doing a special protest on their behalf!

Angie still thought it was cool, though.

We did not fly back on our own. Johnny's wife Julie came too, with both of the children—John, who was born before she met Johnny, and Vito.

Billy and I weren't happy about that. We understood that Johnny wanted to keep his family alongside him as much as he could. But how was it going to work when we went out on tour? From the outset, we always had a rule—no girls on the road. In fact, it was a law that Jerry had laid down back in New York.

"The biggest problem bands have," he'd say, "is when girlfriends come on the road." And it's true, look at Sid and Nancy. Or watch *Spinal Tap*. They get snotty, they try to take over, and to be honest, the band members themselves have a hard enough time putting up with each other without adding girlfriends (or wives) to the mix.

Thankfully, Johnny felt the same, so Julie only joined us on the road a couple of times. Otherwise, she stayed at home, but that situation would quickly wear Billy and medown as well.

Julie and Johnny fought all the time. Johnny had taken the money, Johnny had hidden the dope—you'd come in from an evening out and you never knew what you were going to run into. One night, Julie even called the police on him.

Such battles were never a daily occurrence, but Billy and I quickly grew accustomed to hearing their raised voices—Julia screaming, Johnny wheedling, maybe a door slamming shut. But then they would quiet down, presumably make up, and the next day all would be peace and love again.

This one was different. I never did find out what sparked it. All I know is that

the cops came in to find Julie standing there screaming and Johnny lying on the bed, crying his eyes out and clutching the two kids. The poor cops were doing their utmost to calm them both down, but they hadn't reckoned with Julie's capacity to raise the temperature even higher. All of a sudden she started screaming at them: "Look at his arms! Look at the state of his arms! He's a fucking junkie!"

The cops ignored her. I don't know why. Maybe arresting Americans involved too much paperwork, or perhaps they just didn't want to get involved. But they didn't look at his arms; they didn't cart him off to the station. They just did what they could to calm the pair of them down and then made a very grateful exit. And Billy and I kept our heads down, desperate to get away from the domestic nightmare that was life with the Genzales.

The album was imminent. Despite all of our misgivings, Track had arranged an early October release to coincide with our next UK tour, the biggest we had ever undertaken.

With little more than two weeks to go before we went on the road, I tried to pull everybody together for a rehearsal, or to write some new material, but that wasn't going to happen. Billy was up for it, or at least he wasn't opposed to it, but Johnny couldn't be bothered, and Jerry was still going on about the tapes and how, if something wasn't done to salvage them, he was going to walk.

Track remained resolute. They tried to console us by saying that some of our alternate mixes would be used on planned

European and American pressings of the album. But it was completely up to us what happened next. Either we could shut up and just get on with things. Or they would can the album and send us on our way.

They knew the album was substandard—and if they didn't, then they obviously hadn't listened to a word we'd said, or a note they'd heard, for six months. No, they knew, but their hands were tied as much as ours.

Like us, Track had deadlines and commitments, too. Record release dates are not simply pulled out of thin air; all manner of other considerations go into them, and once set—with distributors, stores, and promotion lined up—it can be a real pain to have to set them again. We had no choice. Like it or not, *L.A.M.F.* would be released on schedule on October 3.

Three days later Jerry left the Heartbreakers.

His timing could not have been more malicious. We had a week before the tour was due to start, but just twenty-four hours before a warm-up show at Bristol Polytechnic. Before he went, though, he delivered a delightfully cogent explanation of the album's acronymic title.

"Where I come from, it used to be a part of the graffiti where some gangs would write their name on the wall, what gang they're in, y' know, 'Little Chico from the Ellery Bop,' 'Big Tony from the Hellburners,' and then after that they'd put 'Like a Mutha Fuckah' or else if they were on war terms and they were fighting rival gangs they'd usually put D.T.K.L.A.M.F—'Down To Kill Like A Mutha Fuckah,' 'cause in its day it was really fuckin' violent. Ahm talkin' 'bout sawn off shotguns, ahm talkin' 'bout great homemade zip guns, I'm talking 'bout a death or two in every gang fight."

The journalist, incidentally, had opened his questioning with his own suggestion. "Let's All Make Friends."

The cover matched the title. We took it when we were back in New York, down in Soho, which was still a factory, sleazoid area. There were so many ideas about what the album sleeve should be, and a lot of arguing on that score; I think everybody threatened to quit the band at some point, as different ideas for the photo came and went. But finally we took that particular set of pictures, and sent them over to Track. They liked that one shot; we agreed, and that was it. It was just a shame that, by the time the record was released, the lineup in the photo was already out of date.

We had no time to mourn Jerry's departure. Somehow, Johnny persuaded Paul Cook to play drums for the Bristol show, with Steve Jones adding guitar. It was never going to be a permanent situation, though, so once we got back to London, we started auditioning.

A few people came along, including Rat Scabies, whose own band, the Damned, had just broken up. He was good, but he wasn't a Heartbreaker. Neither was anybody else we saw. The auditions were over, and we were still without a drummer.

Finally, we asked Leee to find out if there was any way we could get Jerry back as a hired hand.

The fact was, we missed him. Yes, he was constantly causing problems, grumbling and moaning all the time; yes, he hated Leee to the point of siding with Danny Secunda during his attempted managerial coup. We could probably have thought of a thousand reasons why we were grateful that he'd departed.

But we wanted him back regardless, and he agreed. Of course, he charged us a small fortune for his services, probably earning as much per gig as we were getting a week, and walking away with a couple of free Pearl drum kits at the end of the tour. But he was still Jerry, and to be honest, I don't think any of us would have taken a different stance had we been in his position.

He wasn't a permanent solution; he was still adamant that he had left the band and that he was only doing this for the money, which of course placed another problem on the horizon. We were trying to put together a European tour to follow on from the British dates, but that couldn't happen until we knew who our drummer would be.

There was talk of flying back to New York and holding auditions there, but deep down I think we knew it was hopeless. Nobody could truly replace Jerry despite him being the most fucked-up, irrational, paranoid, stubborn person I had ever met. Once he made up his mind, he could not be budged. His drumming was totally instinctual and incredible. He never even had to practice; he was just a natural.

He had the highest personal standards, and he hated himself because he couldn't live up to them. Deep down, he loathed drugs and junkies. Deep down, he craved a virgin girlfriend. Deep down, he was a racist and a homophobe. Every middle-class right-wing phobia and obsession you can think of, Jerry held dear. And he could not live up to a single one of them. He couldn't even be anti-Semitic any longer—his girlfriend was Jewish.

But was it his fault? Never. There was always someone else to blame. It was like having Richard Hell back in the band. Jerry wanted to produce the album, Jerry wanted to select the songs, Jerry wanted to tell us how to play them.

He truly got crazier by the hour, while his moods changed from one extreme to the other in a matter of minutes. He was drug crazy, worse than any of us. It was so bad that I even made a wager with myself—ten to one, Jerry would either have a nervous breakdown or kill himself within the year.

Plus, considering he was not a member of the group (he was very adamant about that fact), he had an awful lot of opinions about it. The only difference was that, although he was still moaning about the album mix, he was no longer blaming Track for all of its problems. And why? Because the new band that he and Esther's brother, Steve Dior, had formed, the Idols, would be cutting some demos for the label soon enough.

I like *L.A.M.F.* I think it's a good album. At the same time, though, I have always been well aware of its faults. I've never been one of those listeners who can forgive an album its sonic flaws just because the "feel" is right. I was disappointed by both of the

Dolls' albums, and I was never a fan of Iggy's *Raw Power* either, not even after everyone started raving about how foresighted the original mix was. *L.A.M.F.* felt the same; only this time, I understood those other artists' frustration.

All manner of excuses, or causes, have been mooted to try and explain what went wrong: everything from the rumored presence of a drunken Kit Lambert at the mastering sessions to that of an inexperienced Danny Secunda.

At one point, Johnny even blamed Jerry for remixing the entire thing behind our backs, after we'd already approved the master, while at least a few of the reviewers piled the responsibility onto Speedy, and that added further friction when Danny Secunda told us to stop complaining about the record because of the damage it was doing to Speedy's reputation.

"Well," we replied, "what about *our* reputation?"

It could have been any of these things; it could have been none of them. It happened, it was horrible, and all we could do was pull ourselves up the best we could, and hope next time worked out better.

If there was a next time. Halfway through the tour, Track entered its final death throes. All of our tour support was withdrawn, and promotion was at an end. We were on our own.

A new single, the album's "One Track Mind," and live recordings of a couple of my songs on the B-side vanished almost without trace; a couple of months later, our third single, "It's Not Enough," barely made it out of the production plant before the label crashed out of existence.

Early in November, with the tour at an end, we were as good as label-less once again.

We weren't panicked. CBS was showing an interest—a lot of interest. Nothing had been confirmed yet, but it was looking promising. We had come to a decision regarding a drummer, too; Terry Chimes, once of the Clash, would see us through the European tour and, if he worked out, maybe the future as well.

Yes, the lack of money was a problem. Now, more than ever, we needed that envelope stuffed with cash that Gail would collect at the end of each evening. But we were playing great, as well as we ever had, and we'd kept it up night after night after night, scouring the country's club scene as we raced toward the climax at the London Rainbow.

Even the interminable journeys between gigs were enjoyable. We'd chat, we'd sleep, we'd read, and we were among friends. Once again, the Banshees and the Models were on board with us, band brothers who supported us as vociferously as we supported them.

The reviews were great. I'd been a little nervous when we set out, painfully aware that we were still delivering much the same set as we'd been playing a year before, when we first arrived in London. But audiences wanted to hear the songs they knew, so every song was greeted like a conquering hero. They wanted to watch Johnny and I having our volume battles onstage, so we gave them to them. Even on those nights when the inevitable delays and distortions curtailed or even collapsed our set, there was not a band in the country to top us.

"The band plays rock and roll like guns fire bullets, like steamrollers flatten tarmac, like thunder rolls," said one review, and that's how it felt onstage. Playing in this band had always been easy, but now it felt effortless.

You never knew what was going to happen from night to night. That might have been the greatest feeling of all. Nothing was scripted. You never knew who was going to fall over or forget the songs, and you certainly never knew what Johnny was going to say between songs, and there were evenings when that was worth the price of admission on its own. Other artists of the age were renowned for insulting their audiences—Johnny Rotten, of course, and the Iggy Pop of past renown, and a host of lesser noname acts who saw hostility as a short cut to notoriety.

Johnny put them all to shame.

It was a relatively new development in his stage persona. All the times I saw the Dolls, I never heard Johnny say much onstage, and it was the same when the Heartbreakers were in New York. We'd make jokes about one another between numbers, but that was as far as it went. He didn't even seem to enjoy introducing songs.

But then he saw what Johnny Rotten was doing, ripping the crowd a new asshole in that sneering, wheedling voice of his, and Johnny decided to do it as well.

"Fucking faggots," he'd sneer. "You don't know good music when you hear it . . . don't you know how to dance?" A bit of a Rotten copy. But then he became more inventive. One time in New York he asked the audience, "What happened? Did all the barbers go on strike?" because they all had long hair. They were all "fucking assholes, fucking faggots"—even if it was a good audience, he would launch indiscriminately in. He just liked doing it.

At first, the rest of us were mortified— "What the fuck are you trying to do?" But then we realized he was really good at it. I always felt that Rotten's diatribes were a put-on, in the same way as he could snap between personalities the moment a journalist entered the room. He had an image, and he was living up to it. It was an act, and if you saw the Pistols often enough, you realized it was a scripted act as well.

Johnny, on the other hand, was usually so out of it that even he didn't know what he was going to say until—or sometimes even after—he said it. There were a few standard lines, renaming the Dolls as the New York Dildos, for instance, but most of it was completely off the cuff. "If I was a comedian and you kids were my audience, you could be great."

It was hilarious, but ultimately, it became ruinous, as the penchant for trash-talking became a part of his offstage persona as well. Right now, however, it was a part of the performance, and we looked forward to it as much as the audience.

I've said before that the loud, caustic Johnny who made his way through the 1980s was very different to the one I'd known at the beginning of the Heartbreakers. That, in the beginning, he was very quiet and meek.

The change came slowly—so slowly that, even once he started laying into the crowd for sins both real and imagined, I never saw where it could lead.

Others did. By early December, writer Jane Suck was asking her readership, "Why is Thunders the most arrogant slob to ever stumble across a stage?"

But it's the same for every performer. The dynamic changes as you fall into an image, and the bigger you become, the more people expect to see it. It becomes inescapable, a self-fulfilling prophecy, and ultimately, a parody. When I stood onstage with Johnny at the last Heartbreakers reunion show of all, in 1990, it was difficult to believe the guy I'd once known was even in the room.

Chapter Nineteen

OVER THE RAINBOW

Although it was not the final gig of the schedule, nobody denied that our appearance at the Rainbow Theatre in London was the climax of the *L.A.M.F.* tour. The place was packed, and most of the city's punk royalty was there. But so were kids who'd followed us since we first touched down in the United Kingdom, and we wanted to give them a show to remember.

You could never get away with it now. Health and Safety would blow a gasket.

Smutty from the Rockats set up a huge plate glass window onstage, and we put a brick through it. We hadn't played a note, and the place was already howling its support. The P.A. that night was appalling, probably because Keith kept falling asleep on the board. It was just one problem after another, but adrenalin and energy carried us through.

Octavio was there—he'd come over from Paris for the occasion and brought some quality dope along with him—and some old friends of mine from college, who were vacationing in London, were there as well. There was a party upstairs at the Rainbow; they sealed off the second-floor balcony after the show and turned it over to us. Then, when that was done, we all went back to Oakley Street.

That's when I proved to Track that Johnny and Jerry were not the only junkies in the band. It was a bit late in the day for them to do anything about it, but Leee did get the phone call from someone in the office, saying, "Excuse me, but I thought you said . . ."

I can't say I know what happened. The booze was flowing, mandies and heroin too, and I could feel myself slipping a little. Nothing that another drink, or pill, couldn't cure, of course, so I kept going and the rest of the night, for me, is less of a blur and more of a total blank. I was still a little stoned from the show, and as soon as the needle went into my arm, I passed out.

For everyone else, on the other hand, it was panic stations. Apparently I started choking. Apparently I was turning blue. Apparently I was out for thirty minutes. That's what I was told. All I know is that I woke up naked in the bathtub, with people throwing ice cubes on me, and emergency techs coming up the stairs. They saw that I was up and alert, said "okay," and didn't take me. But when I came round completely, I couldn't help remembering poor Billy Murcia of the Dolls—Jerry's predecessor. He had an overdose in London and wound up in a bathtub, but he didn't recover consciousness.

There was no time for recriminations, however. The following night, we were playing in Leeds.

The tour wrapped up in Chelmsford on Halloween, and after that, we had a couple of weeks to ourselves. CBS were still interested in us, we were told, and maybe one or two other labels as well. We were rehearsing with Terry Chimes, in readiness for the European gigs (notice it was no longer a tour), and the future auguries were good all around.

Much as happened after Hell left, the problems with Jerry seemed to spark a new wave of creativity in the band. New songs were flowing—beginning with "Too Much Junkie Business."

Johnny appropriated it a little later, but it was actually something I wrote on my own. My original idea was to rewire Chuck Berry's "Too Much Monkey Business," and that was what was on my mind as I wrote the lyrics. But when I finished, I realized it didn't match Chuck's progression. Bo Diddley's "Pills," on the other hand, fit perfectly, and it was a great choice as well because the Dolls had recorded such a great version of that. All I had to do was change the key to A.

Johnny loved the song, adored the title, and he was always jealous that he didn't get to write it. So when it was finally released in the mid-1980s he stuck his name on it as well. People would come up to Johnny to say, "Oh, I love your song"—people like Jim Carroll—and Johnny would just go, "Yeah, yeah, thanks."

"Laughing at You" was another one, but best of all was "Little London Boys," our riposte to a song—"New York"—that Rotten insisted be included on the Pistols' album. And in terms of vehement vitriol, we wiped the floor with it. To be honest, "New York" didn't bother me. It was Rotten being typically Rotten. But Johnny felt that he had to answer back.

I came up with the music for "Little London Boys," and I deliberately structured it like a Pistols song, only instead of a descending riff, I had an ascending one, and it was a little faster.

I was going to write the lyrics as well, but Johnny begged me to let him do it because he took "New York" very personally—and who can blame him for that? He did a really good job, too. I'd already called the song "Little London Boys," so he worked around that, writing it really quickly, helping me knock it into its finished state, and then we were rehearsing and playing it. A few months later, he rerecorded it on his *So Alone* solo album, and in 2018, I revisited it on *Wacka Lacka Boom Bop a Loom Bam Boo.* It's a great song.

But moments like these were a short-lived high. The tour—which ultimately amounted to just a handful of shows in Holland after the bulk of the French leg fell apart—went well, at least until we got to Groningen, in the Netherlands, and our equipment didn't show up.

We cobbled together what we could from whatever was available, but the show was a disaster. Nothing worked, and anything that did function was on the verge of breaking down. We played four songs, apologized to the crowd, and left the stage, hoping they would understand.

Of course they didn't. With the place verging on a riot and with a couple of hundred very pissed off Dutchmen hurling abuse and anything else that was movable towards the stage, we came out and tried again. This time, we got three songs in, but it was still a mess. We left the stage, and I think the audience finally gave up.

The irony is that afterward we went to a local club to wind down and were invited up to play a guest set. It was phenomenal.

It was time to go home, a ferry ride across the sea. Customs grabbed us the moment we got off the boat. Six fucking hours they kept us there while they quizzed us about how long we intended to stay in the country and whether we had enough money to fund our stays—they couldn't (or, more likely, wouldn't) get their heads around the fact that we more or less lived and worked in Britain, with valid work permits and everything else, and had just popped overseas for a few days. When they finally let us go, you could see disappointment etched on their faces.

We spent November cooling our heels. It was clear that Terry was not a natural Heartbreaker, so we played one final gig together at the Vortex—which showed just how desperately we were suddenly sliding, that we'd slipped from the Rainbow to the Vortex in barely a month—and then paid him off, only to hire him back at the beginning of December for a one-off show at the Bataclan in Paris. A fabulous venue, even if it is now world famous for all the wrong reasons.

The Vortex show was strange simply because we were now far too big for the place. As Jane Suck complained: "But for the fact I love Leee Childers and don't want him to take the first plane back to New York, I'd let fly . . . like, why are the Heartbreakers back in the Vortex? That ain't cool, that's dumb."

It was a good gig, though, and so was Paris. Johnny's New York Dolls reputation had once again certainly followed him, and I lost count of the number of times we were told we were "bee-yooo-ti-ful." So, from what I glimpsed of it, was Paris, and I'd been hoping that we'd get to spend some time there.

Unfortunately, the French label that was financing the deal, Barclay, didn't come through with the support money they'd promised. We wound up losing hundreds of pounds and had to leave the morning after the gig.

Even more damaging was the news that CBS wasn't interested in signing us after all, and for the most obvious reason—they'd heard that we were all junkies. A few other companies were still sniffing around, however, including RCA and Virgin (with whom we'd just signed a publishing deal), while Leee managed to convince EMI to let us record some demos with Mike Thorne, the in-house producer who'd been siding with us back at the start of the year.

We recorded three songs: "Little London Boys," "Too Much Junkie Business," and a cover of the Shangri-Las' "Give Him a Great Big Kiss," which had been on Johnny's mind since the early days of the Dolls. But the tape would amount to nothing, and when I looked back over the past twelve months, the feeling of futility was inescapable.

Another Christmas was coming, and we were more or less in precisely the same position that we'd been in twelve months earlier.

The money we got from the publishing deal had gone, most of it into our arms. An Italian tour that was scheduled for the Christmas period had been cancelled, and there wasn't a label in the land that would touch us.

We never had it confirmed, but it appears that certain Track Records personnel had not been reticent about discussing our offstage predilections, and the London music business was small enough that word had filtered into every corner. We weren't quite pariahs, but we were close.

We were also broke. Billy and I had been planning to return to New York for the holidays and to audition a new drummer. But even that was up in the air. We didn't have the money for plane tickets.

We did, in the end, make it, flying out on December 23, and once the festivities were over, we set up a series of auditions at our old rehearsal space on Grand Street and Lafayette, in a second-floor room above a sleazy little diner. We'd been rehearsing there since the beginning, every time we were back in New York, and Philippe lived there for a while. I suppose the best thing you can say about it was that it was adequate. Just.

The guy who rented the place was a friend of John's named Carl. He was always hanging out with the Dolls and then the Heartbreakers; he was taking drugs with us, and I even fucked his wife once. She called me up at my apartment one day, I think just to say hello, and she asked what I was doing. I told her I was washing the kitchen floor, which I was, and she said "I'm in love! I've never heard a guy say that before!" The next thing I knew, she was on her way over!

So we held the auditions, but either the people we saw weren't up to our standards, or they simply didn't want to relocate to the United Kingdom. We finally settled on Spider, the Pure Hell drummer who had sat in for Jerry way back in the last days of the Dolls—Johnny knew him better than the rest of us, but he thought he was as good a choice as any. Billy and I agreed. He wasn't perfect, but he was certainly the best of a bad lot.

We also knew the fact that Spider was black would make an impression. For all its embracing of reggae and dub, and the growing impact of Rock Against Racism, punk in Britain at the time was still predominantly white, just as reggae was predominantly black.

Nobody was asking, "Where are all the black punk bands?" of course, for the same reason not many people demanded more white reggae bands at that time. The crossover between the two musical forms was already so pronounced that it would have been hard to emphasize the linkage any further. But maybe Spider would blaze a new trail.

Billy and I also played a single show at Max's on January 13, an all-star affair featuring Johansen, Sylvain, Lee Crystal, Ivan Kral, Philippe, and my brother Richie. Typically, we called ourselves the Works, which was the nickname given to the hypodermic needles used to inject drugs.

The bulk of our visit, though, was more play than work. Personally, I didn't get much done beyond a lot of worrying, a lot of drugs, and a lot of reading—I even almost finished Proust, at last!

When we first got back, I was staying at my apartment in Brooklyn Heights. Track had kept up the rent payments for the first six months or so; then, when I heard they were falling behind, I offered the place to Richie. That worked well, but shortly after I returned, the building was sold and the new owners made an offer to buy me out.

I took the money and moved into the spare bedroom of my friend, fashion designer Anna Sui—she had a huge apartment, and we'd been friends for years. It was a natural fit, and it also unleashed the phenomenon of the Three Little Pigs onto an unsuspecting Manhattan scene.

The Pigs were Anna, me, and our friend Linda Danielli (later to become Mrs. Johnny Ramone). Together we would tour the sleazier after-hours bars that had recently become popular among the punk crowd, places that stayed open till ten in the morning.

The scene was much as you'd expect—a lot of furtive (and not so furtive) sex and groping, an awful lot of drinking, a certain amount of drugs, and a vast amount of confusion, such as the night at a venue called the Cave, which was notorious at the time for a back room that made the one at Max's look positively sedate. I'm sure I was back there for some prurient reason, when suddenly I heard a commotion at the door. I interrupted whatever I was involved in at the moment, squashed into the corner with some Asian kid, and went in search of the cause. Anna had come in looking for me because she wanted to move on to someplace else, when out of nowhere, a guy leaped on her, insisting that she was a man. "I know you are!" he was screaming, pulling her clothes off as he did so. "I know you're a man!"

We left.

Occasionally, too, I would go through a period thinking I should give up drugs before I killed myself, and I'd wind up spending two days in bed, trying to get straight. It's not easy. The first day you sleep, the second you're sick, and the third you're so bored and so desperate to get high that you'll do anything.

For the most part, though, I killed time playing basketball on the different courts around the city, mostly at a huge playground on the Eighth Avenue side of the Village, behind a school. I visited my parents and hung out with Richie, who was now playing in the otherwise all-girl group the Erasers—they'd just cut their first single, "Funny," and it was funny; I was more impressed when he showed me that than I was by my first sight of my own records.

We wound up spending three months in New York but finally flew back to London on March 28, 1978.

It was the worst possible timing. A few days before I left, but too late for me to change plans, doctors discovered a lump on my mother's breast. It was too early to say whether it was serious— she was scheduled to go into the hospital and have it removed in a few days' time. In the meantime, all I could do was hope, and wait.

I seemed to be doing a lot of that lately.

Chapter Twenty
HEARTS BREAKING

We should have stayed in New York.

We were homeless. Of course Track had stopped paying rent on the Oakley Street flat, and with nobody else to pick it up, we were on our own.

Johnny and Julie had already found a place in Soho, close to Piccadilly Circus, and they agreed to let Spider crash with them while he found his feet.

Billy and I, on the other hand, were left to our own devices. We wound up staying at a friend's house in Kensington; Alain was a Swiss photographer who was going to college in London at the time. He had a pull-out bed and an extra bedroom, and he was adamant that we could stay for as long as we wanted. Or, at least, until he returned to his parents' estate outside Geneva, Switzerland, in the summer, and they stopped paying his rent.

Still waiting to hear whether EMI were interested in the demo we'd recorded before Christmas, and hoping they would be, we hoped we'd not be staying there that long.

What we didn't know, not at first, was that the collapse of Track was only the first ruction. Leee, who himself seemed to be on the way out, filled us in on what had been going on while we were away—how Johnny had put together an impromptu band called the Living Dead, basically the Only Ones plus Patti Paladin, and started playing occasional sets at the Speakeasy.

He wasn't replicating the Heartbreakers, either—"Great Big Kiss" was in his set, sung by Patti, but the bulk of the performance was either new songs or material dating back to the early days of the Dolls. It was as if he'd stumbled upon a whole new direction and at exactly the right time.

The Sex Pistols broke up in January, and with their disband-
ment, punk seemed to have lost its entire momentum. The media
had already grown bored and was amusing itself inventing new
fads and fashions just to see if they could entice any new band
onto the wagon—there was a power pop surge that lasted for
about five minutes; there'd be a Mod movement that would make
it to ten. One of the papers, *Sounds*, was even championing something called, simply, "New Music," whose catchment area appeared to be any band that knew how to play a minor chord. The
Banshees were going to go far in that department.

Punk itself had splintered down political lines, far right versus
far left; disquieting reports of gigs transforming into battle-
grounds were becoming more and more commonplace, and when
I looked back at what the Heartbreakers had achieved across the
past twelve months, it was impossible to discern a single place
where we might fit in.

It went back to the image thing that had been worrying me six
months earlier, but it was also tied into the increasingly divisive
nature of British youth politics.

We'd seen how the country was crumbling; we'd suffered
through the year of industrial action that saw power cuts black
out entire cities and the fire brigade go on strike. We'd seen the
disgusting conditions in which people were expected to live and
read the headlines about soaring unemployment and stagnating
wages.

But what could we do? We were guests in the country—visitors,
foreigners. For us to raise our voices in protest at any of these
things not only felt disingenuous, but it would be positively
phony. So we concentrated on being no more than we were—a
great rock 'n' roll band—and left the politics to everybody else.

There was the Clash, so outspoken on the far left; there was
the Jam, lionizing the virtues of the English working class; there
was the Pistols, or what was left of them (Cook, Jones, and Vicious
were remaining together while they completed a movie), still

sticking two fingers up at "the establishment"; and there was a vast coterie behind them who could at least point to their support of Rock Against Racism as proof of their intentions.

And there was the Heartbreakers, rank outsiders.

I didn't doubt that Johnny would survive. The time he had spent in the United Kingdom had done nothing to diminish the power of his mystique nor the fervor of his most besotted acolytes. Journalists, musicians, anybody who had ever considered, in a wholly unironic way, the purchase of a T-shirt emblazoned with the legend "too fast to live, too young to die"—they clung to Johnny like bats in a belfry, desperately hoping that just a few scraps of his glamour would rub off on them.

While things were going well for the band, we laughed at these people, or about them. It wasn't malicious; it was more disbelieving, that same sense of unreality that I experienced the time I watched that journalist posturing in our Pimlico flat, demanding that we agree that he looked just like Keith Richard before rushing to ask if there was anything Johnny needed. A cup of tea, a slice of cake, an armful of smack.

It was pitiful, but it was also ironic because those were the people who would ensure Johnny's survival, at least for however long it took before the music scene came to its senses again. And, while Billy and I were far away, one more had drifted into his orbit, a bug-eyed publicist with delusions of managerial grandeur, whispering in Johnny's ear, "Hey, you don't need those other guys . . . you're the star . . . you should go solo." And Johnny, whose own share of the gig money had never been enough, started listening. By the beginning of May, 1978, it was all over. The Heartbreakers had broken up.

I'm not going to say that Billy and I didn't have a clue what was going on. We hadn't spoken once with Johnny while we were in New York—transatlantic phone calls were prohibitively expensive, and we were scarcely the letter-writing kind. But we heard whispers, and when Leee got in touch, which he tried to do fairly regularly, he would mention that Johnny had played a few one-off shows with different musicians.

So I knew Johnny had been busy while we were gone, and knew, as I wrote in my diary at the time, that he'd been "making quite a bit of money." But I also believed, and I wrote this as well, that while there was a "possible future," it was all much too vague for that to happen now. "He still needs us," I wrote.

He didn't.

There never was a falling out with Johnny, and you can't even say we drifted apart. He never made any effort to contact us once we returned to London, but we made no effort to contact him. I don't believe I even had his phone number for a long time.

It doesn't matter, though. Overnight our world changed.

Spider had barely arrived in London before he returned to New York; he had not played one single show with us.

Leee and Gail upped and moved to California and took the Rockats with them; later, when that band broke up, they drove back to New York, where Gail and Smutty were married.

Johnny released a solo single called "Dead or Alive," which was basically the same chords as "One Track Mind," only played a little slower, and then signed a solo deal with a brand-new label called Real—later, they'd sign another name from my past, that American girl who'd so pissed me off when she strummed my guitar without permission, Chrissie Hynde and the Pretenders.

Billy and I hung out.

We had already agreed we were going to remain in London, and having no rent to pay made that decision even easier to stick to. And it's not as if we were completely idle. In fact, one of the first phone calls I received was from Sid Vicious, still uncertain about life in the new zombie Pistols, asking if I wanted to form a band with him.

I said no. For a start, he was too unreliable, and I really didn't enjoy playing behind a bad singer. He was still with Nancy Spungeon, too, and that was someone I really didn't want to be in close quarters with.

Another call—Ed Hollis, producer for Eddie and the Hot Rods, another band that seemed to be slightly out at sea in the new musical climate, but who I'd always enjoyed going to see. Did Billy and I want to cut a single?

This time, I said yes.

We chose two songs: "Too Much Junkie Business" and a cover of Gary U. S. Bonds's "Seven Day Weekend," which the Dolls used to perform. Hollis called in Henri Paul Tortosa, a French guitarist who was working with Johnny around the same time (he plays on "You Can't Put Your Arms Around a Memory"), and Steve Nicol from the Hot Rods, and we had a couple of weeks of commuting between Kensington and the Island Studios in Hammersmith while we recorded it. (Interestingly, Ed and Steve had also been involved when Johnny recorded "Dead or Alive" at the same studio.)

It was a great single, but Island Records, who we assumed would be releasing it, passed, and it wouldn't see the light of day until 1983, when it came out on the French label Skydog. So much for getting a buzz out.

I don't remember how much, if anything, we were paid for the sessions. To be truthful, I have no idea how we survived at all. I usually had a little money that I saved from when we were making it—I didn't spend it all like Johnny did. But it wasn't much, and it didn't last.

I think we fell back on charity, to be honest, and hope. There was an awful lot of hope. I'm hazy on the details, but there were rumors afoot that Johnny was talking about reforming the Heartbreakers to record a second album. It never happened, though— too many people were whispering too many things in his ear, and he started work on *So Alone* instead.

Billy and I struggled on. We found people who would pay for stuff for us. We'd go to parties and eat there; we'd go to shows and, because there was a degree of celebrity clinging to us, we didn't have to buy our own drinks too often. Drugs were supplied by anybody who would share their own stash, usually the junkies hanging around Warwick Gardens, which was a regular shooting gallery at that time.

If we missed the last tube and couldn't get back to Kensington, we'd find somebody who'd allow us to crash for the night. It was hand-to-mouth the whole time, but really, I don't know how anybody survived at that time. All the kids we knew were living in squats and were probably either selling drugs or their bodies to get by.

We did have a reunion with Johnny. He was playing a show at the Speakeasy on my birthday, April 22, so we joined him onstage for his second set, playing through a clutch of numbers that felt like old friends now. It was just a one-off, though, and we never even discussed a repeat performance. But shortly after that, Johnny got in touch to ask if we fancied helping out on a couple of studio sessions.

In the studio with Steve Lilywhite, he was mainly relying on Paul Cook and Steve Jones to keep things going and then calling in other friends when they were required—Paul Gray from the Rods, Phil Lynott of Thin Lizzy, Mike Kellie and Peter Perrett from the Living Dead, Steve Marriott, and more.

We knew he was recording "Little London Boys," but when I heard it, I couldn't say I was especially impressed—it was all right, but it sounded much better live. Now he wanted to tackle "Give Him a Great Big Kiss" as well, and Steve Jones just wasn't cutting it; he couldn't get his head around that fifties backbeat. So Johnny called in Billy and me instead, and it came out great.

We also joined him for a version of "So Alone" that didn't make the album, but if anybody ever wants to know what a second Heartbreakers album might have sounded like (and why couldn't we have used Paul Cook on drums?), those are the tracks I'd point them to.

As for the rest of what became *So Alone*, it's hard to say. That album was as different to *L.A.M.F.* as *L.A.M.F.* was to the album people expected us to make when we first went into the studio. It's by far the best Johnny ever sounded in the studio, at least as a solo artist, and *So Alone* deserves every one of the plaudits that now rain down whenever its name is mentioned.

L.A.M.F., on the other hand . . . . With hindsight, and the benefit of the various live recordings that I've heard, *L.A.M.F.* didn't even *begin* to approximate what we sounded like.

At their best, on their night, in the moment and on the edge, the Heartbreakers really could break hearts. Every component in its right place, every riff nailed down and solo locked tight, every lyric defiant, every hair in place, the Heartbreakers remain the greatest band I have ever seen, heard, or dreamed of.

We just couldn't make it count when we needed to.

Chapter Twenty-One

CLEAN-UP TIME

Billy and I didn't leave London right away; in fact, it was mid-summer before we finally conceded defeat. Prior to that, there had always been different distractions or people to hang out with—a couple of girls from New York that we knew, Henri Paul, different musicians.

But Alain was going back home to Switzerland. Of course he was giving up the apartment as well, and that was it for us.

I did spend a few weeks in Geneva with Alain, waiting while Island made their minds up about "Seven Day Weekend," and it was great; I even cleaned up while I was there. But then it was back to London, boredom, and frustration and, inevitably, back to Warwick Gardens. Finally I called my parents and asked them to loan me the money to buy a plane ticket home. It was August 1978 and who was the first person I ran into? Johnny.

He was still recording, but he had returned to New York for whatever reason and was looking to play some shows. Or, at least, looking to make some money for drugs. Playing shows was the easiest way he knew of doing that. As it was for Billy and me, too. I don't remember whose idea it was to play the first Heartbreakers reunion gig, but it was probably Johnny's.

It was as if no time had passed. Any residual bad feelings that might have lingered on from the breakup were gone. Basically, we were all strung out, we were all in town, and we all needed money. Especially Johnny. No matter how much he could make in England from recording or touring, it would be gone within a week or even a day of him getting it, and sometimes even faster than that. A Heartbreakers gig simply made sense.

Jerry was still in London, and I don't think we would have invited him along even if he hadn't been. The mood between the three of us was good, and Jerry's incessant moaning would have torn that to shreds. Instead we brought in Lee Crystal again and played a couple of shows at Max's—of course!—over the Friday and Saturday of August 18 and 19.

The shows weren't great. We hadn't had time to rehearse too much, and we maybe winged it more than we should have. The reviewer for the *Village Voice* certainly wasn't impressed. But the crowd seemed happy, and Tommy Dean certainly was. He immediately booked us for another two shows, a month later, and suggested that he record them as well.

More gigs, more money. A live album—even more money. We said yes, and this time we did rehearse; we brought in Ty Stix, who we knew from hanging out at Max's and who was playing with Cheetah Chrome from the now-broken-up Dead Boys.

Ty was a solid drummer, but he was also a guy who liked to take downers a lot, so sometimes he'd be a little slow on the beat. You can hear it on the ensuing album, where we left on a couple of mistakes because they add to the atmosphere. There's one at the beginning of "All by Myself"; we started and then had to stop again because, ironically, the beat was way too fast. But Johnny already had an explanation in hand. "We never said we were the most professional band in the world."

Most times, though, Ty was fine, and it was better than having a speed freak as a drummer.

He knew the material as well, so we had two or three get-togethers to break him in, and all went well. So well that we lined up another show at Max's for November *and* went out on what you could call the Heartbreakers' first and only American tour—as far north as Toronto and out west to the Whiskey in Los Angeles and the Mabuhay in San Francisco.

The tour did not pass completely trouble free. In fact, it got off to what could have been a disastrous start when Billy got busted for having some pot wrapped up in one of his socks as we made our way into Canada. They kept him overnight at the airport, but thankfully he was released the following morning.

We did the gigs in Toronto and Hamilton, and that's where we met Long John Baldry, who'd been a major player on the British blues scene back in the early sixties. He threw a huge party at his house and spent the night trying to pick up Johnny.

When we crossed the border out of Canada, it was Johnny's turn to be stopped by customs after they spotted the giant abscesses on his arms. One of them looked like a baseball. Of course they searched the rest of us—full strip searches—and I happened to have some Darvocet painkillers on me. Finally they let us go with a fifty-dollar fine.

Los Angeles was memorable, too, particularly on the day when, on the way to that evening's gig, Billy and I walked into Johnny's room at the Tropicana to find him sitting on the toilet with three girls in the bathroom with him and water flooding out of a broken faucet.

Johnny was half asleep, but that didn't quell the girls' ardor. One was crouched between his legs, trying to suck his cock. Another was kissing his face and caressing his chest. And the third girl, who couldn't find a spare piece of body to maul, was humping his guitar.

As gently as we could, we prized Johnny (and his guitar) free of the ladies and led him out to the van. I'm still not convinced he had any idea what had been going on while he dozed.

All told, it was an enjoyable tour, and there was more to come in November—a couple of gigs opening for Blondie at the Palladium and the Paradise, in Boston, and another couple of headliners at Max's.

But that was it, we swore. The money was great; the audiences loved us. The *Live at Max's* album, recorded by Peter Crowley on the Rolling Stones Mobile, sounded great (it came out the following July), and the crowds at the California gigs were sensational—seriously, we could have stood onstage and not played a note, and the adulation would still have knocked us off our feet.

But Johnny's solo album was imminent, and it would receive some of the best reviews of his entire career. The November show at Max's, I wrote in my diary, "was the last one," and added, "The Heartbreakers are finally finished . . ."

And then, on a new line, "I think."

Tony Machine, most recently a Dollette, was our drummer for the occasion, and again it sounded good. But to be painfully truthful, that really wasn't a consideration. We did the shows for the payday, pure and simple, and I made that point in my diary, as well: "I'd still do some New York gigs because we make so much bloody money." The only real drawback was, "John's still in the twilight zone." Meaning, no matter how divorced from reality his drug intake had rendered him in the past, now he'd traveled even further out, nodding out in the middle of conversations, forgetting where (and maybe even who) he was, flying off the handle at the most imagined slight. I still considered him my friend. But maintaining that relationship was becoming very hard work indeed.

Besides, I was already playing again in my own right, guesting with other bands and musicians, and putting together a band of my own, a slow process which also came with a hefty whack of *déjà vu* as I wrestled with the perennial problem of finding a drummer.

While that saga dragged on, I was also filling in with Howie Pyro's band, the Blessed, a gloriously ramshackle teenaged band that made up in chemistry and presence for *everything* they lacked in terms of actually being able to play their instruments.

I'd known the band for a couple of years by now, since the summer of 1977, when the Heartbreakers returned to New York City. They were just little kids at the time, but they were definitely the flavor of the month.

I stopped by to see them play a few shows at Max's and CBGB, and they had all these Andy Warhol type of people hanging out with them. They were such pretty boys, and the art freak vampires and pedophiles were running after them, while all these society photographers and designers were trying to hang out with them. They were generating a buzz in New York.

The Heartbreakers did a couple of shows with them, and I was also friends with the girl who managed them, Eileen Polk. So when they had a fight with their guitar player and he left, she called me and asked if I'd do Max's with them because, she said, "they need a guitar player double quick." I said, "Sure, it'll be fun."

Musically they were pretty basic, but they had a lot of charisma. I took them to the same rehearsal space that we used, I put some rock 'n' roll into their songs, and we played a few gigs together. Then, when it was time for me to return to London, I put them in touch with one of my guitar player friends, Jean Francois (we called him "JF"), who would later join me in an early version of the Waldos.

Now I was back with them, and I must admit that it did feel strange playing in a band in which I was the oldest member by some twelve years—I wasn't yet thirty, but that statistic alone could have left me feeling ancient. Thankfully, it didn't. I remained with the band for a good few months; in fact, in August 1979, we even recorded a single at a studio in Bayside, Queens. It was produced by Dave Eng, the same guy who later did the Waldos' first single, "Crazy Little Baby," in 1991.

Around this same time, I started seeing a guy who played in another New York band who was much the same age as my Blessed bandmates, and I was having the time of my life. We'd met at the Mudd Club just before New Year's, and it was almost a month before we spent our first night together. Almost a month, incidentally, during which I was clean.

For the first time since Carol, nearly two years before, I felt content in my love life, and for the first time since . . . *I don't know when* . . . I was feeling secure in a band. I didn't need the Heartbreakers—or, it seemed, any of the extras that came with them.

But I did need to answer the phone when it rang a couple of weeks into the new year, and with the twisted inevitability that seemed the hallmark of my life at the time, it was Carol. It was January 1979, and I hadn't heard from her since April, 1977.

She was coming to the States to visit Jim Price in Los Angeles, and she asked if she could stop over in New York City to see me. Of course I said yes, and because my parents were out of town on vacation, I even invited her up to their place in Floral Park. One of the kids was with her (Jim's son stayed back in LA with his dad), and I remember how we'd park the boy with his uncle, who also lived in the city, while we went out to buy drugs, which was an astonishing experience for Carol—we'd drive into these derelict neighborhoods, she'd wait in the car while I ran into an abandoned building, and then I'd emerge minutes later with the stuff. She couldn't believe how fast the process was.

Carol stayed in New York for five or so days and then returned to the United Kingdom, and that was basically the last time I ever spoke to her. I did get a letter from her in the '90s, but I don't think I ever replied to her. She was the first girl I ever got truly involved with, the first I ever fell in love with, and I spent almost two years pining for her. I hate to use the term, but her visit to New York City finally gave me closure.

As it transpired, all of these fresh starts turned out to be false starts—Carol, the Blessed, everything. The only things that remained constant in my life, at least for now, were the Heartbreakers and the never-ending cycle of reunion shows, which would have been more accurately titled rent parties. Because that's what they were. We used to get together to play a show to pay the rent for a month or a couple of months

"Rent party" is an old term. Young kids used to throw a party in an apartment and charge people five or ten dollars to get in so that it would help to pay the rent for the next month or so.

So, March, 1979—Johnny was back in town and needed money. Jerry was back as well, and for all our resolutions the previous fall, we gave him a call, and there we were, back at Max's. Tommy recorded it again, and there was talk of releasing a live EP high-lighted by a positively epic and gorgeously ramshackle version of "So Alone," which would have been the title track to Johnny's album if only he'd included it on there!

In the end, the EP didn't come out. Tommy closed the Max's label instead. But the tapes would appear soon enough, and so would the Heartbreakers. In fact, we'd do reunion gigs more or less every time Johnny was back in town—around once a year, because of course he was here, there, and everywhere, and each time, it was good money.

It gave the media a laugh, as well. As Richard Grabel of *New Musical Express* remarked when the next one came around: "The Heartbreakers have abandoned the conceit of billing each of their now regular appearances at Max's as a 'farewell' gig and it looks a safe bet that they will be around for a while.

"For all their foibles, there is an endearing quality about this band of losers that makes us keep forgiving their sins and rooting them on. Because when things come together for them—when they're not fighting, when they can make it to the stage without stumbling over—they can still work an uncomplicated rock 'n' roll magic."

But I was growing tired. Tired of living with different people in the city, or moving out to Floral Park to stay with my father. Tired of being in a band that really hadn't been a band for three years.

My mother had passed away by now—I was still in London, at Leee's, I believe, when I got the call to say she'd been diagnosed with breast cancer and would be undergoing both a mastectomy and a lengthy period of chemo, but it was already too late. She died in January 1980, and that loss, too, played into my sudden disaffection with the way I was living.

So when, sometime around 1981, maybe 1982, my father raised the possibility of finding jobs for both Richie and me, I was immediately intrigued.

A friend of his, from back in his days in retail banking, was looking for people to run financial data for the computing company where he worked. We were interviewed, and perhaps to my surprise, they hired us both. We put on our suits and headed for Wall Street.

It was straightforward work, but it was fascinating. Of course it was the very early days of computers, at least so far as either business or the public were concerned, so anybody who knew their way around one—as we did—was going to be in demand.

Basically, the company would hire out both computers and operatives to different banks, to work on corporate takeovers, keeping a computer record of who had sold their stocks, who had exchanged it, and so on. Our job was to gather together all the information that came through, key it into the computer, add up all the stocks, convert them into the new stocks, cash, bonds, whatever was required, and then provide the banks with a report, so they could write the checks.

For example, if someone had ten shares of a company that was being bought for ten dollars a share, then they were entitled to a hundred dollars cash. If they had a hundred shares, they were entitled to a thousand dollars. And so on. There were other more complex transactions, but that was the gist of it.

I started out as a temp, and it wasn't a big thing. But it got me interested in the world of finance. I didn't know anything about it when I started—the only thing I ever knew about money was that I never had enough and always wanted more. But the more I learned, the more fascinating it seemed. Stocks, bonds, warrants, mutual funds, and hundreds more types of securities. I'd always thought the music industry was a big world, but finance was even bigger.

I was a good worker and a fast learner, and after a year or two of temping, they took me on full time. From there I jumped over to a regular brokerage firm, and that really opened things up for me.

That was when the learning curve really steepened. I thought I knew stuff, but I soon discovered that I had only ever been exposed to one tiny area of brokerage operations. There were many other types of activities that were completely different, so I had to learn what they were all about, and again, the more I learned, the more I wanted to know.

By now I'd moved out of Anna's apartment and was living with a girl I'd met recently. She came to a few shows, she was cute, and although my feelings for her were never as intense as they were with Carol, we got on really well. She had a great apartment, too, and even better, it was effectively rent free—the building's residents were on what was called "rent strike," refusing to pay the landlord until whatever legal deadlock they were involved in was resolved, so between my wages and hers, there was quite a lot of money floating around.

Unfortunately, I really only knew of one way of spending it.

People always talk about how being a junkie screws up your life. What they don't say so much about is how easy it is for your habit to screw up other people's, and she was—I suppose you'd have to say—my victim.

When I met her, she had little interest in drugs. She'd snort coke occasionally and smack rarely, but with me shooting it up every day and not even trying to hide it, she just tumbled into my world.

That apartment on Twenty-Second Street, close to Gramercy Park, became a shooting gallery. All manner of people were dropping by at any hour of the day or night—Johnny came by one time to score some coke from her, and unbelievably, he tried to pay with fake ten-dollar bills. And when I say "fake," I mean something a kid might have drawn. Not even a blind man would have been fooled. They weren't even cut to the right size!

My friend did get out of it. Her brother worked for a tech company up in Boston, and he sent her the money to go into a rehab clinic out in Minnesota—her roommate was Natalie Cole—and she did get straight. I last saw her sometime around 1988, and she was still taking pills, but that was all. I am so thankful that she made it.

I had also reconnected with Diane, my girlfriend from the early days of the Heartbreakers, although it was our past romance that reunited us as opposed to anything current.

Shortly before Hell left the band, in April 1976, Diane gave birth to her son Damian. I'll be honest and say, I was sure that I was his father—the first time I saw the boy, I thought, "He's got my nose." Diane would not say, however. She had gone through the pregnancy alone, and she intended raising her son alone as well. A father would only get in the way.

Damian was around four years old when he started asking questions. So one day Diane got in touch and I still remember her cautiously saying, "I've got something I need to tell you."

"I think I know what it is," I replied, and that was it. I was a father.

Diane still didn't want anything from me beyond whatever I was willing—or, given my drug use, able—to give, but every couple of months I'd visit, and it was wonderful being there to watch Damian grow. Even if it was, as it turned out, for just a few years.

I was still playing music throughout this period and still available for those sporadic Heartbreakers reunions. In fact, the only time when I faced any conflict whatsoever—and really, it was no conflict—came in 1984, when we were suddenly confronted with the possibility of a return to the United Kingdom. In fact, a lot was in the air at the time, although I'm not convinced that any of the musicians were party to it. But you know how these things are. . . .

Leee Black Childers still represented us; he and Gail were both back in England now, working with Angie Bowie, and Leee was still managing the latest incarnation of the Rockats. He even endured a reunion with Jerry when he joined the band for a time.

In the course of negotiating a deal for that band with Jungle Records, Leee happened to mention that he also owned the master tapes to both *L.A.M.F.* and a couple of Speakeasy shows that Track had recorded, alongside a heap of demos and mixes.

Jungle jumped. A separate deal with Johnny and his current management, a New York coke dealer named Chris, paved the way for Johnny to oversee a complete remix of *L.A.M.F.* with Tony James alongside him, while another deal apparently called for a

Heartbreakers reunion tour and an accompanying video and drifted vaguely around the possibility of a new studio album.

Chris was an interesting guy with some very interesting contacts. I remember Johnny and I driving back to New York City from Rhode Island one night in early 1982, end of February, beginning of March. We reached the city at eight in the morning, and we wanted to get high, so we stopped at Chris's place, a nice loft in Tribeca, and who should be sitting there with him? John Belushi, with his nose literally streaming with blood from doing coke all night, but utterly irrepressible, sitting there firing off jokes and funny stories.

He left to return to LA that same morning. And that was the week he died.

That apartment was a surreal place, but I was there a few times because Johnny was now living on the floor below. Chris used to keep bags of money just lying around, literally spilling twenty-dollar bills onto the floor, and there were all these people sitting around, completely stoned, who'd just help themselves as they walked out or went to the bathroom or whatever. They'd just slip a bill into their shoe or into a pocket. Even I helped myself to one once.

Johnny, Billy, and Jerry came over to Europe first, flying to Paris for a movie project they were involved with, Patrick Grandperret's *Mona et Moi*. I was working; my two-week vacation wouldn't begin for another few days, so Henri Paul completed the "band" in the movie.

I arrived in time for a gig at the Gibus club in Paris, and then it was back to the United Kingdom for a few warm-up shows, and then the Lyceum. And every morning, we'd be knocking on Chris's door to receive our daily dose of coke and dope. It was actually very well organized!

We didn't spend that much time together, outside of whatever band activities we needed to attend to—rehearsals, mostly, and maybe some promotional things that I've forgotten. Even at our lowest ebb in London, the Heartbreakers were never a social club, forever running around together. Billy and I spent the most time together, just hanging out or going to clubs. Johnny, though, would be here, there, and everywhere, probably trying to score, for the most part, and we had our own circles of friends and acquaintances, too.

It was the same now. The cities we visited, I'd be up and out, exploring whatever took my interest. I'd maybe see the others in the hotel lobby at some point, but we wouldn't really connect until it was time to go to the venue.

The warm-ups went well. Unfortunately, the Lyceum—where, of course, the cameras were rolling for that contracted video— was forgettable, and not only because Johnny compounded whatever he'd taken that day with eight large vodkas immediately before he went onstage.

What I best recall, regrettably, is the rambled rant about black homosexuals which Johnny dropped into "So Alone." He played pretty well that night, but if you watch the video, you can see me standing there, just rolling my eyes as he burbled on. Johnny always had a tendency to ramble on that song, but this was extreme even by his standards.

I flew back to New York immediately after the show, although a Heartbreakers of sorts did continue on for a while, with either Sylvain or Henri Paul replacing me on guitar, and then as a three-piece which imploded bitterly on a British tour that summer of 1984. It couldn't have lasted any longer.

There were other impromptu reunions, however. I played a few shows around New York with Johnny, with Jerry on drums and their regular guitar player, Luigi Scorcia, relegated to bass for the occasion. I also guested a few times with Jerry's new band, the Jerry Nolan Group; I remember one at the Rat, in Boston, where I was onstage for the entire set.

The first band that I started after the Heartbreakers originally broke up was called the Hurricanes, but that didn't last long. I then formed the Heroes. My brother Richie was on board along-side me, Barry Apfal played, and there was also a drummer, Billy Rogers, who played with the Heartbreakers a few times in their latter days.

That band died too, but it also sort of morphed into the Waldos. I disbanded the Heroes, and then six months later I shuffled the lineup a little bit and started the Waldos. And Johnny would always make a point of coming to see us play when he was around. Partly to say hello, and partly so he could piss me off.

No matter where we were gigging, he would always jump up onstage with us for a number or two. But whereas most "special guests" wait until the end of the show and then jump up to give the audience an extra farewell thrill, Johnny would join us near the start.

First he'd make his way to the front of the stage, usually during our first number, just to make certain the entire club knew he was there. Only when he was assured of that would he jump onstage, play a few songs, and then walk off, leaving us in front of a crowd who had already experienced the biggest thrill of the evening and who knew it, as well. And the only reason he did it was to annoy me, because he knew the effect he'd have as well as I did.

It was becoming increasingly obvious that I needed to make a decision. Heroin or finance.

I was living in Flushing at the time, sharing a place with my brother Richie. It was actually our older brother's apartment, but when our father decided to leave Floral Park and move down to the Jersey Shore with his two sisters, our brother bought the family home, and we took his place. And though it wasn't an everyday occurrence, I quickly fell into a routine. I'd leave the house early, drive into Williamsburg to score, and then take the train into work and shoot up in the bathroom. I would then repeat the process in reverse on the way home.

Or else I'd be running out at lunchtime to buy drugs,

I doubt that I was the only one, either. Just like you see in the movies these days, Wall Street was awash with coke at the time—there was one girl in my office who was dealing it, and she'd send it through the interoffice mail system!

I didn't know any junkies where I worked, apart from a few friends who I'd helped find jobs down there, but coke was everywhere, and pot and hash were big as well. Company parties would be unbelievable—there would be lines of people outside the bathroom, all these Fortune 500 companies, the entire work force lined up to shoot or snort some coke.

At the same time, though, I just didn't want to be a part of that world anymore.

A couple of things decided me.

The first was a very close call. One lunchtime, I went out to score and I got picked up in a sting operation. I was in jail for two and a half days. Fortunately, my brother Richie worked just a couple of blocks away and went into the office to pick up my bag and tell them that I'd been in an accident.

I stuck to that story when I returned to work and somehow I got away with it. But I knew it was not an experience, or a risk, that I ever wanted to take again.

The other thing was Richie.

I've mentioned before that we had always been close, growing up listening to much the same music, many of the same guitarists, learning to play our instruments together. When I was playing with the Demons, and the early days of the Heartbreakers, he was already in a whole lot of bands around Floral Park, and sometime after we went to England, he made that transition onto the New York scene.

He played in a few bands—the Erasers, the otherwise all-girl group with whom he cut his first single; the Voodoo Shoes, with Donna Destri (Jimmy's sister); and the Senders for a time, as well. And every time I came back from London, I'd bring him a stash of clothes from Sex, mohair sweaters, things like that.

Unfortunately, he also got involved with dope, and soon, we were going out and copping together, even after he joined me on Wall Street—I think he was working for American Express at the time. But he was also looking to go clean, and because his health insurance covered rehab, he was able to go straight.

It was while he was in the rehab center that he called me, saying one of the counselors wanted to talk to me. I went along, and the guy was halfway decent. But basically what he was saying was that I couldn't continue living with Richie because I was still a junkie and it was going to be hard enough for him to stay off the dope without me continuing to use. But this guy also claimed he "knew" that there was no way I would be able to stop using without a lot of help, and that was the message he kept drilling into me. "You'll never do it. You'll never clean up." And that pissed me off so much that I made up my mind there and then. "I'll show you."

That was in spring 1988, and by the end of May—Memorial Day, in fact—I was clean, and I've never looked back. Well, once. Two or three months later, Richie and I both decided to try it one last time, and for me, that *was* the last time.

The detox had been fairly gruesome, even though I knew what to expect because I had tried to stop so many times before. I took whatever I had, but I also remembered the stomach cramps that I'd just been through, the sweats, the methadone, the couple of months of feeling like crap. There was no way I was going to go back to it.

And as soon as I got straight, my Wall Street career started picking up. One of my bosses took a liking to me and sort of mentored me as I learned all this shit. Within four years of cleaning up, I was in charge of a department of twenty-five people, and two years after that, I was supervising the entire settlement operation of 125 people. I was even investing in stocks by myself.

Then things started to change. Big banks started to take over all of the indie brokerage firms like ours. We got bought by one bank, and that one got bought out by another, and suddenly all of the vice presidents were being laid off. That was in 2001. I managed to get another job at an asset management firm in 2002, but the following year, that was taken over by Lehman Brothers, and of course they famously went bankrupt in 2008, the biggest bankruptcy filing in American history.

Fortunately, the asset management company was able to buy itself back from the Lehman estate, and I remained with them until I retired in early 2015.

All the while, though, I was still doing gigs and even inviting people from the office along to see them. It must have been like a modern-day *Dr. Jekyll and Mr. Hyde*—straight Wall Street banker by day, mad punk rocker by night—and I had the clothes closet to prove it. On one side, I arranged all my work suits and ties, and on the other side, all my beat-up stage clothes.

EPILOGUE

The best rumor about myself that I ever heard was that I had died in the September 11 attacks on the World Trade Center. Some local newspaper in Connecticut actually printed it. Also, my old high school newspaper had an issue a few years back where they also listed me as deceased. I called them up with the old Mark Twain line 'rumors of my demise have been greatly exaggerated . . .' and they printed an apology in the next issue. They had gotten me mixed up with my brother Richie, who also went there."

—Walter Lure

Shortly before he passed away, Nils Stevenson asked me to write a few lines for a book he and his brother Ray were putting together, *Vacant—A Diary of the Punk Years*.

It was the first time I'd sat down to seriously contemplate that year and a bit that the Heartbreakers spent as brothers in Britain, and I had my opening sentences before I even started to think about it.

"It was the best of times, it was the worst of times, only none of us could tell the difference because we were so out of it all the time. We did everything we weren't supposed to, and we did it with a vengeance."

That was 1977. A decade later and we were still doing it. Only now we were a little bit older, a little bit slower and, if you watch the Lyceum video, a little bit more burned out. We were still "doing it with a vengeance." We just weren't quite so vengeful anymore.

The eighties drifted on and so did the Heartbreakers. Jerry was generally around for most of the reunions, but Billy disappeared following the breakup of the three-piece Heartbreakers in the summer of 1984, and I didn't see him again for about twenty-five years.

We kept it going, though, but there were certainly moments when it was touch and go, a lot of nights when Johnny was totally fucked up and he couldn't keep himself together, lying unconscious in the dressing room with bubbles coming out of his mouth, and we'd have to start the show without him.

Even then, though, we knew he'd manage to wake himself up and be onstage for the second or third number. Or he'd come out and just keep playing the wrong song, over and over, until finally we had to pull the plug on his amp. He didn't notice. So across the last few years, it was a toss-up whether Johnny would be together enough to play and hold up his end onstage. Many nights he did, but on others it was a mess.

The final Heartbreakers reunion was at the Marquee, on the West Side, in November, 1990. Tony Coiro from the Waldos played bass—he'd worked with Johnny a few times during the 1980s, so we had a good chemistry going. Jerry and I were both straight as well, which was a relief because on the occasions when Jerry turned up at Waldos gigs, offering to sit in with us, he could barely play the drums anymore. He'd been on methadone so long that he couldn't even play "Get Off the Phone." He didn't have his chops.

Johnny was as bad as I'd ever seen him—during rehearsals, he could only play two or three songs before he'd need to run to the bathroom to shoot up some shit.

I kept my qualms to myself and allowed the *Village Voice* to set the stage for the show: "It may be just a rent party, like their several farewell shows ten years ago [and every other reunion we'd played since then!], though that doesn't mean they won't take you some place. We saw Nolan walking down Broadway a couple weeks ago and he still looks like a star. Thunders might be another story, but here's hoping."

A thousand people turned out to see us, and I don't know what they were hoping for—probably the same onstage OD they'd been dreaming of for a decade-plus of Johnny gigs. Like Sylvain Sylvain once said, there's "a certain charisma about a guy that everybody thinks is about to drop dead."

But once we were out in front of them and Johnny came to life, we played a really good show. I'd been convinced that somebody would be unconscious or we'd forget the songs, but it was all right. Johnny was in fairly good shape. He threw one of his temper tantrums, I think over either money—he wasn't getting paid enough—or drugs—he wanted more before he went onstage. But it wouldn't be Johnny without that.

Six months later, on April 23, 1991, Johnny was dead.

So much has been written about his death and the manner of his passing—wild rumors, sheer speculation, incredible conspiracies. Such things go with the territory, I suppose—you only have to look at the bizarre and often baffling notions that sprung up around the deaths of Jim Morrison, Sid Vicous, and, a few years after Johnny, Kurt Cobain, to know that some people will never be satisfied with the "official" story.

All I can say is that I don't know. I'd not seen or heard from Johnny in six months; I didn't even know he was in New Orleans. I have no idea who he was hanging out with, who he'd crossed, and who he'd pissed off.

I do know, however, that his thirty-eight years on earth had taken a massive toll on his body; that he did not look after (or even acknowledge) his health; and that I myself had spent the past seventeen years waiting for the call that would tell me he had gone. That didn't diminish the shock I felt when the call did finally arrive, but at least now I knew I'd never have to dread those words again.

A few weeks later, on June 19, there was a memorial gig at the Marquee.

All of our friends were there, Johansen and Sylvain, Tony Machine, Lenny Kaye, Cheetah Chrome, sundry Senders. I played a set with the Waldos; Jerry did something with Patti Paladin and Stevie Klasson. And that was the last time I saw Jerry until I went to see him in the hospital, shortly before he died on January 14, 1992. He was already in a coma.

Tony Coiro accompanied me on that final visit. Three years later, in 1995, Tony, too, passed away. He had been having problems with his stomach over the summer, and that September, he was diagnosed with liver cancer. He was dead by Christmas; he pretty much withered away.

Tony's death was just one more in what felt like a never-ending conveyor belt. A year after Jerry, just as the Waldos released our first album, *Rent Party*, we lost our drummer, Charlie Sox, to an accidental overdose.

He was never really strung out, but he dabbled every now and then behind our backs because, while most of us had been involved in drugs at some point, we had all stopped by then. We didn't know that he was using. He just OD'd one day.

A few weeks after Tony died, we held a memorial show at the Continental Divide, and if I wanted to be horribly sentimental (which I don't), I'd say that I'd lost a friend, but I gained—or regained—a son.

Somewhere in the mid-1980s, I lost touch with Diane and Damian. It wasn't deliberate, but it was my own doing; I was so strung out so much of the time, fighting just to keep myself together for work and the occasional gig, that I simply couldn't think straight.

Time had no meaning to me; one day bled into another, and I'd think I should call, or visit, but put it off until the next day, and before I knew it, days had become months and months had become years until there came a time when I didn't even know how to get back in touch. The address I had was no longer theirs, the phone number was long out of service, and in those days before the internet and social media made it so easy to connect with lost friends and lovers, it was just one dead end after another.

Backstage at Tony's memorial, I happened to notice a young man standing off to one side, just looking at me. He walked over and I felt . . . it's hard to explain. Recognition is too strong a word. I just felt something. Something that he confirmed the moment he opened his mouth. "Walter. Do you remember Diane?"

It was Damian, grown now—nineteen, nearly twenty years old. And I didn't know if he was going to punch me in the face or give me a hug. Thankfully, he shook my hand and we sat down for a chat.

We've been friends ever since—maybe not a conventional father and son, but close. We visit, we spend time together, we talk on the phone, and when he married in 2008, I even saw Diane again, for the first time in almost two decades. And the first thing I said to her, or one of them, anyway, was to thank her for doing such a great job raising her son. Our son.

And today I am a grandfather with two beautiful grand-daughters.

Back in the 1990s, however, the fates had not yet finished with me. In 1997, I lost my brother Richie.

He and I had gotten straight together, and I thought it would last. Tragically, I was wrong. Around 1992 or 1993, I got him a job with the company I was working for, and he started playing in a band again, the Sea Monsters. But of course that meant he was hanging around the clubs again, and slowly he found himself being pulled back in.

He got fired from the job because he was taking too many days off. He was in the hospital for weeks with a spinal infection. He was kicked out of the band because he was too stoned to do any-thing. Finally I persuaded him to go back into rehab, and for a while it looked as though he was turning the corner. They even found him a place at a halfway house out in Arizona; he got a job with a brokerage firm out there, and he seemed to be doing well.

But there were problems. I know of at least one occasion when he got seriously beaten up by one of the other guys in the halfway house; he lost the job—why, I never discovered. Suddenly he was back on smack again. And one day in October 1997, our brother received the call from the local police. Richie had been found dead in his room, where apparently he'd been lying for several days. His body was so decomposed that it was cremated before it was returned to us.

Officially it was an overdose. But, bearing in mind what had happened at the halfway house, I do sometimes wonder if there was more to the story. . . .

Whatever happened to Richie, it was horrific—one of the worst experiences I have ever lived through—and it was the final straw. Things had become too crazy, and I just thought, "Fuck this!"

I didn't know how, but somehow I couldn't help feeling that I was responsible. People were dropping like flies around me, and the one thing they had in common was that they all knew me.

It was time to get out, to retire from music, to stop killing people. But there were all these people who kept begging me to keep the Waldos going.

The Japanese kids who play with me now in my New York version of the group were in a band called the Hip Nips. I became friends with them, and they were dying to play with me. Then Todd Youth from Murphy's Law convinced me to do a band called the Lures, and for a while I had two bands. One was called the Waldos and one was called the Lures, and we played basically the same songs with one or two differences in the sets.

One of the Japanese guys, EZ, played in both of them, and that kept me going because I was really ready to stop. Then it just ended up being the Waldos because Todd had his own thing starting up. I have kept going, however, with the Waldos ever since, and thankfully, they have all managed to stay alive. We even recorded another album, 2018's *Wacka Lacka Loom Bop a Loom Bam Boo*, and I'm proud to say it received some of the best reviews I've ever had!

I mentioned that Billy would resurface again, but that was not a happy story either.

Apart from one call sometime during the 1990s, when he wanted to know if there was any money due to him from royalties, I'd not heard anything of him since he and Jerry left Johnny's three-piece Heartbreakers in 1984, during their final British tour; apparently he had a Swedish girlfriend and opted to remain in the United Kingdom. From there, he told me, he had gone in to rehab in Ohio, which is where he fell in with some religious cult and became a preacher.

From there, he moved to south Jersey, some place around Cherry Hill, and married; he was still a preacher but also working as a counselor for drug addicts, and when he showed up at one of the Max's reunion shows I was playing at the DeLancey around 2009 or 2010, he looked halfway decent. He even still had his hair, albeit it was white.

So far as I could tell, he was off drugs, but he had contracted AIDS and Hepatitis C, and he'd lost half of one leg in a car accident. His body was breaking down. He was a fucking mess.

It was good to see him, though, and a few months later he called me to ask if I'd be interested in getting a band together.

I wasn't. I was still working, and the only time I toured was when I took the Waldos out for a week during my annual vacation. But a year or two later I was in London, playing the Purple Turtle in Camden, and he showed up again.

Apparently some local entrepreneur had learned that he was still around, brought him to London, and was setting him up in a band with Steve Dior. They came backstage, this obnoxious middle-aged guy with bleached blond hair who wore a leather jacket and introduced himself as the manager, and Billy—who was fucking wrecked.

He'd gained weight, his teeth were gone, and they'd dressed him up as a pirate, of all things. When he talked, it sounded as though something had gone seriously wrong with his brain. He'd aged two decades since the last time I saw him.

It got worse. The manager suggested Billy join me onstage for "Chinese Rocks"—he did, but he'd forgotten how to play it. It was a mess, and so was the tour they'd booked for him. Apparently they played one gig in London and it was so bad that they cancelled the rest and dropped him.

The poor guy was stuck in London, though, for another two or three weeks because his flight home had been booked for the end of the tour and he didn't have the money to change it. He didn't have any place to stay—he was crashing at various people's houses, and the whole thing was an absolute disaster. And the next thing I heard was when he passed away in 2014.

Which means, aside from Hell—who was there at the beginning but has managed to steer clear of everything since—I am the sole surviving member of the Heartbreakers. And I remain proud of all that we accomplished.

The songs were great, and they still hold up well today, some forty years later. I realized that a couple of years ago when I got together with Jesse Malin of D Generation, Clem Burke from Blondie, and Wayne Kramer of the MC5, to play a couple of *L.A.M.F.* anniversary gigs.

I'd known them all for years—Clem from the New York scene and Wayne from when he worked with Johnny in Gang War in the eighties—and we had played together a few times. The only one I didn't know was Tommy Stinson from the Replacements, who we brought in to play bass and sing a couple of songs.

In terms of experience, Jesse was the "new kid," but I'd known him for years as well, since back when he was a teenager, playing a New Year's gig at an old deli on Avenue B and Sixth that somebody had rented for a party.

It was Charlie from the Waldos and I, plus a guitarist I couldn't remember, and Jesse, who was somebody Charlie knew. I remember I had to rush there after working late—I was stuck in the office until almost midnight and drove like a devil to get from Thirty-Third and Ninth over to the Lower East Side. I probably needn't have bothered. There were mobs of people heading for Times Square and barely anybody at the deli. But that was where I met

Jesse for the first time, and over the years, we'd run into one another all the time.

In fact, it was Jesse who suggested the *L.A.M.F.* gigs in the first place—three shows at the Bowery and one at Webster Hall. Two nights of rehearsal beforehand, every gig sold out, T-shirts flying out of there like crazy.

There were teething troubles. I didn't know Tommy, so I don't know, either, whether he was trying too hard to behave like Johnny at the first gig, or if he was just toasted. Whatever the reason, there were a few issues.

But the second night was fantastic, everything clicked, and there's a CD and DVD of the night to prove it.

It went so well, in fact, that we decided to do it again the following year, 2017, which of course was the fortieth anniversary of *L.A.M.F.* Jesse called, saying, "Let's do it again with some different people."

Clem was on board, of course, and Glen Matlock's name came up for bass because he was there at the time, a part of the original scene. We thought about Steve Jones as well, but he rarely leaves Los Angeles these days, but then Billy Joe Armstrong from Green Day was approached, and he was thrilled. I'd not known he was such a Heartbreakers fan, but he was. He knew all the songs.

So that would have been great, but then Green Day fired their entire management team that September, and Billy ended up have to back out because there were too many business issues that he had to deal with.

But then Jesse remembered opening up for Social Distortion sometime when he was a teenager, and how he and Mike Ness got talking after the show and discovered a mutual love of the Heartbreakers. So we got in touch with him and he agreed right away to do the shows—six of them spread between New York City and the West Coast—LA, San Diego, San Francisco—and they all sold out. Everyone was sober! I think that, alone, confirms the lasting power of *L.A.M.F.*, and also, the Heartbreakers that made it.

Yes, we only did one studio album and later a few live releases. No, we probably didn't live up to our potential. But the fact that I'm still playing this stuff four decades later, and people are still paying to hear and see it, says it all. There was definitely more to that music than meets, or met, the eye back then.

Maybe you could compare it to those shooting-star type of artists who blaze so brightly, but briefly—the Sex Pistols, the New York Dolls, James Dean, and God knows how many others; there's a lot of them in all the different art fields. I've even heard us being described as icons, if that's anything to write home about, but either way, I'm definitely glad it happened.

I also always say that if the album hadn't gotten so many bad reviews back then, and it had sold a lot more—yes, if, if, if—I probably wouldn't be here now.

Yes, I probably thought I'd have a longer career in the music business than I did, but it just didn't happen. And I do reflect fondly on that time —I probably had the most fun of my entire life, and we were on top of the world.

I don't really have regrets, either—just sort of "what ifs . . . ?" People still send messages about how much they loved us back then and how they still like all the songs, so I'm well aware of the quality of our work. I knew it was good, but there are millions of artists who are good and don't get anywhere, so at least we had our brief run.

But I also believe that if we had gotten any bigger back then, we all might have died a lot earlier, given our proclivities at the time, and I include myself in that. One of the main reasons I survived was the fact that I had to go out and get a job. Johnny, Billy, and Jerry never had to do that—Johnny never worked a day in his life at a regular job.

Nice work if you can get it, I guess, but it comes with one hell of a price.

JOHNNY THUNDERS & THE HEARTBREAKERS DISCOGRAPHY

It's a mess, isn't it? So many labels, so many live albums, so many mixes, so many fans saying this, that, or the other pressing is the best—the cassette, the first remaster, the box set . . . there have been so many different releases that I can't keep track of them, and I'm not even going to try. But here's what I think you should at least listen to. . . .

—Walter Lure, August 2018

July 7, 1975—Live at CBGB
Goin' Steady—Can't Keep My Eyes on You—Flight—Hurt Me—You Gotta Lose—Stepping Stone—New Pleasure—Blank Generation—I Wanna Be Loved
On CD *What Goes Around*

November 16, 1975—Live at Mothers
Love Comes in Spurts—Chinese Rocks—Pirate Love—Can't Keep My Eyes on You—Hurt Me—So Alone—New Pleasure—Blank Generation
On CD *Live at Mothers*

January 23, 1976—SBS Studios, Yonkers
Pirate Love—I Wanna Be Loved—Goin' Steady—Flight—Love Comes in Spurts—Hurt Me—Can't Keep My Eyes on You—Chinese Rocks—Blank Generation—You Gotta Lose
Tracks 1–4 on CD *L.A.M.F.—Definitive Edition*
Tracks 5–8 on Richard Hell CD *Time*

October 1976—Jay Nap Studios
Born to Lose—Do You Love Me—Can't Keep My Eyes on You—It's Not Enough—I Love You—Take a Chance—Get Off the Phone (backing track only)—I Wanna Be Loved (backing track only)
Tracks 1–8 on CD *Down to Kill*

February–March 1977—Essex Studios, London
Chinese Rocks (5 mixes—2/20/77)
Born to Lose (8 mixes—2/21/77)
Let Go (mix—2/22/77)
All by Myself (mix—2/22/77)
**Tracks 1–3 (unknown mix) on CD *L.A.M.F. (The Lost '77 Mixes)*
(Special Edition)**
**Track 2 (mix 4 "after curry"—2/20/77) on CD *L.A.M.F.—Definitive
Edition***

March 15, 1977—Live at the Speakeasy (Two Sets)
Chinese Rocks—All by Myself—Let Go—Can't Keep My Eyes on
You—I Wanna Be Loved—Do You Love Me—Get Off the Phone—
Going Steady—I Love You—Born to Lose—All by Myself (2) —Chinese
Rocks (2) —Get Off the Phone (2) —I Love You (2) —
I Wanna Be Loved (2)
Tracks 1–10 on LP *D.T.K.—Live at the Speakeasy*
Tracks 11–15 on CD *Down to Kill (Complete Live Speakeasy)*

March 21, 1977—Ramport Studios, London
Going Steady—Baby Talk—Do You Love Me—Born to Lose—Chinese
Rocks—Pirate Love—It's Not Enough—One Track Mind
16-track 2-inch multi-track reference tape

March 1977—Ramport Studios, London
Born to Lose (mix 3/22/77)
Born to Lose (mix 4—3/22/77)
Chinese Rocks (mix 3—3/22/77)
Chinese Rocks (mix "second choice"—3/22/77)
I Wanna Be Loved (unknown date)
Get Off the Phone (unknown date)
Tracks 1–6 on CD *L.A.M.F.—Definitive Edition*

April 1977—Ramport Studios, London
Baby Talk (rough mix—4/22/77)
Can't Keep My Eyes on You (rough mix—4/22/77)
Going Steady (rough mix—4/22/77)
Track 2 on CD *L.A.M.F.—Definitive Edition*

April 22, 1977—Ramport Studios, London
All by Myself—Let Go—Get Off the Phone—Can't Keep My Eyes on
You—I Love You
2-inch tape prepared for mixing, 4/22/77

May 1977—Olympic Studios
All by Myself (mix 1—5/16/77)
All by Myself (mix 2 "solo loud"—5/16/77)
Get Off the Phone (mix—5/16/77)
Get Off the Phone (mix—5/16/77)
Goin' Steady (mix 1 "rough"—5/19/77)
Goin' Steady (mix 2—5/19/77)
Tracks 2, 4, 5 on CD *L.A.M.F.—Definitive Edition*

May 20, 1977—Single (Track Records)
Chinese Rocks/Born to Lose

May 24, 1977—Trident Studios
Baby Talk (mix 1—5/24/77)
Baby Talk (mix 2—5/24/77)
Baby Talk (mixes 3–5—5/24/77)
Goin' Steady (5 mixes—5/24/77)
Track 2 on CD *L.A.M.F.—Definitive Edition*

June 1977—Ramport Studios
It's Not Enough (mix 1 "vocals, drums up"—6/1/77)
It's Not Enough (mix 2—6/1/77)
It's Not Enough (mix 3—6/1/77)
One Track Mind (mixes 1–4—6/1/77)
One Track Mind (mix 5—6/1/77)
Tracks 1, 2, 5 on CD *L.A.M.F.—Definitive Edition*

Baby Talk (mixes 1–6—6/5/77)
Baby Talk (mix 7 "next best"—6/5/77)
Baby Talk (mix 8—6/5/77)
Goin' Steady (mixes 1–3—6/5/77)
Tracks 2, 3 on CD *L.A.M.F.—Definitive Edition*

Pirate Love (mix 1—6/7/77)
Pirate Love (mix 2—6/7/77)
Pirate Love (mixes 3, 4—6/7/77)
Track 3 on CD *L.A.M.F.—Definitive Edition*

All by Myself (mixes 1–4—6/8/77)
All by Myself (mix 5—6/8/77)
Pirate Love (mix 1—6/8/77)
Pirate Love (mix 2—6/8/77)
Pirate Love (mixes 3–5—6/8/77)
Tracks 2, 4 on CD *L.A.M.F.—Definitive Edition*

Can't Keep My Eyes on You (mixes 1, 2—6/10/77)
Can't Keep My Eyes on You (mix 3—6/10/77)
Can't Keep My Eyes on You (mix 4—6/10/77)
Let Go (2 mixes—6/10/77)
Let Go (mix "varispeed"—6/10/77)
I Love You (2 mixes—6/10/77)
Tracks 2, 5 on CD *L.A.M.F.—Definitive Edition*

I Love You (mix 1—6/11/77)
I Love You (mix 2—6/11/77)
I Love You (mixes 3–5—6/11/77)
Let Go (mixes 1–6—6/11/77)
Let Go (mixes 1–2—6/?/77)
Let Go (mix 3—6/?/77)
Let Go (mixes 4, 5—6/?/77)
Tracks 2, 6 on CD *L.A.M.F.—Definitive Edition*

I Love You (mixes 1–7—6/22/77)
I Love You (mix 8—6/22/77)
Do You Love Me (mix 1—6/22/77)
Do You Love Me (mixes 2–4—6/22/77)
It's Not Enough (mix "bright rough")—6/27/77)
One Track Mind (mixes 1–6—6/27/77)
One Track Mind (mix 7—6/27/77)
One Track Mind (mix 8—6/27/77)
All by Myself (unknown date)
Tracks 2, 3, 5, 7, 9 on CD *L.A.M.F.—Definitive Edition*

July 1977—Ramport Studios
Pirate Love (mixes 1–5—7/2/77)
Pirate Love (mix 6 "new voice"—7/2/77)
Pirate Love (mix 7—7/2/77)
Let Go (mixes 1–3—7/2/77)
Let Go (mix 2 & 1 edit—7/2/77)
Baby Talk (mixes 1, 2—7/22/77)
Born to Lose (mix—7/22/77)
Chinese Rocks (mix—7/22/77)
Do You Love Me (mix—7/22/77)
I Love You (mix—7/2/77)
Goin' Steady (mix—7/22/77)
Tracks 2, 5, 9, 11 on CD *L.A.M.F.—Definitive Edition*

March–July (?), 1977—Ramport Studios
All by Myself
Do You Love Me
Goin' Steady (backing track)
Baby Talk (backing track)
Pirate Love (backing track)
Born to Lose (backing track)
Chinese Rocks (backing track)
**Tracks 1–7 unknown mixes on *L.A.M.F. (The Lost '77 Mixes)*
(Special Edition)**

August 1977—Live at the Village Gate, New York
Chinese Rocks—Pirate Love—Get Off the Phone—All by Myself—Let
Go—Can't Keep My Eyes on You—Chatterbox—One Track Mind—
Take a Chance with Me—Born to Lose—Boppin' the Blues—Do You
Love Me—I Wanna Be Loved
On CD *L.A.M.F. Live at the Village Gate, 1977*

September 1977—Advision Studios
Baby Talk (mix—9/10/77)
Going Steady (mix—9/10/77)
One Track Mind (mix "dry, clean"—9/10/77)
Baby Talk (mix—9/15/77)
Goin' Steady (mix—9/15/77)
Tracks 3, 4, 5 on CD *L.A.M.F.—Definitive Edition*

October 1977—LP L.A.M.F. (Track Records)
Chinese Rocks—Born to Lose—Let Go—All by Myself—Get Off the
Phone—Can't Keep My Eyes on You—I Love You—Goin' Steady—Baby
Talk—I Wanna Be Loved—It's Not Enough—Pirate Love—One Track
Mind

October 28, 1977—Single (Track Records)
One Track Mind—Can't Keep My Eyes on You (live)—One Track Mind
(live)

November 20, 1977—Live at the Rainbow, London
Boppin' the Blues—Chatterbox—Chinese Rocks—Pirate Love—Get Off
the Phone—All By Myself—Let Go—Can't Keep My Eyes on You—I
Love You—Born to Lose—One Track Mind
**An audience tape purportedly recorded on this date circulates on
the Internet.**

December 8, 1977—Live at the Bataclan, Paris
All by Myself—Let's Go—Can't Keep My Cock in You [sic]—I Love
You—Too Much Junkie Business—London Boys—Give Her a Great Big
Kiss—Born to Lose—One Track Mind—Do You Love Me—I Wanna Be
Loved—Take a Chance with Me—Baby Talk—Chinese Rocks
On CD *Vive La Revolution*

December 13, 1977—Riverside Demos
London Boy
Too Much Junkie Business
Give Him a Great Big Kiss
Tracks 1, 2 on CD *Down to Kill*

March 24, 1978—Unreleased Single (Track Records)
It's Not Enough—Let Go

**Spring 1978—Basing Street Studios (The Heroes—Walter Lure/
Billy Rath)**
Too Much Junkie Business
Seven Day Weekend
Tracks 1, 2 on Skydog single and CD *Down to Kill*

July 1, 1978—Basing Street Studio (Johnny Thunders Session)
Give Him a Great Big Kiss
So Alone
Track 1 on LP *So Alone*
Track 2 B-side (and CD bonus track)

September 16, 1978—Live at Max's Kansas City
Milk Me—Chinese Rocks—Get Off the Phone—London Boy—Take a
Chance—One Track Mind—All by Myself—Let Go—I Love You—Can't
Keep My Eyes on You—I Wanna Be Loved—Do You Love Me
On LP *Live at Max's Kansas City*

1979—Single (Beggars Banquet)
Get Off the Phone (live at Max's Kansas City)
I Wanna Be Loved (live at Max's Kansas City)

1979—Live at Max's Kansas City
All by Myself—Pirate Love—Too Much Junkie Business—Don't Mess
with Cupid—So Alone
On CD *Live at Max's Kansas City Vols 1 & 2*

1982—Single (Jungle Records)
Chinese Rocks (live at the Speakeasy 1977)
All by Myself (live at the Speakeasy 1977)

1983—Single (Jungle Records)
Let Go
Born to Lose
Chinese Rocks
On 12-inch single *Vintage 77*

March 25, 1984—Live at the Lyceum, London
Pipeline—Personality Crisis—One Track Mind—Too Much Junkie
Business—Do You Love Me—Just Because I'm White—Copy Cat—Baby
Talk—Born to Lose—All by Myself—In Cold Blood—Seven Day
Weekend—So Alone
**On LP and VHS (later CD/DVD) *Live at the Lyceum Ballroom.* The
Lyceum sound check is featured on DVD in the box set *Down to
Kill.***

1984—*L.A.M.F* Remixes
Chinese Rocks—Born to Lose—Let Go—All by Myself—Get Off the
Phone—Can't Keep My Eyes on You—I Love You—Goin' Steady—Baby
Talk—I Wanna Be Loved—It's Not Enough—Pirate Love—One Track
Mind
On LP *L.A.M.F. Revisited*

1994—*L.A.M.F. (The Lost '77 Mixes)* (Special Edition—2CD)
For details see above

2005—*Down to Kill* 2CD + DVD Box Set
For details see above

2012—*L.A.M.F.—Definitive Edition* (4CD Box Set)
For details see above

2017—*L.A.M.F. (The Lost '77 Mixes)*
Disc 1 of above, remastered 2017

Appendix Two

WALTER LURE DISCOGRAPHY

1979—The Blessed Single (Daven Records)
Deep Frenzy
American Bandstand

December 21, 1980—Johnny Thunders Live at the Silverbird, Detroit
Pipeline—London Boy—Too Much Junkie Business—Chatterbox—All by Myself—Let Go—So Alone—Do You Love Me—Get Off the Phone—Chinese Rocks
On CD *Thunderstorm in Detroit*

March 13, 1982—Johnny Thunders Live at Irving Plaza, New York City
In Cold Blood—Too Much Junkie Business—Alone in the Crowd—Pipeline—Just Another Girl—Sad Vacation—Baby I Love You, I Really Do—Who Needs Girls—Born to Lose
On CD *In Cold Blood*

1991—The Waldos Single (Baylor Records)
Crazy Little Baby
Cry Baby

1994—The Waldos LP *Rent Party*
Cry Baby—Love That Kills—Sorry—Seven Day Weekend—Never Get Away—Golden Days—Flight—Countdown Love—Busted—Crazy Little Baby—Crazy 'Bout Your Love—Party Lights

1995—The Waldos Session
Let Go
On CD *A Tribute to Johnny Thunders: I Only Wrote This Song for You*

1994—Live at CBGB
Ballad of Johnny Thunders—Countdown Love—Rocking in New York City—Leave Me Alone—Who Killed John Lennon?—They Loved You to

Death—Far Away Place—Ballad of Johnny Thunders—So Alone—
Chinese Rocks—Too Much Junkie Business—So Alone
On CD *Rick Blaze & Walter Lure Live in New York City*

2005—Live at Continental, New York City
Sorry
I Wanna Be Loved
Track 1 on CD *Live at Continental: Best of NYC Volume One*
Track 2 on *Volume Two*

April 14, 2007—Live at Wild at Heart, Berlin
One Track Mind—Sorry—Never Get Away—Cry Baby—Get Off the
Phone—Busted—Let Go—London Boys—Take a Chance—I Wanna be
Loved—Born to Lose—Chinese Rocks—Too Much Junkie Business—
Do You Love me
On CD *Walter Lure Live in Berlin*

2009—Born to Lose: A Tribute to Johnny Thunders
Jet Boy (the Waldos)
Short Lives (Walter Lure)

2011—The Waldos, Live at the Bell House, Brooklyn
Get Off the Phone—Never Get Away—All by Myself—Cry Baby—
Golden Days—London Boy—Countdown Love—Can't Keep My Eyes
on You—Party Lights—Pirate Love—Born to Lose—Too Much Junkie
Business—Chinese Rocks
On LP *Walter Lure & the Waldos Live in Brooklyn*

2014—Guest Appearance with the Jim Jones Revue, Forum, London
Chinese Rocks
On CD *The Last Hurrah—Live at the Forum*

**2016—Last Ditches LP *Spilt Milk* (with Randy Pratt, Binky Phillips,
Bobby Rondinelli)**
Excuse Me—That's What We Do—Where Am I?—So So So—Itchin' For
a Fight—I Wanna Be Loved—Monkey on My Back—I Made a Mess—I
Get That a Lot—N-O Spells No—A Think About You—Kiss This—
Throw the Dog a Bone

November 15/16, 2017—Live at the Bowery Electric, New York City
Born to Lose—Baby Talk—All by Myself—I Wanna Be Loved—It's Not
Enough—Chinese Rocks—Get Off the Phone—Pirate Love—One Track
Mind—I Love You—Goin' Steady—Let Go—Can't Keep My Eyes on
You—Do You Love Me
On CD *L.A.M.F. Live at the Bowery Electric*

2018—The Waldos LP *Wacka Lacka Loom Bop a Loom Bam Boo*
Crazy Kids—Damn Your Soul—Where Were You (On Our Wedding
Day)?—London Boys—Lazy Day—Take a Chance on Me—Wham Bam
Boo—Bye Bye Baby—She Doesn't Love You—Little Black Book—Don't
Mess with Cupid—You Talk Too Much

INDEX